CHINESE SEASONS

Books by
Nina Simonds

Classic Chinese Cuisine
Chinese Seasons

CHINESE
SEASONS

· · · · · · · · · · · · · · ·

Nina Simonds

Houghton Mifflin Company   Boston   1986

Library of Congress Cataloging-in-Publication Data

Simonds, Nina.
  Chinese seasons.

  Bibliography: p.
  Includes index.
  1. Cookery, Chinese. 2. Menus. 3. Festivals — China.
I. Title.
TX724.5.C5S589   1986   641.5951   86-7336
ISBN 0-395-36802-2

Printed in the United States of America

M 10 9 8 7 6 5 4 3 2 1

Design by Nancy Belford/Calligraphy by Johanna Chao

Some of the material in this book has appeared in a different form in *The Pleasures of Cooking* and *Gourmet* magazine.

This one's for Don . . . and for Debby.
This book is theirs almost as much
as mine.

Acknowledgments

When I wrote my first book, I discovered that producing the manuscript was the easy part. It was the acknowledgments that gave me the most trouble. Since space was limited, I could acknowledge only a few people, yet so many friends, relatives, students, and colleagues had provided immeasurable support and love through the years. I now find myself in the same position, and I simply *cannot* go on at length. So, I offer my warmest thanks to you all (you know who you are anyway!) and apologize that I cannot list everyone by name.

There are, however, a few who must be mentioned. Don Rose, my sweetheart, was always there for support as well as to taste and edit. My best friend and fellow cook, Debby Richards, tirelessly (and always cheerfully) brainstormed about food and tested more recipes. And Martyn Richards was always — or almost always — ready for more testing and tasting.

At Houghton Mifflin, I offer my warmest thanks to Linda Glick Conway, my faithful editor; Nan Talese, editor in chief (and spiritual leader); Sarah Flynn, my ever-meticulous manuscript editor; and Bob Overholtzer, art director, for his support and contribution to the design of this book.

Special thanks are also in order for Harriet Wasserman, my agent, for her sound advice, support, and humor.

Over the past few years, I have had the pleasure and luck to have worked regularly with several publications. I must express my gratitude to my colleagues at the *Boston Globe* (in particular Patti Doten, Jan Freeman, and Michael Larkin); *The Pleasures of Cooking* (especially Carl Sontheimer, Cecily Brownstone, and Suzanne Jones); *Gourmet* magazine (most notably Zanne Zackroff and Kemp Miles); and the *Washington Post* (especially Phyllis Richman, Bob Kelleter, and Tom Sietsema).

Of course, thanks are also due to my family for their support and love (thanks to my brother Wobbit and his toll-free number), as well as to some special friends: Rosalie and Bob Quine, Mat Shaffer, Rachel Blumenstein, and Stella and Pickering Lee.

The illustrations on the part title pages are reprints of paintings by Qi Baishi, who is considered by many to have been the greatest classical modern Chinese painter. He was born in Hunan province in 1863 and died in Beijing in 1957. Grateful thanks to Duo Yun Xuan Publications, Shanghai, for the reprints, and to Wu Tung, curator of Asiatic Art at Boston's Museum of Fine Arts, who graciously provided information about these works.

Last, I must give credit to Nancy Belford, my gifted designer, who worked long and hard to please my sense of aesthetics and function. It was Nancy who created and shaped the unique and graceful design of this book. Johanna Chao's flowing calligraphy further complements and enhances the graphics. Finally, I would like to thank Ruth Bauer. It is Ruth's vibrant and beautiful watercolor that graces the cover of *Chinese Seasons*.

Contents

Introduction

In China, it is the distinct seasonal dishes that mark the passage of time on the calendar. The New Year is heralded by coils of freshly made pork sausage and slices of sticky, steamed sweet-rice cake. Crisp, deep-fried spring rolls announce the coming of spring. Summer is signaled by the appearance of cone-shaped rice dumplings known as *zong-zi*, which are wrapped in bamboo or lotus leaves and prepared for the Dragon Boat Festival. And plump crabs and chrysanthemum cakes confirm the arrival of autumn.

The importance of this culinary calendar was made apparent to me from the moment I arrived in the Orient. I was nineteen and had journeyed to Taiwan to study Mandarin and Chinese cuisine. My plane arrived in the middle of the night, but my Chinese surrogate father and mother, who had never met me and had only a dated high school graduation picture with which to identify me, were at the airport to meet me and take me to their home.

We sat in the living room and they welcomed me, shyly and somewhat formally, with the serving of tea and moon cakes. The conversation was a little awkward, since my Chinese was minimal and their English was limited, but we managed to communicate; we talked about the moon cakes. They told me that they had just celebrated the Festival of the Harvest Moon, otherwise known as the Moon Festival, and that moon cakes were the traditional holiday specialty. Moon cakes, they said, were especially treasured because they played a critical role in helping the Han Chinese overthrow their Mongolian rulers during the Yüan dynasty (1271–1368). My hosts also explained that there were many different kinds of moon cakes, with both sweet and savory fillings, and that each year friends, relatives, and business associates would mark the holiday by exchanging boxes filled with moon cakes. I was encouraged to eat as many as I liked, because they had received far too many — and before very long we would be celebrating another holiday and enjoying its traditional dishes.

For the Chinese, food has always played a prominent role in life's daily routine as well as in the observation of its milestones. The rituals of all Chinese holidays, weddings, and birthdays inevitably involve the preparation of food. Most of these dishes have been defined and shaped by the seasonal offerings. From the beginning of Chinese civilization, the taste of the gastronomical calendar was determined largely by the land and its products.

This culinary agenda was established in ancient China. Archeological records dating back to the Sung dynasty (960–1279) contain exhaustive descriptions of the seasonal foods, confirming their importance in early China. In his essay on food during the Sung dynasty in *Food in Chinese Culture*, edited by K. C. Chang, Michael Freeman further confirms this fact:

For country folk, the seasonal markers were, of course, changing tasks: plowing, seeding, transplanting, harvesting, and so on, through the year. But for the city dweller, work was not seasonal, or at least far less so, so that time was marked by the cycle of fruits and vegetables available in the markets and by the special foods consumed at festivals.

At the time of the Ch'ing-ming festival, fifteen days after the spring equinox, the people of [the ancient capital] Kaifeng [in eastern China] made jujube swallows with dough and strung them on willow branches above their doors. . . . As summer approached, apricots and cherries appeared in the market. . . . Autumn was also the best time for jujubes [red dates]. . . . As winter arrived, the people of Kaifeng began to eat preserved ginger, goose pears, quince, and crabs and clams. Time and, thus, memory was suffused with impressions of food.

The cycle continues, and these same seasonal, festival foods are prepared today just as they were in ancient China. The stories behind many of these dishes are part of the legacy of age-old customs and traditions. They serve as a valuable insight into the cultural heritage of the Chinese. Many of them are recounted on the following pages, and I hope they will provide further understanding of China and its people.

The seasonal holiday dishes that are presented in the first menu in each section of this book not only define the Chinese calendar, they illustrate the basic tenets of classic Chinese cuisine. These traditional foods also serve as a springboard for the innovative recipes that follow.

For any cook, a firm grasp of the fundamentals of a cuisine is necessary before one can begin to create new recipes. Just as a French chef should fully comprehend classic French cooking before embarking on nouvelle cuisine, so too must a Chinese cook be familiar with his own classic roots before delving into culinary invention.

The new recipes represent a marked departure from classic Chinese cuisine. Some involve combining traditional Chinese cooking methods with our own local, seasonal ingredients. Others are the product of a fusion of French ingredients and technique with other ethnic influences. These dishes may be considered "new," but they all adhere to the basic philosophy of classic Chinese cooking: use the freshest available ingredients with seasonings and cooking methods that accentuate and complement their inherent flavors.

These dishes also exemplify a creative culinary trend that is at its peak in this country and is now making its way into China as well. As foreign products are being introduced to all parts of China, chefs are using their training and imagination to produce unusual dishes that further expand the repertory of Chinese cuisine.

Chinese Seasons represents not only an effort to pay homage to past traditions and customs but also an attempt to celebrate and anticipate those of the present and future.

Nina Simonds
Spring 1986

A Note of Explanation

The Chinese seasonal gastronomic calendar unfolds on the following pages. The book begins with spring and Ch'ing Ming, or the Festival of Pure Brightness, and then proceeds through summer and fall to winter, which culminates in Chinese New Year and the Lantern Festival.

Since it is assumed that this book will be used primarily by cooks living in the United States and Canada, the division of seasons and their respective Chinese festivals incorporates influences from both Chinese and Western calendars. This consideration is mainly due to the availability of seasonal ingredients. Although Chinese New Year and the Lantern Festival are regarded as spring holidays in China, they occur in late January and early February, when winter products predominate. Accordingly, both holidays are included in the winter section of this book.

Each of the four seasonal sections opens with an introduction to the most significant Chinese festival of that season, describing the holiday's history, customs, and rituals. The first menu represents a selection of traditional holiday specialties combined with classic seasonal dishes. The second menu, which digresses from the traditional repertory of Chinese classics, features local seasonal foods coupled with Chinese and French ingredients and techniques.

Although the menus in each chapter conform to the basic guidelines used by Chinese cooks in general meal planning, I have adapted the traditional menu format to a cross between a banquet and a home-style meal. Whereas a traditional Chinese banquet menu might easily contain twelve to fourteen dishes, most festival meals in this book involve the preparation of three to four recipes. This lighter menu format reflects the simplicity usually desired by the Western home cook, while maintaining the elegance and refinement associated with a banquet menu. The menus are by no means absolute, and cooks should feel free to mix and match, inserting appropriate dishes from other sections of the book to create new meals.

The third part of each seasonal section contains recipes for dishes appropriate for that time and season. For summer, an extensive selection of salad dishes is offered, while varied casserole and soup recipes are presented for wintertime eating. These dishes also may be inserted, where appropriate, in the menus. On the other hand, many are admirably suited to being served simply by themselves.

The Chinese Seasonal Calendar

The traditional Chinese calendar is lunar-based. As in the West, twelve moons define the twelve months of the year. Chinese holidays fall on certain days, depending on the lunar cycle, and the Gregorian date usually varies each year. Accordingly, Chinese New Year, which is observed on the first day of the first lunar month of the year, may fall anywhere from January 26 to February 6. (During a Chinese leap year, the date may be even later.)

Chinese seasons, conversely, are ruled by the sun. In China, the annual calendar is divided into twenty-four fifteen-day intervals, which make up the agricultural calendar. The primary events of this calendar are the two solstices and two equinoxes, and the seasons begin exactly midway between the solstices and equinoxes: August 8 marks the beginning of autumn on the Chinese seasonal calendar (as compared to September 22 on the Western calendar); and November 8, rather than December 21, heralds the arrival of winter.

Obviously, the Chinese calendar differs quite a bit from ours. In parts of China that lie in the temperate zones, the actual climatic conditions and temperatures are at odds with those of the traditional Chinese seasonal cycle. Still, the ancient Chinese believed that this calendar reinforced the interrelationship between man and nature, and it is observed today with as much conviction as it was in earlier times.

The twenty-four cycles, which are known as "joints and breadths," are outlined in the Chinese agricultural almanac. As shown in this chart, cycles with similar conditions share the same description, and for a few, no description is available.

English Name		Chinese Name
Spring's Beginning		Li Ch'un
Rain Water		Yu Shui
Awakening of Insects	春	Ching Che
Division of Spring		Ch'un Fen
Pure Brightness		Ch'ing Ming
Grain Rain		Ku Yu
Summer's Beginning		Li Hsia
Ripening Grain		Hsiao Man
Grain in Beard	夏	Mang Chung
Arrival of Summer		Hsia Chih
Slight Heat		Hsiao Shu
Great Heat		Da Shu
Autumn's Beginning		Li Ch'iu
Stopping of Heat		Ch'u Shu
White Dew	秋	Pai Lu
Autumn Equinox		Ch'iu Fen
Cold Dew		Han Lu
Frost's Descent		Shuang Chiang
Winter's Beginning		Li Tung
Slight Snow		Hsiao Hsueh
Great Snow	冬	Da Hsueh
Winter Solstice		Tung Chih
Slight Cold		Hsiao Han
Great Cold		Da Han

Gregorian Calendar	Description
February 5	If the day is clear and bright, plowing will be easy.
February 20	There should be no more snow, but rain showers may be expected.
March 7	The first thunder, due on this day, will wake the hibernating dragon.
March 22	For the health of the countryside, rain should fall.
April 6	If south winds blow, the harvest will be successful.
April 21	This is the right time to sow wheat.
May 6	The beginning of hot weather.
May 22	The winter wheat may be harvested soon.
June 7	If the rain tarries, prayers are said, lest the ground become too dry.
June 22	The garlic is ripe and should be picked.
July 8 July 24	If the heat is not great during this time, the grain will not be of good quality.
August 8 August 24	Should rain fall on Ch'u Shu, it will be hard to pick the crops.
September 8	The dry weather begins.
September 24	If white clouds are abundant, there will be a good harvest for late crops.
October 9	The first leaves will fall from the trees.
October 24	The first film of ice.
November 8	
November 23	
December 7	
December 22	The Emperor makes a sacrifice at the Temple of Heaven.
January 6	
January 21	

SPRING

● ● ● ● ● ● ● ● ● ● ● ● ● ● ● ● ●

春

The first thunder

due on this day

will wake

the hibernating dragon

. . . .

CH'ING MING, OR THE FESTIVAL OF PURE BRIGHTNESS

Traditionally, the New Year's Festival is the first holiday that heralds the advent of spring. In many parts of China, however, as well as in the Western Hemisphere, wintry conditions still prevail. For this reason, Ch'ing Ming, or the Festival of Pure Brightness, which is celebrated on the third day of the third moon, or one hundred sixty days after the winter solstice, is much more evocative of spring.

In ancient China, this holiday, which is also known as the First Feast of the Dead, was considered a pagan celebration of life's renewal. Youths and maidens bedecked with garlands of flowers danced together across the countryside.

Ch'ing Ming's origin, like Easter, centers around the resurrection of the dead. The Chinese believe that the departed are still very much alive, exerting an influence over the destinies of the living and the forces of nature. These souls remain near their ancestral gravestones. On this holiday, the dead are honored: their graves are tidied and both sumptuous and humble offerings are presented to win their favor.

Farmers often set out a few bowls of rice with the following appeal: "Your children have come today with gifts of food. Forgive us that we cannot offer you a rich repast. Forgive and come eat."

Some families' offerings are more elaborate: freshly killed whole chickens braised in soy sauce and bowls brimming with the choicest fruits of the season are among the customary gifts. Once these delicacies are placed on the tombs, and the necessary incantations made, many Chinese sample these offerings, picnicking informally near the graves. Others prefer to return home with their food to enjoy a meal traditionally dedicated to the spirit of reunion.

Ch'ing Ming also precedes, by one day, the holiday known as the Cold Foods Festival, or the Holiday of Prohibited Smoke, and the two occasions are usually celebrated at the same time. No fires are lit on the day of the Cold Foods Festival; the holiday food is prepared beforehand and eaten at room temperature.

This custom is said to have originated during the Chou dynasty, around 635 B.C. A minister named Chieh Tzu-t'ui, after faithfully serving the state of Chin, was overlooked by the reigning duke. Angered and humiliated, Chieh retired from office and fled to the country. Messengers were sent to retrieve him, but they failed to find him. In desperation, they set fire to the woods in an effort to smoke Chieh out. Once the fire had receded, they discovered Chieh's body near a grove of destroyed willows. Overcome with grief, the people built a temple in Chieh's honor and buried him on the mountainside.

In deference to Chieh's memory, on the appointed day each year, the stoves in many Chinese households remain unlit. Assorted cold, stir-fried foods wrapped in pancakes, which are called *amoy popia* in eastern China, are the traditional holiday dish. Some families also hang a willow branch above the front door and at various spots in the house. It is believed to be a good omen, warding off evil influences and wicked spirits.

MENU I

Red-Cooked Chicken Wings

Spicy Sichuan Cucumbers

Amoy Popia

Red-Cooked Chicken Wings

紅燒栗子鷄

3 pounds chicken wings

Red-Cooking Mixture
1 cup soy sauce
½ cup rice wine
3 to 4 cups water
3 tablespoons sugar
6 pieces dried orange peel, about 3 inches long and 1 inch wide
2 cinnamon sticks

1 tablespoon sesame oil

This classic dish, which is enjoyed all over China, is ideal for picnics or buffets. The rich, soy sauce–based braising mixture not only shades the food a handsome mahogany color but preserves it as well. Besides chicken wings, almost any food — such as a whole chicken, pork loin, beef brisket, hard-boiled eggs, bean curd, or chicken livers — can be cooked in the same manner. The braising mixture may be replenished and reused over and over again.

1 Rinse the chicken wings lightly and drain thoroughly. Using a sharp knife, cut off the wing tips.

2 In a large, heavy pot, combine all the ingredients of the **red-cooking mixture** and stir to dissolve the sugar. Heat until boiling. Reduce the heat to medium and simmer for about 30 minutes, uncovered.

3 Add the chicken wings and simmer them for 45 minutes, uncovered, over medium-low heat, stirring occasionally. Turn off the heat and let the chicken wings stand in the cooking liquid until they have cooled to room temperature. Remove with a slotted spoon and toss lightly in the sesame oil. Serve at room temperature or chilled. *Serves six.*

春

Spicy Sichuan Cucumbers

麻
辣
黃
瓜

1½ pounds pickling, Kirby, or
gourmet seedless cucumbers
1 tablespoon salt

Spicy Sichuan Dressing
½ cup sesame oil
1 teaspoon Sichuan
peppercorns
6 dried red chili peppers, cut
into ¼-inch lengths and
seeds removed
4 strips dried orange or
tangerine peel, about 1½
inches long and ½ to 1 inch
wide
6 cloves garlic, thinly sliced
2 tablespoons Chinese black
vinegar
1½ tablespoons sugar

In Sichuan province, pickles such as these spicy cucumbers are made with the pungent seasonings of red pepper, orange peel, and Sichuan peppercorns. The cucumbers will keep for at least a week if refrigerated, but they do intensify in flavor. Daikon radishes, carrots, and zucchini can also be preserved in the same manner, all with excellent results.

1 Rinse the cucumbers lightly and drain thoroughly. Trim the ends and cut each cucumber in half lengthwise. Using a spoon, scoop out the seeds and discard. Cut each half lengthwise into slices about ¼ inch thick and 3 inches long. Place the slices in a mixing bowl, add the salt, and toss to coat. Let stand for 1 hour at room temperature and pour off any water that has accumulated. Lightly rinse the cucumbers in cold water, drain thoroughly, and pat dry. Place the slices in a bowl. Meanwhile, assemble the ingredients for the spicy Sichuan dressing.

2 To make the **spicy Sichuan dressing**: Heat a wok or a heavy saucepan, add the sesame oil, and heat until smoking. Add the Sichuan peppercorns, chili peppers, and dried orange peel. Remove the pan from the heat and cover. Let stand for 20 minutes. Strain the oil, removing the seasonings and pressing them to extract as much oil as possible. Discard the seasonings and mix the oil with the sliced garlic, black vinegar, and sugar. Stir to dissolve the sugar.

3 Add the dressing to the cucumber slices, toss lightly to coat them, cover with plastic wrap, and chill for 8 hours before serving, tossing occasionally. The cucumbers will keep for up to a week in the refrigerator, but the spiciness will increase with age. *Serves six.*

Amoy Popia

春
捲

18 Shanghai spring roll
  wrappers or *lumpia* skins
½ cup coarsely chopped
  peanuts
1 tablespoon sugar
½ cup hoisin sauce
1 recipe Stir-Fried Vegetables
1 recipe Stir-Fried Shrimp
1 recipe Stir-Fried Pork (page
  10)

Amoy popia *is an unusual name for a type of multi-filling spring roll dish served in eastern China. The* amoy *in the name stands for the capital city of the eastern province Fujian, and the* popia *refers to the thin, lacy wrapper — otherwise known as a spring roll wrapper or* lumpia *skin. Unlike the more familiar deep-fried spring rolls, the skins for* amoy popia *are steamed. This version incorporates three separate stir-fried mixtures, which are then combined and wrapped in the spring roll wrappers. For those less ambitious souls, one or two of the stir-fried mixtures may suffice.*

1 Separate the spring roll wrappers and arrange them, slightly fanned out, on a heat-proof plate. Cover with a damp cloth until 10 minutes before serving.

2 In a small bowl, combine the chopped nuts and the sugar. Place the hoisin sauce in a small serving bowl, next to the peanuts.

3 Place the plate containing the wrappers in a steamer tray and cover. Fill a wok with water level with the bottom edge of the steamer tray and heat until boiling. Place the steamer tray over the boiling water and steam the wrappers for 10 minutes. Keep covered until ready to serve.

4 Prepare one or all of the stir-fried mixtures. To serve, arrange them on the table with the wrappers, the peanuts, and the hoisin sauce. Each diner places a wrapper on his plate, spreads it with some of the hoisin sauce, and sprinkles it with the peanuts. A heaping tablespoon of vegetable, shrimp, or pork mixture is placed in the center, rolled up, and eaten with the fingers. ***Serves six.***

Stir-Fried Vegetables

1 small head Chinese cabbage
  (Napa), weighing about 1
  pound
4 or 5 medium-sized carrots,
  peeled and cut into
  matchstick-size shreds

1 Remove the core and any wilted or tough outer leaves from the cabbage and cut the leaves into matchstick-size shreds. Prepare the vegetable seasonings and the vegetable sauce.

Vegetable Seasonings
1 tablespoon minced garlic
3 tablespoons minced dried
  daikon radish (Chinese
  turnip), rinsed lightly and
  drained

1 tablespoon rice wine
  (optional)

Vegetable Sauce
¾ teaspoon salt
2 tablespoons rice wine
1 teaspoon sugar
3 tablespoons chicken broth
1 teaspoon cornstarch

3 tablespoons safflower or
  corn oil

2 Heat a wok, add the oil, and heat until very hot. Add the **vegetable seasonings** and stir-fry for about 15 seconds, until fragrant. Add the cabbage shreds and carrots, and stir-fry over high heat for 1½ minutes, until slightly tender. (Add the tablespoon of rice wine if the mixture is too dry.) Add the **vegetable sauce** and toss lightly until it thickens. Transfer the mixture to a serving platter and serve with the wrappers and the other stir-fried dishes.

. . . .

Stir-Fried Shrimp

1½ pounds medium raw
  shrimp, peeled

Shrimp Marinade
2 slices gingerroot, smashed
  lightly with the flat side of a
  cleaver
1½ tablespoons rice wine
½ teaspoon sesame oil

2 teaspoons minced
  gingerroot
3 cups thinly sliced water
  chestnuts, blanched briefly
  in boiling water, refreshed
  in cold water, and drained
  thoroughly
3 large eggs, lightly beaten

Shrimp Sauce
1 teaspoon salt
1 teaspoon sesame oil
½ teaspoon sugar
½ teaspoon freshly ground
  white pepper
3 tablespoons chicken broth
1 teaspoon cornstarch

¼ cup safflower or corn oil

1 Score each shrimp along the length of the back and remove the vein. The scoring will allow the shrimp to "butterfly" when cooked. Rinse the shrimp and drain thoroughly. Wrap the shrimp in a linen dishtowel and squeeze out as much moisture as possible. Place the shrimp in a bowl. Prepare the **shrimp marinade** by squeezing the gingerroot slices in the rice wine and sesame oil repeatedly for several minutes to impart the flavor. Add the marinade to the shrimp, toss lightly to coat, and let stand for 20 minutes. Discard the gingerroot slices and drain the shrimp.

2 To prepare the egg sheets, rub a nonstick frying pan or a well-seasoned wok with an oil-soaked paper towel. Heat the pan until a few drops of water sprinkled on the surface evaporate immediately. Pour a quarter of the beaten eggs into the pan and tilt the pan so that a thin pancake is formed. Cook until the pancake is light golden; then flip it over. Cook for a few seconds and remove. Prepare three more egg sheets in the same manner. Cut the egg sheets into matchstick-size shreds. Prepare the shrimp sauce.

3 Heat a wok, add the oil, and heat until very hot. Add the shrimp and toss lightly over high heat until the shrimp curl and change color. Remove and drain. Remove all but 3 tablespoons of oil from the pan.

4 Reheat the oil and add the minced gingerroot. Stir-fry for 10 seconds, until fragrant. Add the sliced water chestnuts and stir-fry for 15 seconds. Add the **shrimp sauce** and toss lightly until the mixture starts to thicken. Add the shredded egg sheets and the cooked shrimp. Toss lightly to coat with the sauce and transfer to a platter. Serve with the wrappers and the other stir-fried dishes.

. . . .

Stir-Fried Pork

1½ pounds boneless center-cut pork loin

Pork Marinade
1 tablespoon soy sauce
1 tablespoon rice wine
1 teaspoon sesame oil
1 tablespoon water
1½ teaspoons cornstarch

8 dried Chinese black mushrooms, softened in hot water, stems removed, and caps shredded
4 cups leek or scallion greens, cut into matchstick-size shreds
6 cups fresh bean sprouts, rinsed lightly and drained thoroughly

Pork Sauce
1½ tablespoons soy sauce
1 tablespoon rice wine
1 teaspoon sesame oil
½ teaspoon sugar
3 tablespoons chicken broth
1 teaspoon cornstarch

½ cup safflower or corn oil

1 Remove any fat or gristle from the pork loin. Cut the pork, across the grain, into paper-thin slices, and cut the slices into matchstick-size shreds. Place the shreds in a bowl, add the ingredients of the **pork marinade,** toss lightly, and let marinate for 20 minutes. Prepare the pork sauce.

2 Heat a wok and add the oil. Heat until very hot, add the pork loin, and stir-fry over high heat, stirring constantly, until the shreds change color and separate. Remove with a slotted spoon and drain. Remove all but 3 tablespoons of oil from the pan.

3 Reheat the oil until very hot. Add the black mushrooms and stir-fry for about 30 seconds, until fragrant. Add the shredded leeks or scallions and stir-fry for about 1 minute, or until just tender. Add the bean sprouts and continue stir-frying over high heat for 30 seconds. Add the **pork sauce** and toss lightly until the sauce thickens. Transfer to a platter and serve with the wrappers and the other stir-fried dishes.

MENU II

Tea-and-Anise-Flavored Chicken Livers

Steamed Asparagus in a Ginger-Lemon Dressing

Shredded Ham and Chicken in a Light Mustard Dressing with Pancakes

Loquats and Strawberries Sweetened with Plum Wine

Tea-and-Anise-Flavored Chicken Livers

1½ pounds fresh chicken livers

Anise-Tea Mixture
6 cups water
½ cup China black tea leaves, tied up in a square of cheesecloth
¼ cup rice wine
¼ cup soy sauce
4 whole star anise, smashed lightly with the flat side of a cleaver
6 slices gingerroot, smashed lightly with the flat side of a cleaver

This recipe is a take-off on the classic dish known as "tea eggs." In the traditional dish, hard-boiled eggs are cooked in the flavorful braising mixture. In this adaptation, chicken livers are used. The tea and soy sauce in the cooking mixture color, flavor, and preserve the livers. An unusual variation of this dish may be made by using hard-boiled quail eggs. Fresh quail eggs are available at many well-stocked Chinese supermarkets; their flavor is preferable to that of the canned variety, which tend to have a very strong, gamy flavor.

1 Drain the chicken livers and rinse lightly. Drain again. Using a sharp cleaver or knife, separate at the natural division. Heat 2 quarts of water until boiling and blanch the livers in the water for about 2 minutes. Remove and drain. Discard the water.

2 In a heavy pot, combine the ingredients of the **anise-tea mixture.** Heat until boiling and reduce the heat to low. Simmer 20 minutes, uncovered, so that the flavors will blend. Add the chicken livers; once the liquid reaches a boil, continue simmering for 15 minutes. Remove the pan from the heat and let the livers cool in the anise-tea mixture. When they are cool, remove the livers from the liquid and cut them into thin slices. Serve at room temperature or cold. *Serves six.*

Note
You may reuse the anise-tea mixture; it will keep indefinitely in the refrigerator. The seasonings should be replenished with every other use.

Steamed Asparagus in a Ginger-Lemon Dressing

3 pounds fresh, tender
asparagus

Ginger-Lemon Dressing
1 tablespoon finely grated
gingerroot
⅓ cup freshly squeezed
lemon juice
⅔ cup safflower or corn oil
1 tablespoon sesame oil
1 teaspoon salt
¼ teaspoon freshly ground
white pepper

Here is a vegetable dish very much in keeping with the spirit of this spring festival. The ginger-lemon dressing is beautifully seasoned to accent the fresh, delicate flavor of the asparagus. Other vegetables such as sun chokes, broccoli, and cauliflower would also be complemented by this delicate dressing.

1 Snap off the tough stem ends of the asparagus and rinse the stalks lightly. Drain well. Line a steamer tray with cheesecloth, a wet linen dishtowel, or parchment paper and arrange the asparagus in the tray. Cover.

2 To prepare the **ginger-lemon dressing,** place the gingerroot and lemon juice in a bowl. Slowly, in a thin stream, add the oil, beating vigorously with a whisk or a fork. As soon as the mixture starts to emulsify, add the oil more quickly. Fold in the sesame oil, salt, and pepper.

3 Fill a wok with water level with the bottom edge of the steamer tray and heat until boiling. Place the steamer tray containing the asparagus on top and steam for 9 to 10 minutes, or until the asparagus are just tender. While the asparagus are still hot, toss them lightly in the ginger-lemon dressing. Chill briefly before serving, or serve at room temperature. ***Serves six.***

Shredded Ham and Chicken in a Light Mustard Dressing with Pancakes

2 cups cooked chicken breast meat cut into matchstick-size shreds

1½ cups cooked ham cut into matchstick-size shreds

2 cups shredded carrots

1 cup shredded celery

2 cups fresh bean sprouts, rinsed lightly and drained thoroughly

Mustard Sauce

1 tablespoon mustard powder

2 tablespoons hot water

½ cup plum sauce

3 tablespoons clear rice vinegar

2 tablespoons sesame oil

1 tablespoon soy sauce

1 teaspoon salt

1 tablespoon sugar

1 recipe Mandarin pancakes (page 40), optional

This delectable salad of shredded ham and chicken may be served wrapped in Mandarin pancakes or by itself. The spicy plum and mustard sauce complements the smoky flavor of the ham and delicate taste of the chicken. If you take this dish on a picnic, carry the dressing separately and add it to the salad just prior to serving.

1 Arrange the chicken, ham, carrots, celery, and bean sprouts in separate concentric circles or piles to form a decorative pattern on a large platter.

2 To prepare the **mustard sauce,** begin by mixing the powdered mustard and hot water to form a smooth paste. Cover and let stand for 10 minutes. (This will bring out the flavor of the mustard.) Add the remaining ingredients and mix to form a smooth sauce. Transfer the sauce to a decorative serving dish. Before serving, add the mustard sauce to the salad and toss all the ingredients lightly to coat. Spoon some of the mixture into a Mandarin pancake, roll up, and eat. You may also serve the salad without the pancakes with the mustard sauce poured on each serving. *Serves six.*

Loquats and Strawberries Sweetened with Plum Wine

2 15-ounce cans loquats in
  syrup
1 quart fresh, ripe
  strawberries
1 cup plum wine
¼ cup finely minced or
  shredded candied
  gingerroot

Fruit is always served at the end of a formal Chinese meal, and this refreshing salad is a fitting ending to this holiday menu. Any cut-up ripe, fresh fruit may be substituted for the strawberries, and arbutus (otherwise known as Chinese strawberries) or lychees may replace the loquats. All are available in syrup in Chinese supermarkets. The combination of fresh and preserved fruit, both Western and Chinese, gives the dish an unusual yet pleasing flavor.

Place the loquats, with their syrup, in a bowl. (If they are very big, cut them in half crosswise.) Hull the strawberries, cutting away any bad spots. Rinse lightly and drain. Cut the larger strawberries in half and place in a bowl with the loquats. (If the strawberries are not very ripe, add sugar to taste.) Add the plum wine and toss. Let macerate for 1 hour, tossing occasionally. Serve in bowls placed over crushed ice and sprinkle the fruit with candied gingerroot. **Serves six.**

BIRTHDAYS

For most cultures, springtime symbolizes rebirth and renewal. For the Chinese, the same belief exists. On New Year's Day, a holiday that signals the coming of spring, all Chinese informally celebrate their birthdays as well. They acknowledge the passage of another year and increase their ages accordingly.

As an individual ages in China, birthdays become a more noted event. The elderly command more respect as they grow older, and birthday festivities become more elaborate with the passing years. The sixtieth birthday is considered a milestone, and usually some type of elaborate banquet is planned. From then on, every ten years, birthdays are commemorated with increasing fanfare.

In ancient China, the infant mortality rate was so high that a newborn baby was not even considered a bona fide member of society. Still, a birth, particularly that of a boy, was cause for joyous celebration. Red-dyed eggs were sent to relatives and friends, announcing the baby's arrival. As soon as the infant could be taken out, it was brought to a temple and presented with offerings, to ensure the favor of the gods. The first official birthday was observed only at the end of one month.

For this first birthday, known as *man yue*, or "full month," relatives and friends, bearing gifts of money, clothing, and food, would gather to feast on longevity noodles and other delicacies. Everyone would pause to admire the mother and child.

Another traditional activity was *man ko*, or "filling of the mouth." The maternal grandmother would carry a basket containing steamed breads in the shape of the Chinese character for happiness. She would then hold several of the buns while the mother of the newborn child took generous bitefuls and, in doing so, filled her mouth to capacity with "happiness." In some parts of China, particularly in the south, a steamed fresh or salty duck egg was given to the baby so that it would inherit some of the qualities of the "red" yolk — specifically those of enthusiasm and diligence.

No further special notice was then taken of a birthday until a man or a woman was wed. In ancient China, the traditional age of betrothal was sixteen for a man and fourteen for a woman. Birthdays then assumed a greater importance and parents-in-law sent gifts of clothing and food.

The most important birthdays for a man were at the ages of twenty-one, thirty-one, and the other odd numbers that marked the beginning of a decade. For a woman, the even numbers at the opening of a decade were observed. On these occasions, close relatives and friends gathered to eat and drink.

Many of the old birthday customs are still observed today. New Year's Day is the universal birthday for all Chinese, since the holiday marks the passage of one year and the arrival of the next. On this day, according to custom, children bow low before their parents, out of respect. Some buy sweetmeats of dried fruit, boil them in water, and present the fragrant liquid as an offering for their parents to drink.

The sixtieth and seventieth birthdays customarily are major affairs when the entire family gathers with friends at home or in a restaurant for a celebration banquet. Longevity noodles are an essential part of the birthday feast. The noodles, which are long and white, suggest a wish that the person may live as long a life as the noodles and have hair as white. Steamed buns, in the shape of a peach and tinted a rosy color, are also presented, since they symbolize the magic peaches of immortality. And for the day, the birthday person is given the temporary title of Long Life God.

春

MENU I

Spicy Coin-Shaped Roasted Pork

Steamed Whole Fish with Black Bean Sauce

Stir-Fried Noodles with Chicken and Leeks

Longevity Buns

Spicy Coin-Shaped Roasted Pork

燒
金
錢
肉

2½ pounds center-cut pork
  loin, or pork tenderloin

Pork Marinade
3 tablespoons sweet bean
  sauce
1 teaspoon chili paste
3 tablespoons soy sauce
2 tablespoons rice wine
1 teaspoon sesame oil
1½ tablespoons sugar
1 tablespoon minced
  gingerroot
1 tablespoon minced garlic

10 to 12 bamboo skewers,
  about 10 inches long

*A sixtieth birthday is real cause for celebration in the
Orient, and when my Chinese surrogate mother's father
approached that milestone a sumptuous banquet was
planned. It was an extraordinary twelve-course meal, and
several dishes remain firmly etched in my memory. This
spicy dish, which carries with it a wish for prosperity, is
one of them.*

1 Trim any fat or gristle from the pork and discard.
Cut the meat lengthwise, with the grain, into long
strips 2 to 3 inches wide. Cut, across the grain, into
slices about ¼ inch thick. Place the slices in a bowl.
Prepare the **pork marinade** by mixing the ingredients together to form a smooth paste. Add the marinade to the pork slices and toss lightly to coat. Let
marinate for at least 1 hour at room temperature, or
overnight in the refrigerator, if possible. Soak the
bamboo skewers in cold water to cover for 1 hour.

2 Preheat the oven to 425 degrees, or heat the
broiler. Loosely thread the pork slices onto the
skewers. Place on a baking sheet and bake, turning
several times and basting with the marinade, for 20
minutes, or until the outside of the meat is dark
brown and the inside is cooked. Alternatively, broil
the meat for 10 minutes on each side. Serve with
steamed buns (page 68). ***Serves six.***

Steamed Whole Fish with Black Bean Sauce

1 whole 3- to 3½-pound firm-
fleshed fish, such as sea
bass, red snapper, pike, lake
trout, or baby haddock

Fish Marinade
2 tablespoons rice wine
1 teaspoon salt
2 slices gingerroot, smashed
lightly with the flat side of a
cleaver

½ pound ground pork

Meat Seasonings
1 tablespoon soy sauce
1 tablespoon rice wine
1 teaspoon sesame oil

Fish Seasonings
2 tablespoons fermented black
beans, rinsed, drained, and
minced
2 tablespoons minced
scallions
1 tablespoon minced garlic

Fish Sauce
6 tablespoons chicken broth
2 tablespoons soy sauce
2 tablespoons rice wine
1 teaspoon sugar
1½ teaspoons cornstarch

2 tablespoons safflower or
corn oil

*For the Chinese, a whole fish represents bounty and
abundance and it is considered de rigueur for any special
occasion, particularly a birthday or wedding. The head of
the fish, as custom dictates, always faces the guest of
honor. If a whole fish is unavailable, fillets may be substituted and the cooking time decreased accordingly.*

1 Ask the fishmonger to clean the fish through the
gills, leaving the head and tail intact. Rinse the fish
lightly and pat dry. Pinch the gingerroot slices in
the **fish marinade** repeatedly for several minutes to
impart the flavor. Holding the cleaver at a 45-degree
angle to the fish, make long scores crosswise, at in-
vervals of an inch, on one side of the fish. Rub the
fish marinade into the scores and all over the fish.
Let marinate for 20 minutes. Place the ground pork
in a bowl, add the **meat seasonings,** toss lightly,
and let stand for 20 minutes. Prepare the fish seasonings and the fish sauce.

2 Place the fish on a heat-proof platter that will fit
in your steamer, or in a steamer tray lined with aluminum foil. Heat a wok, add 1 tablespoon of oil,
and heat until very hot. Add the ground pork and
cook, stirring constantly to separate the meat.
When the meat changes color, remove it and drain.
Reheat the pan, add the other tablespoon of oil,
and heat until very hot. Add the **fish seasonings**
and stir-fry for about 10 seconds, until fragrant;
then add the **fish sauce.** Cook the mixture, stirring
constantly, until thick. Add the cooked meat, toss
lightly, and spoon the sauce over the fish.

3 Fill a wok with water level with the bottom edge
of the steamer tray and heat until boiling. Place the
fish in the tray over the water and cover. Steam for
15 to 20 minutes, until the fish meat flakes when
prodded with a fork. Transfer to a platter and
serve. ***Serves six.***

Stir-Fried Noodles with Chicken and Leeks

鷄
肉
炒
麵

1½ pounds boneless chicken breast meat, skin removed

Chicken Marinade
1½ tablespoons soy sauce
1½ tablespoons rice wine
1 teaspoon sesame oil
1½ teaspoons cornstarch
1 tablespoon water

½ cup safflower or corn oil
½ pound thin egg noodle clusters, such as vermicelli
1 teaspoon sesame oil

Minced Seasonings
1 tablespoon minced garlic
1 tablespoon minced gingerroot

10 dried Chinese black mushrooms, softened in hot water, stems removed, and caps shredded
3 cups leeks or Chinese chives, cut into julienne strips about 1½ inches long
3 cups fresh bean sprouts, rinsed lightly and drained thoroughly

Noodle Sauce
1½ cups chicken broth
3 tablespoons soy sauce
2 tablespoons rice wine
1 teaspoon sesame oil
1 teaspoon sugar
¼ teaspoon freshly ground black pepper
1 teaspoon cornstarch

In the West, a birthday party would be incomplete without the presentation of a birthday cake. In the Orient, a huge platter of noodles assumes the role of a birthday cake. Noodles symbolize longevity, and it would be inexcusable for a Chinese birthday menu not to include a noodle dish. This one is a type of lo mein: the soft, cooked noodles are tossed in a sauce studded with shredded meat and assorted vegetables. Beef or pork may be substituted for the chicken.

1 Remove any fat or gristle from the chicken and cut the meat into matchstick-size shreds, about 1½ inches long and ¼ inch thick. Place in a bowl, add the **chicken marinade,** toss lightly to coat, and let marinate for 20 minutes. Prepare the other ingredients, including the minced seasonings and noodle sauce. Place near the stove.

2 Heat until boiling 2 quarts of water with 1 tablespoon of the safflower or corn oil. Add the noodles and cook until just tender, or *al dente,* about 3 to 5 minutes. Drain in a colander. Rinse lightly under warm water, drain thoroughly, and transfer the noodles to a bowl. Add the sesame oil, toss lightly to coat, and set aside.

3 Heat a wok, add the remaining oil, and heat until very hot. Add half the chicken shreds and toss lightly over high heat until the chicken pieces change color and separate, about 3 to 4 minutes. Remove with a slotted spoon and drain. Reheat the oil and stir-fry the remaining chicken shreds, remove, and drain. Remove all but 3 tablespoons of oil from the wok.

4 Heat the oil until very hot. Add the **minced seasonings** and the shredded black mushrooms. Stir-fry over high heat for 10 to 15 seconds, until fragrant. Add the leeks or chives and stir-fry for about 1 minute, or until slightly limp. Add the bean sprouts and the **noodle sauce.** Stir and cook until slightly thickened. Add the cooked noodles and chicken. Toss lightly to coat and transfer to a serving platter. Serve immediately. *Serves six.*

Longevity Buns

Basic Yeast Dough
3 cups all-purpose flour
2 tablespoons sugar
1¼ cups warm water
½ tablespoon active dry yeast
1 tablespoon safflower or corn
  oil

Filling
1 pound chopped pitted dates
2 cups hot water
½ cup unsalted butter, cut
  into eight pieces
1½ tablespoons lemon juice
1 teaspoon vanilla extract
1 teaspoon ground cinnamon

1 teaspoon baking powder
Red food coloring

Longevity buns are so named because they carry with them a wish for a long life. The steamed buns, which are stuffed with a rich date paste, are created in the shape of peaches, a fruit that symbolizes immortality for the Chinese. Longevity buns may be prepared in advance and resteamed for 10 minutes until hot; and they freeze beautifully. They are excellent served as an unusual dessert, as in this birthday menu, or as a snack with tea.

1 To make the **basic yeast dough,** begin by placing the flour in a mixing bowl or on a flat surface, and make a well in the center. Dissolve the sugar in the warm water and add the yeast. Mix gently and let stand for about 10 minutes, until it foams and forms a head. (This is proofing the yeast.) Add the yeast mixture and the oil to the flour. Slowly incorporate the liquid into the flour, mixing to a rough dough. On a lightly floured surface, knead the dough until the mixture is smooth and homogeneous. Place in a lightly greased bowl, cover with a damp cloth, and let rise in a warm place, free from drafts, for 3 to 4 hours, or until tripled in bulk.

2 To make the **filling,** place the dates and the water in a heavy saucepan. Heat until the water is boiling. Turn the heat to low and cook uncovered, stirring occasionally, for 15 to 20 minutes, or until the water has evaporated, leaving a thick paste. Add the butter and continue cooking, stirring constantly, until the mixture comes away from the sides of the pan. Remove the pan from the heat and add the lemon juice, vanilla extract, and cinnamon. Stir to combine the ingredients and chill until cool.

3 Punch down the dough and turn it out onto a lightly floured surface. Flatten the dough, making a slight well in the center, and add the baking powder to the center. Bring up the edges of the dough to enclose the baking powder and pinch to seal. Knead the dough to incorporate the baking powder evenly. Cover with a cloth and let rest for 20 minutes. Form the dough into a long, snakelike roll about 1½ inches in diameter. Cut the roll into twenty-four pieces. With a cut edge down, use your fingers to flatten each piece into a 3-inch circle. The edges should be thinner and the center thicker. Place a heaping tablespoon of the date filling in the center of the dough skin. Gather up the edges to enclose the filling and pinch to seal. Roll the bun into a round ball. Lightly stretch the top of the bun to a point (to form the top of the "peach"), and using a ball of cotton, brush some red food coloring on the bun to create a blush. Lightly score the "peach" lengthwise, from the bottom to the point. Arrange the finished buns, about 1 inch apart, in steamer trays that have been lined with wet cheesecloth or with parchment paper punched with holes. Let rise for 15 minutes. (Freeze any leftover date paste for future use.)

4 Fill a wok with water level with the bottom edge of the steamer tray and heat until boiling. Place one tray of buns over boiling water, cover, and steam over high heat for 15 to 20 minutes, or until the buns are puffed and springy. Steam the remaining buns in the same manner. To reheat, steam the buns for 10 minutes over high heat. *Makes twenty-four buns.*

MENU II

*Composed Salad with Spring Lamb in a
Sesame Vinaigrette*

Spicy Chinese Cioppino

*Steamed Zucchini Noodles with a Spicy
Dressing*

Strawberry-Lychee Ice

Composed Salad with Spring Lamb in a Sesame Vinaigrette

2 pounds boneless leg of lamb, shank portion

Lamb Marinade
1½ tablespoons soy sauce
1 tablespoon rice wine
1 teaspoon sesame oil
½ tablespoon cornstarch

2 heads leafy lettuce, stems removed, rinsed lightly, and drained
6 tablespoons safflower or corn oil
½ cup sesame oil
½ cup minced scallion greens
4 firm tomatoes, peeled, seeded, and chopped
¼ cup wine vinegar or tarragon vinegar
1 teaspoon salt
½ teaspoon freshly ground black pepper
¼ cup minced fresh parsley

This dish imitates the form of a classic Chinese cold platter. There is the vegetable underlayer, the meat or seafood garnish on top, and, finally, some type of spicy dressing. In this case, the ingredients and formula are Chinese, but the dish bears a strong similarity to a nouvelle cuisine warm composed salad. Beef or pork may be substituted for the lamb, and to give the dish more of a Chinese slant, shredded cabbage may be used instead of the leafy lettuce.

1 Trim away any fat or gristle from the lamb, separating the muscles of the meat. Cut, across the grain, into paper-thin slices that are approximately 1½ inches long and 1 inch wide. Place the slices in a bowl, add the **lamb marinade,** toss lightly, and let marinate for at least 20 minutes.

2 Cut the lettuce crosswise into strips about ¼ inch wide. Arrange the strips in mounds on serving plates, leaving a slight depression in the center.

3 Heat a wok or a deep, heavy skillet, and add the oil. Heat until very hot, about 400 degrees. Add half the lamb and cook, stirring constantly, until the meat changes color and the pieces separate. Remove with a slotted spoon and drain. Reheat the oil, add the remaining lamb, and cook, stirring constantly, until the meat changes color and the pieces separate. Remove and drain. Clean out the pan.

4 Reheat the pan, add about 2 tablespoons of the sesame oil, and heat until hot. Add the lamb and toss for about 1 minute. Remove the lamb and arrange it on the serving plates, in the center of the lettuce. Clean the pan thoroughly and dry.

5 Reheat the pan, add the remaining sesame oil, and heat until very hot. Add the scallions and toss lightly until fragrant, about 15 seconds. Add the chopped tomatoes and toss lightly, for about 10 seconds. Add the vinegar and cook, stirring constantly, for about 1 minute, until the liquid is reduced slightly. Add the salt and pepper and stir well. Portion the tomato mixture over the lamb pieces and sprinkle parsley on top. Serve immediately. ***Serves six.***

Spicy Chinese Cioppino

2 tablespoons sesame oil
⅓ cup safflower or corn oil
1 tablespoon minced garlic
1 tablespoon minced
   gingerroot
2 cups chopped onion
¾ chopped green pepper
1 heaping teaspoon chili
   paste, or to taste
1½ cups peeled, seeded, and
   coarsely chopped tomatoes
1 tablespoon tomato paste
2½ cups clam juice
1 cup rice wine
2 teaspoons chopped fresh
   basil
1½ teaspoons salt
½ teaspoon freshly ground
   black pepper

Seafood Marinade
¼ cup rice wine
5 slices gingerroot, smashed
   lightly with the flat side of a
   cleaver

1½ pounds haddock, scrod,
   or red snapper fillets, skins
   removed
1 pound medium raw shrimp,
   peeled and deveined
12 ounces crabmeat, picked
   over to remove any pieces
   of cartilage
½ cup minced fresh parsley
   or coriander (Chinese
   parsley)

Cioppino has always been one of my favorite seafood stews, so it seemed natural to deviate from the classic recipe slightly, adding such Chinese flavorings as sesame oil, chili paste, and gingerroot to create the rendition below. As with any seafood dish, the fish must be absolutely fresh for optimum flavor. If haddock is unavailable, any firm-fleshed meaty fillet will do. This soupy stew is excellent the first time, and even better when reheated on the second and third days.

1 In a 6-quart casserole or Dutch oven, combine the oils and heat until very hot. Add the garlic, gingerroot, onions, green pepper, and chili paste. Sauté for about 10 minutes, until soft. Add the tomatoes, tomato paste, clam juice, rice wine, basil, salt, and pepper, and bring to a boil. Reduce the heat to low and simmer, uncovered, for 10 to 15 minutes.

2 While the mixture is cooking, combine the **seafood marinade** ingredients and pinch the gingerroot slices repeatedly in the rice wine for several minutes to impart the flavor. Rinse the seafood lightly and drain thoroughly. Cut the fish fillets into pieces about 2 inches square and place them in a bowl. Add half the marinade and toss lightly to coat. Place the shrimp and crabmeat in another bowl, and add the remaining marinade. Toss lightly to coat and let the seafood stand for 10 minutes. Discard the gingerroot slices in the marinade.

4 Add the fish pieces, shrimp, and crabmeat, as well as the marinade, to the tomato mixture. Simmer for 15 minutes, partially covered, over medium-low heat. Remove and ladle into bowls. Sprinkle with the chopped parsley and serve. ***Serves six.***

Steamed Zucchini Noodles with a Spicy Dressing

2 pounds fresh zucchini, ends trimmed, rinsed lightly, and drained thoroughly

Spicy Dressing
¼ cup soy sauce
1 tablespoon rice wine
1 tablespoon clear rice vinegar
2 teaspoons sugar
1 tablespoon minced scallions
1 tablespoon minced garlic
2 tablespoons sesame oil
1 teaspoon chili paste (optional)

The shredded zucchini in this dish resembles jade-green longevity noodles (hence the name), making it a suitable vegetable for this birthday meal. Carrots or sweet potatoes are also excellent shredded, steamed, and served in this spicy dressing.

1 Cut the zucchini, lengthwise, into quarters. Using the shredding disk of a food processor, or a vegetable grinder, cut the zucchini into long, thin shreds. (They may slightly resemble thin vermicelli noodles.) Arrange the "noodles" on a heat-proof plate and place in a steamer tray. Cover the steamer tray.

2 Fill a wok with water level with the bottom edge of the steamer tray and heat until boiling. Place the steamer tray over the water and steam the zucchini for 3 to 5 minutes, or until barely tender. While the zucchini is steaming, prepare the **spicy dressing.** Remove the zucchini and very lightly squeeze out any excess moisture. Transfer the zucchini to a serving dish, add the dressing, and toss lightly to coat. Serve warm. Alternatively, let the zucchini marinate in the dressing, toss lightly occasionally (draining out any excess moisture), and serve at room temperature. *Serves six.*

Strawberry-Lychee Ice

2 quarts fresh, ripe
  strawberries
2 tablespoons granulated
  sugar, or to taste
1 15-ounce can lychees with
  syrup
⅔ cup Grand Marnier
Ice and rock salt for freezing

Although ice cream — made with milk or cream — is not generally prepared in China, fruit purées, both fresh and frozen, are very popular. For those who prefer a dessert requiring less time and effort than this ice, the strawberry purée with diced lychees may be served simply over crushed ice.

1 Hull the strawberries and rinse lightly. Drain and pat dry. Place the strawberries in a bowl. Drain the lychees, reserving the syrup and adding it to the strawberries. Cut the lychees into large dice and place them in a bowl. Add half the Grand Marnier to the strawberries and half to the lychees. Toss lightly and let the mixtures stand for 1 hour at room temperature.

2 In a food processor fitted with the steel blade, purée the strawberries. Remove and combine with the diced lychees. Prepare an ice cream maker, according to the manufacturer's instructions, with salt and ice. Transfer the strawberry-lychee mixture to the ice cream maker and process until the mixture is firm and slightly stiff. Remove and place briefly in a freezer to further firm up the mixture. Shortly before serving, remove from the freezer to soften. Alternatively, you may freeze the mixture in an ice tray until slightly stiff, remove from the freezer, stir, and freeze again before serving. ***Makes approximately 2 quarts.***

CHINESE ROLL-UPS

Most Americans know them as egg rolls — stout, deep-fried concoctions made of flour-egg-and-water wrappers stuffed with barbecued pork, occasionally shrimp, a generous amount of cabbage, and celery. The classic Chinese rendition, known as a spring roll, is delicately long and thin, made with a lacy flour-and-water skin, and stuffed with a combination of shredded pork, shrimp, Chinese black mushrooms, and bean sprouts. Both dishes — adapted and traditional — are representative of the extensive category of pick-up foods that might best be described as *juan*, or roll-ups. They are small food packages or rolls consisting of meat, seafood, and vegetable fillings wrapped in a thin, crêpe-like skin.

Chinese roll-up dishes are eaten year round, but they are traditionally associated with spring, when vegetables and other fresh products are just coming into their prime season. Deep-fried spring rolls are one of the traditional foods served for Chinese New Year, a holiday that signals the advent of spring. With their slim oblong shape and golden exterior, they are said to resemble a bar of gold, and they imply a wish for prosperity and good luck for the coming year.

Some roll-ups — like the classic Chinese spring roll — are deep-fried until delicately crisp and golden brown. Others are steamed — with a rice-flour, egg-crêpe, or basic flour-and-water skin. Still others may be stir-fried dishes, or layered seafood, meat, and vegetable salads served at room temperature with Mandarin pancakes. The stuffing and skins vary from region to region in China, and they are served as hors d'oeuvres, *dim sum*, or complete meals in themselves.

The Chinese roll-up known in eastern China as *amoy popia* is served on another spring holiday, Ch'ing Ming, or the Festival of Pure Brightness. Lacy flour-and-water wrappers are stuffed with assorted stir-fried meat, seafood, and vegetable fillings. Since no fires are lit on this holiday, the food is all prepared in advance and eaten at room temperature. The skins used for making *amoy popia* (see page 8) are the same as those used by all Chinese in the Orient to make spring rolls, but they are steamed rather than deep-fried. They are exquisitely thin and delicate — unlike most of the standard egg roll skins available in this country.

Most Chinese markets in the Orient have a spring roll maker. He is usually surrounded by piles of freshly made skins. By skillfully manipulating a soft blob of flour-and-water dough in one hand and then rubbing it in a circular motion over the surface of a very well seasoned griddle, he forms a thin skin. It cooks in a matter of seconds, creating a paper-thin wrapper. The dried skins are then peeled off and sold by the pound to customers who use them to make Chinese roll-up dishes.

These same delicate flour-and-water skins are available frozen in this country at most Oriental grocery stores. They may be circular or square and are labeled Shanghai spring roll wrappers or *lumpia* skins. Look for tightly sealed, nonfrosty packages, avoiding those with freezer burn. Once defrosted, the wrappers should be carefully separated and covered with a damp towel to prevent them from drying out. The defrosted wrappers will keep for up to a week in the refrigerator.

Once fried, Shanghai spring roll wrappers tend to be crisper and more delicate than other spring roll wrappers. The more familiar square flour-egg-and-water spring roll wrappers can be found in many supermarket produce sections and are acceptable if the thinner skins are not available. For certain stir-fried dishes, such as *amoy popia* and assorted salads, where the wrappers are steamed, Mandarin pancakes — although much thicker — may be substituted.

Besides flour and water, other ingredients are used for roll-up skins. Whole beaten eggs are often fried to form a thin, crêpe-like skin. Wheat starch, cornstarch, or rice flour is mixed with water to make a batter that is then poured into a mold and steamed, or fried to create a flat sheet. Even a dried skin made from scalding soybean milk, known as a bean milk skin, is frequently favored.

SPRING Roll-ups

Fillings for these dishes are equally varied. Pork, shrimp, bean sprouts, Chinese cabbage (Napa), dried black mushrooms, and Chinese garlic chives are all stuffed into a skin for traditional spring rolls. Cantonese spring rolls may contain a similar mixture, or a variation with chicken, bamboo shoots, and bean sprouts. Vegetarian spring rolls, redolent with sesame oil, are often stuffed with carrots, bean sprouts, dried black mushrooms, and cellophane noodles.

Perhaps one of the greatest advantages of the Chinese roll-up concept is that it readily lends itself to improvisation. Almost any type of meat, seafood, or vegetable may be used in the filling and wrapped in a skin. And some of the finished rolls may be made in advance and reheated, or served at room temperature.

CHINESE ROLL-UPS

Traditional Spring Rolls

Chicken Spring Rolls

Vegetarian Spring Rolls

Cantonese-Style Spring Roll Wrappers

Cantonese-Style Spring Rolls

Mandarin Pancakes

Stir-Fried Beef with Leeks

Spicy Stir-Fried Lamb with Sweet Bean Sauce

Cold Tossed Rainbow Vegetables with Pork

Stuffed Cabbage Rolls

Steamed Egg Rolls

Rice Noodle Wrappers

Rice Noodle Rolls

Traditional Spring Rolls

上海春捲

1 pound boneless center-cut
   pork loin

Pork Marinade
1 tablespoon soy sauce
1 tablespoon rice wine
1 teaspoon sesame oil
1 teaspoon cornstarch
1 teaspoon water

½ pound medium raw
   shrimp, peeled and
   deveined

Shrimp Marinade
1 tablespoon rice wine
½ teaspoon salt
¼ teaspoon sesame oil

6 cups safflower or corn oil

4 cups shredded Chinese
   cabbage (Napa)
3 cups Chinese chives or
   scallion greens, cut into
   1-inch pieces
4 cups fresh bean sprouts,
   rinsed lightly and drained
   thoroughly
2 tablespoons rice wine
6 dried Chinese black
   mushrooms, softened in hot
   water, stems removed, and
   caps shredded

Sauce
1 tablespoon soy sauce
1 tablespoon rice wine
½ teaspoon salt
¼ teaspoon freshly ground
   black pepper
1 teaspoon cornstarch

30 Shanghai spring roll
   wrappers or *lumpia* skins

Paste
¼ cup flour
4 tablespoons water
1 egg, lightly beaten

When I was studying classic Chinese cooking in Taipei in the early 1970s, one of my teachers was a Sichuanese master chef who was equally adept at turning out robust fiery dishes and delicately seasoned ones. He was also a master at making perfect spring rolls. One of his secrets was that he always squeezed the liquid out of the filling before wrapping it in the skins so it would not leak through the wrapper during deep-frying. It is a procedure that I follow to this day. This recipe is an adapted version of that chef's classic. Like many other fried foods, spring rolls may be prepared in advance and reheated in a 350-degree oven for 10 to 12 minutes before serving.

1 Remove any fat or gristle from the pork loin. Cut the meat across the grain into paper-thin slices, and cut the slices into matchstick-size shreds. Place the pork shreds in a bowl, add the **pork marinade,** toss lightly to coat, and let marinate for 15 minutes. Rinse the shrimp, drain, and pat dry. Cut into small dice, place in a bowl, and add the **shrimp marinade.** Toss lightly to coat, and let marinate for 15 minutes. Prepare the sauce and the paste.

2 Heat a wok, add 3 tablespoons of oil, and heat until very hot. Add the Chinese cabbage, and stir-fry until just wilted, about 1½ minutes. Add the Chinese chives or scallions, the bean sprouts, and the 2 tablespoons of rice wine. Stir-fry for another minute over high heat and remove with a handled strainer. Drain off the liquid and spread the mixture out on a tray to cool.

3 Reheat the wok, add 3 tablespoons of oil, and heat until very hot. Add the pork shreds and stir-fry over high heat, stirring constantly until they separate and change color. Remove and drain. Reheat the pan and add 2 tablespoons of oil. Heat until very hot. Add the diced shrimp and toss lightly over high heat until they change color. Remove and drain. Wipe out the pan, add 2 tablespoons of oil, and heat until very hot. Add the shredded black mushrooms and toss lightly over high heat for 30 seconds, until fragrant. Add the cooked pork and shrimp, and the **sauce.** Stir-fry briefly until the sauce has thickened. Remove the mixture and spread out on a platter to cool. Once it is cool, combine it with the cabbage–bean sprout mixture.

4 Arrange one spring roll wrapper flat on a counter, like a diamond. (Cover the others with a damp cloth to prevent them from drying out.) Grab a portion of filling and squeeze out any excess liquid. Place the filling in a line across the lower third of the wrapper, and using your finger, spread some **paste** on the opposite edge. Starting at the nearest point, roll the spring roll wrapper over to completely enclose the filling. Fold in the two sides and continue rolling over so that the last fold seals in the two sides. Press lightly to seal. Repeat for the remaining wrappers and filling.

5 Heat a wok, add the remaining safflower or corn oil (a little less than 5½ cups), and heat to 375 degrees. Add five or six of the spring rolls and deep-fry in the hot oil, turning constantly, until golden brown and crisp. Remove with a slotted spoon and drain on absorbent paper. Continue frying the remaining rolls, drain, and serve with plum sauce and hot mustard. *Makes about thirty rolls.*

Chicken Spring Rolls

鶏絲春捲

1½ pounds boneless chicken
  breast meat, skin removed

Chicken Marinade
1 tablespoon soy sauce
2 tablespoons rice wine
½ teaspoon salt
1½ teaspoons cornstarch

6 cups safflower or corn oil

Minced Seasonings
1 tablespoon minced scallions
2 teaspoons minced
  gingerroot
8 dried Chinese black
  mushrooms, softened in hot
  water to cover, stems
  removed, and caps
  shredded
4 cups fresh bean sprouts,
  rinsed lightly and drained
2 cups matchstick-size shreds
  bamboo shoots, blanched
  briefly in boiling water and
  drained

Sauce
3 tablespoons soy sauce
3 tablespoons rice wine
1½ tablespoons sesame oil
½ teaspoon salt
½ teaspoon freshly ground
  black pepper

20 Shanghai spring roll
  wrappers or *lumpia* skins

Paste
¼ cup flour
4 tablespoons water
1 egg, lightly beaten

In most dim sum *parlors, the Cantonese offer a flavorful variation on the spring roll theme with a delicate stuffing of chicken, bamboo shoots, black mushrooms, and bean sprouts. While serving these elegantly thin rolls, the waiter generally snips them into thirds with sharp scissors and gives them a generous dousing of Worcestershire sauce. The same ritual may be followed before serving these spring rolls. Beef or pork may be substituted for the chicken if desired.*

1 Trim any fat from the chicken meat. Holding a cleaver or a sharp knife parallel to the cutting surface, cut the chicken breasts in half through the thickness. Cut the halves into matchstick-size shreds. Place the shreds in a bowl, add the **chicken marinade,** toss lightly, and let marinate for 15 minutes. Prepare the minced seasonings, the sauce, and the paste.

2 Heat a wok or a deep skillet, add ½ cup of the oil, and heat until very hot. Add half the chicken shreds and stir-fry over high heat until the shreds change color. Remove with a handled strainer and drain. Reheat the oil, add the remaining chicken shreds, stir-fry until they change color, remove, and drain.

3 Remove all but 3 tablespoons of oil from the wok and reheat until very hot. Add the **minced seasonings** and the black mushroom shreds and stir-fry for about 15 seconds, until fragrant. Add the bean sprouts and the bamboo shoots, and stir-fry over high heat for 1 minute. Add the **sauce** and stir-fry until the mixture is slightly thickened. Remove with a handled strainer and drain thoroughly. Spread the mixture on a tray and let it cool.

4 Arrange one of the spring roll wrappers flat on a counter, like a diamond, and place a portion of the filling across the lower third of the skin. (Cover the other wrappers with a damp cloth to prevent them from drying out.) Rub some of the **paste** on the opposite point. Starting at the closest point, roll the spring roll skin over to completely enclose the filling. Fold in the two sides and roll over again so the last fold seals in the two sides. Press lightly to seal. Repeat for the remaining spring rolls.

5 Heat a wok, add the remaining 5½ cups of oil to the pan, and heat to 375 degrees. Add five or six spring rolls and deep-fry in the hot oil until golden brown, turning constantly. Remove with a handled strainer and drain on absorbent paper. Deep-fry the remaining spring rolls as directed. Remove and drain. Serve warm or at room temperature with plum sauce and hot mustard. *Makes about twenty rolls.*

Vegetarian Spring Rolls

2 ounces bean threads (cellophane noodles), softened in hot water for 10 minutes
12 dried Chinese black mushrooms, softened in hot water for 10 minutes
3 cups shredded carrots
2 tablespoons rice wine
4 cups Chinese chives or scallion greens, cut into 1-inch pieces
6 cups fresh bean sprouts

Minced Seasonings
1½ tablespoons minced garlic
1 tablespoon minced gingerroot

Sauce
¼ cup soaking liquid retained from dried mushrooms
1½ tablespoons soy sauce
2 tablespoons rice wine
1 teaspoon sesame oil
¼ teaspoon freshly ground black pepper
½ teaspoon cornstarch

6 cups safflower or corn oil
20 Shanghai spring roll wrappers or *lumpia* skins

Paste
¼ cup flour
4 tablespoons water
1 egg, lightly beaten

Vegetarian cooking, as most Chinese vegetarian dishes illustrate, need not be bland and predictable. These crisp rolls, with their fragrant stuffing of carrots, bean sprouts, black mushrooms, and chives, further confirm this.

1 Drain the bean threads and cut them into 3-inch pieces. Drain the black mushrooms (reserving ¼ cup of the soaking liquid); remove the stems and discard. Shred the caps. Prepare the minced seasonings, the sauce, and the paste.

2 Heat a wok, add 3 tablespoons of the oil, and heat until very hot. Add the **minced seasonings** and stir-fry for about 15 seconds, until fragrant. Add the shredded mushrooms and stir-fry for another 10 seconds. Add the carrots and the 2 tablespoons of rice wine. Stir-fry for about 1 minute, until just tender, and add the Chinese chives or scallions, bean sprouts, and bean threads. Toss lightly over high heat to mix, and add the **sauce.** Cook until the bean threads have absorbed all the liquid and the mixture is fairly dry. Remove and spread out on a tray to cool.

3 Arrange one spring roll wrapper flat on a counter, like a diamond. (Cover the others with a damp cloth to prevent them from drying out.) Grab a portion of filling and squeeze out any excess liquid. Place the filling in a line across the lower third of the skin, and using your finger, spread some paste on the opposite edge. Starting at the nearest point, roll up the skin a little to enclose the filling.

Fold in the two sides and continue rolling over so that the skin forms a tight package and completely encloses the filling. Repeat for the remaining skins and filling.

4 Heat a wok, add the remaining safflower or corn oil, and heat to 375 degrees. Add about five or six of the spring rolls and deep-fry in the hot oil, turning constantly, until golden brown and crisp. Remove with a slotted spoon and drain on absorbent paper. Continue frying the remaining rolls, drain, and serve with plum sauce and hot mustard. *Makes about twenty rolls.*

Cantonese-Style Spring Roll Wrappers

2 cups all-purpose flour
½ teaspoon salt
1 large egg, lightly beaten
½ cup cold water

These days, most supermarket produce sections carry some form of spring roll wrappers, made with eggs, flour, and water. With the aid of a pasta machine, however, the wrappers can be made easily at home. While these spring roll wrappers are not as delicate as lumpia *skins, they may be used in spring roll dishes other than Cantonese-style spring rolls.*

1 Mix the flour and salt in a large mixing bowl. Lightly beat the egg and water together. Make a well in the flour and add the egg and water. Mix together the ingredients to form a rough dough. (Add a little flour if the dough is too wet.) Turn the dough out onto a lightly floured surface and knead for about 5 minutes, until smooth and homogeneous. Cover with a cloth and let rest for 30 minutes.

2 Using a pasta machine, set the dial on the lowest setting (for the thickest pasta), and feed the dough into the machine. Sprinkle the dough with flour and fold in half. Turn the machine to the next setting and feed the dough through again. Sprinkle again with flour and fold over. Continue feeding the dough through the machine (do not fold any further), turning the machine up a notch each time, until the second-to-last setting. Place the dough on a lightly floured surface and cut it into 6-inch squares. Set the squares aside for 5 minutes to firm up; then use as directed in the recipe for Cantonese-style egg rolls. *Makes sixteen to eighteen wrappers.*

Cantonese-Style Spring Rolls

1½ pounds barbecued pork loin (see page 40), cut into ¼-inch dice
½ pound medium shrimp, boiled, deveined, and cut into ¼-inch dice
6 cups shredded Chinese cabbage (Napa) or Savoy cabbage
3 tablespoons rice wine
4 cups chopped celery
3 cups scallion greens cut into ½-inch lengths

Sauce
1½ tablespoons soy sauce
1 tablespoon rice wine
1 teaspoon sesame oil
½ teaspoon salt
½ teaspoon freshly ground black pepper
1 teaspoon cornstarch

6½ cups safflower or corn oil
1 recipe Cantonese-style spring roll wrappers (page 38)

Paste
¼ cup flour
4 tablespoons water
1 egg, lightly beaten

The traditional spring roll, with its slender shape and generous stuffing of pork, shrimp, and black mushrooms, has little to do with the ersatz version found in many Cantonese-American restaurants. Too often, these so-called egg rolls are long on cabbage and celery and short on barbecued pork and shrimp. Still, I must admit to having a weakness for well-made egg rolls. They may not be authentic, but, as a child, I loved them. This recipe is my slightly refined version of the adapted classic.

1 Place the filling ingredients, including the sauce, near the stove, so they will be within easy reach. Prepare the paste.

2 Heat a wok, add 3 tablespoons of the oil, and heat until very hot. Add the cabbage and 1 table-spoon of the rice wine. Stir-fry for about 1½ minutes over high heat, until slightly wilted. Add the celery, the scallion greens, and the remaining rice wine. Stir-fry for another minute. Add the barbecued pork, the shrimp, and the **sauce.** Toss lightly over high heat until the sauce thickens. Remove and spread out on a tray to cool.

3 Arrange an egg roll wrapper flat on the counter. (Cover the others with a damp cloth to prevent them from drying out.) Grab a portion of the filling and squeeze out any excess liquid. Place the filling across the lower third of the skin, leaving an inch or two along the outside edge. Using your finger, spread some **paste** along the opposite edge. Starting at the edge closest to the filling, roll over the skin to enclose the filling. Fold in the two sides toward the center, and continue rolling over so that the skin forms a tight, thin package and the edge is sealed. Repeat for the remaining skins and filling.

4 Heat a wok, add the remaining safflower or corn oil, and heat to 375 degrees. Add five or six of the egg rolls and deep-fry in the hot oil, turning constantly, until golden brown and crisp. Remove with a slotted spoon and drain on absorbent paper. Continue frying the remaining rolls, drain, and serve with plum sauce and hot mustard. *Makes about eighteen rolls.*

Barbecued Pork

1½ pounds pork loin,
  trimmed
1½ tablespoons hoisin sauce
1 tablespoon soy sauce
1 tablespoon rice wine
2 teaspoons sugar
1 tablespoon minced garlic

Marinate the pork loin for 30 minutes in a mixture of the remaining ingredients. Then bake in a preheated 350-degree oven for 35 to 45 minutes. Remove, cool, and use as directed.

Mandarin Pancakes

薄

餅

2 cups all-purpose flour
1 cup boiling water
¼ cup sesame oil

Mandarin pancakes are best known in the United States as an accompaniment to Peking duckling and mu shu pork. *In northern China, Mandarin pancakes are served not only with these dishes but also with numerous stir-fried meat and vegetable combinations, functioning as a staple in place of rice. These unusual pancakes are especially convenient for entertaining, since they may be prepared in advance and reheated before serving.*

1 Place the flour in a mixing bowl. Slowly add the boiling water, mixing with a wooden spoon to form a rough dough. Let the dough cool slightly and turn out onto a lightly floured surface. Knead for about 5 minutes, until smooth and elastic. Cover with a damp cloth and let rest for 30 minutes.

2 Cut the dough in half and form each half into a long snakelike roll about 1½ inches in diameter. Cut each roll into twelve pieces. Cover the dough pieces with a damp cloth to prevent them from drying out. Place one piece, with a cut side down, on a lightly floured surface. Using the palm of your hand, flatten it slightly, and with your fingers, press the circle into a 2-inch round. Repeat the same process for another piece of dough. Brush the surface of one dough circle with sesame oil, using enough oil to be generous but not so much that it runs over the edges. Place another circle on top and lightly pinch the edges together to create a double circle. Repeat this step for all the dough pieces; you will have twelve double circles. Using a small rolling pin on a lightly floured surface, roll out each double circle to form a pancake 6 inches in diameter.

3 Heat a well-seasoned 12-inch heavy skillet until very hot. (A bit of water sprinkled on the surface of the pan should evaporate immediately.) If the pan has a tendency to stick, rub the surface lightly with an oil-soaked cloth, then wipe out the pan. Place a pancake in the pan and fry for 1 minute, twirling in a circular motion with your fingertips until it puffs in the middle. Turn it over and fry for another 30 seconds, twirling again. Remove and lightly slap the pancake down on the counter. Let cool for a few seconds and carefully peel the two pancakes apart. Fold each one into quarters, with the cooked side in. Repeat for the other pancakes and arrange them in a circular pattern in a steamer that has been lined with cheesecloth or parchment paper. Cover with a damp cloth to keep them moist. Before serving, steam for 10 minutes over high heat. To reheat, steam for 5 to 10 minutes. *Makes twenty-four pancakes.*

. . . .

Stir-Fried Beef with Leeks

葱
爆
牛
肉

2 pounds eye-of-the-round roast or flank steak

Beef Marinade
3 tablespoons soy sauce
2 tablespoons rice wine
1 tablespoon sugar
1 teaspoon sesame oil
1 tablespoon water
1 tablespoon cornstarch

Beef Sauce
2 tablespoons soy sauce
2 tablespoons rice wine
2 teaspoons Chinese black vinegar
1 tablespoon sesame oil
1 cup safflower or corn oil
6 cloves garlic, very thinly sliced
5 cups shredded leeks, rinsed thoroughly and drained

Few pairings of foods are more distinctly northern Chinese than beef or lamb with scallions or leeks. And this dish, with its fragrant sauce, is perfect for wrapping in Mandarin pancakes, a traditional northern staple. Steamed rice would also go nicely, but the quantity of sauce to flavor the rice should be increased.

1 Remove any fat or gristle from the meat. Using a sharp knife or cleaver, cut the beef, across the grain, into paper-thin slices. Cut the slices into strips 1½ inches long by 1 inch wide. Place the meat in a bowl, add the **beef marinade,** toss lightly to coat, and let marinate for at least 1 hour. Drain the beef and add the marinade to a bowl containing the beef sauce.

2 Heat a wok or a heavy skillet and add the oil. Heat the oil until very hot, about 400 degrees. Add half the beef strips and stir-fry, tossing constantly, until they change color. Remove and drain. Reheat the oil and add the remaining strips of beef. Stir-fry until they change color and separate. Remove and drain. Remove all but 3 tablespoons of oil from the pan.

3 Reheat the oil until very hot and add the sliced garlic and leeks. Toss lightly over high heat until the leeks become slightly limp. Add the **beef sauce** and cook briefly until boiling. Add the beef strips and toss to coat over high heat. Remove to a platter and serve with Mandarin pancakes (page 40). *Serves six.*

Spicy Stir-Fried Lamb with Sweet Bean Sauce

2½ pounds boned leg of lamb, shank portion

Lamb Marinade
2 tablespoons soy sauce
1½ tablespoons rice wine
1 teaspoon sesame oil
1 tablespoon minced garlic
2 teaspoons minced gingerroot
1 tablespoon water
1 teaspoon cornstarch

1 cup plus 2 tablespoons safflower or corn oil
3 cups shredded leeks or scallion greens

Lamb Sauce
2 tablespoons sweet bean sauce
2 tablespoons soy sauce
1½ tablespoons rice wine
1 teaspoon chili paste (optional)
1½ tablespoons sugar
5 tablespoons water

In ancient China, lamb was a meat spurned by many because of its strong, gamy flavor. Since the Chinese word for lamb, yang, also means kid, goat, and mutton, one could never be certain what was being served. Accordingly, vibrant seasonings are generally used to flavor the meat's sauce. Many people who have tasted this dish find it hard to believe they are eating lamb. For those who are partial to other meats, beef, pork, or chicken may be substituted.

1 Remove any fat or gristle from the lamb. Separate the muscles and remove the white membrane from the meat. Cut the meat, across the grain, into very thin slices. Arrange the slices in a row, overlapping slightly, and cut them into matchstick-size shreds. Place the shreds in a bowl, add the **lamb marinade,** toss lightly to coat, and let marinate for at least 30 minutes at room temperature. Prepare the lamb sauce.

2 Heat a wok, add the cup of oil, and heat to 400 degrees. Add half the lamb shreds and stir-fry over high heat until they separate and change color. Remove with a slotted spoon and drain. Reheat the oil and stir-fry the remaining lamb. Remove and drain. Remove the oil from the wok and clean out the wok.

3 Reheat the wok, add the 2 tablespoons of oil, and heat until very hot. Add the shredded leeks and stir-fry over high heat until fragrant, about 1½ minutes. Remove and arrange on a serving platter.

4 Reheat the pan and add the **lamb sauce.** Cook over high heat, until it thickens slightly. Add the stir-fried lamb shreds, toss lightly to coat, and arrange the lamb over the leeks. Serve with Mandarin pancakes (page 40). *Serves six.*

Cold Tossed Rainbow Vegetables with Pork

2½ pounds pork butt or
   shoulder
2 tablespoons safflower or
   corn oil

Braising Mixture
2 cups water
⅓ cup soy sauce
½ cup rice wine
3 tablespoons sugar
1 whole star anise, smashed
   lightly with the flat side of a
   cleaver
1 cinnamon stick
3 scallions, smashed lightly
   with the flat side of a
   cleaver
3 slices gingerroot, smashed
   lightly with the flat side of a
   cleaver

2 medium red bell peppers,
   cored, seeded, and cut into
   matchstick-size shreds
2 cups snow peas, ends
   snapped and veiny strings
   removed, sliced lengthwise
   in half
2 cups scallion greens cut into
   1-inch lengths
1 cup fresh enoki mushrooms,
   stem ends trimmed, rinsed,
   drained, and cut into 1-inch
   pieces

Dressing
2 tablespoons soy sauce
1½ tablespoons rice wine
1½ tablespoons clear rice
   vinegar
1½ tablespoons sugar
2 teaspoons minced garlic
2 teaspoons minced
   gingerroot
¼ teaspoon freshly ground
   black pepper

3 tablespoons sesame oil

*In northern China, Mandarin pancakes are frequently
served with cold tossed salads containing shredded cooked
meats and vegetables. This is an example of such a dish.
It may be served by itself without the pancakes as an
opening cold platter for a multicourse meal. With the
pancakes, the dish becomes a light lunch or dinner
in itself.*

1 Trim the pork of any excess fat or gristle. Cut the
meat, lengthwise, into strips 1½ to 2 inches thick.
Heat a wok or skillet and add the safflower or corn
oil. Heat until very hot and sear the meat until
golden brown on all sides. Remove and drain.

2 In a heavy pot, heat the **braising mixture** until
boiling. Reduce the heat to low and simmer for 20
minutes. Add the seared pork loin and bring the
mixture to a boil. Reduce the heat to medium-low
and simmer for 1 hour, until the meat is tender and
the sauce has reduced to a thick glaze. Remove the
meat and let cool to room temperature. Remove the
seasonings from the reduced braising mixture.
When it is cool, cut the meat into thin julienne
strips, return it to the reduced braising mixture,
and toss lightly to coat. Place the prepared vegetables near the stove and prepare the dressing.

3 Heat a wok, add the sesame oil, and heat until
very hot. Add the red peppers, snow peas, scallions, and enoki mushrooms. Toss lightly over high
heat for about 1½ minutes. Add the shredded
braised pork and the **dressing**. Toss lightly over
high heat to coat. Remove and transfer to a serving
platter. Serve with Mandarin pancakes (page 40).
Serves six.

Stuffed Cabbage Rolls

1 small head Chinese cabbage
(Napa) or Savoy cabbage
1½ pounds ground pork or
beef

Meat Seasonings
2 tablespoons minced
scallions
1 tablespoon minced
gingerroot
1 tablespoon minced garlic
2½ tablespoons soy sauce
2 tablespoons rice wine
1 teaspoon sesame oil
¼ teaspoon freshly ground
black pepper
1 tablespoon cornstarch

Braising Mixture
1½ cups chicken broth
¼ cup rice wine
1½ tablespoons soy sauce
1 teaspoon sugar
1 teaspoon cornstarch

1½ tablespoons Chinese black
vinegar
1 tablespoon finely shredded
gingerroot

Stuffed cabbage leaves are popular in the cuisines of a number of cultures, Chinese among them. The sweet yet hearty flavor of this vegetable perfectly complements ground meat and seasonings. Like other stuffed cabbage dishes, this one improves with age.

1 One by one, carefully remove the cabbage leaves from the head, and holding a cleaver or knife parallel to the cutting surface, trim off any stem so that the whole leaf is uniform in thickness. Heat 2 quarts of water until boiling and drop the leaves, a few at a time, into the water. After 1 minute, remove with a slotted spoon and immediately immerse in cold water. Remove, drain, and set aside.

2 Lightly chop the ground meat for a few minutes until light and fluffy. Place in a large bowl, adding the **meat seasonings.** Stir vigorously in one direction and throw the mixture lightly against the inside of the bowl to combine evenly. Prepare the braising mixture.

3 Arrange a portion of the meat mixture across the center of a cabbage leaf. Roll over the leaf, turn the side edges toward the center, and finish rolling the leaf to form a compact package in which the filling is completely enclosed. Repeat for the remaining filling and cabbage leaves.

4 Arrange the cabbage packages, seam side down, in a casserole or Dutch overn. Pour the **braising mixture** on top. Place over medium-high heat and partially cover. When the mixture reaches a boil, reduce the heat to low, and simmer, partially covered, for 1 hour. The sauce should be reduced to the consistency of very heavy cream. If not, uncover, turn up the heat, and continue cooking for a short time. Before serving, sprinkle the top with the Chinese black vinegar and the ginger shreds. *Serves six.* (Reheat leftovers slowly over low heat for about 15 minutes, until hot.)

Steamed Egg Rolls

豬
肉
蛋
捲

Egg Sheets
2 tablespoons cornstarch
¼ cup cold water
6 large eggs, lightly beaten
  until frothy

2 tablespoons safflower or
  corn oil

1 pound ground pork
½ pound medium raw
  shrimp, peeled

Meat Seasonings
3 tablespoons minced
  scallions
2 teaspoons minced
  gingerroot
2 tablespoons soy sauce
1 tablespoon rice wine
1½ teaspoons sesame oil
2 tablespoons cornstarch

1 egg, lightly beaten

1 tablespoon safflower and
  corn oil
6 dried Chinese black
  mushrooms, softened in hot
  water to cover, stems
  removed, and caps cut into
  matchstick-size shreds
3 cups fresh bean sprouts,
  rinsed lightly and drained

Sauce
1 cup chicken broth
2 tablespoons rice wine
¾ teaspoon salt
½ teaspoon sugar
1 teaspoon sesame oil
1½ teaspoons cornstarch

In this country, "egg rolls" are a Cantonese-American version of the spring roll. In the Orient, they are a simple crêpe made of cornstarch, egg, and water and stuffed with a variety of meat and vegetable fillings. Steamed, as in this recipe, or deep-fried, these egg rolls are unusual and delicious.

1 In a mixing bowl, stir the cornstarch and water to form a smooth paste. Add the eggs and beat lightly to form a smooth batter.

2 With a paper towel or a cloth dipped in the 2 tablespoons of oil, wipe the surface of a 10-inch nonstick frying pan or a well-seasoned wok or skillet. Heat the pan until hot and remove from the heat. (To test the temperature of the pan, lightly sprinkle some water on the surface. If it evaporates immediately, the pan is ready.) Spoon or pour about 2 tablespoons of the egg batter into the pan. Tilt the pan immediately to form a thin, circular pancake about 10 inches in diameter. Place the pan back over the heat and cook briefly until set and a pale golden color. Flip the egg sheet over and cook very briefly. Remove and prepare thirteen more egg sheets in the same manner.

3 Lightly chop the ground pork for a few minutes and place in a bowl. Using a heavy knife or a food processor fitted with the steel blade, chop the shrimp coarsely. Add the ground shrimp to the pork, add the **meat seasonings,** and toss lightly, stirring the mixture vigorously in one direction to combine the ingredients.

4 Arrange one egg sheet flat on a counter and place a 1-inch-wide strip of the pork mixture across the lower half of the egg sheet. Spread the outer edge of the egg sheet with some of the beaten egg, and starting at the closest edge, roll up the egg sheet to enclose the filling. Repeat for the remaining egg sheets and filling. Arrange the rolls, seam side down, on a lightly oiled heat-proof plate. Place in a steamer tray and cover.

4 Fill a wok with water level with the bottom edge of the steamer tray and heat until boiling. Place the steamer tray over the boiling water and steam for 15 minutes over high heat. Transfer the rolls to a serving dish or platter. Prepare the sauce.

5 Heat a wok, add the tablespoon of oil, and heat until very hot. Add the shredded black mushrooms and stir-fry over high heat for 20 seconds, until fragrant. Add the bean sprouts and toss lightly for 15 seconds. Add the **sauce** and heat until boiling and thickened. Pour over the rolls and serve. ***Makes about fourteen rolls.***

. . . .

Rice Noodle Wrappers

沙
河
粉

2 cups all-purpose flour
½ cup wheat starch
1 teaspoon salt
⅓ cup safflower or corn oil
2 tablespoons sesame oil
3 cups water

In professional Cantonese dim sum *kitchens, the method of making rice noodle wrappers is somewhat reminiscent of crêpe making in France. A bit of batter is poured onto a hot surface and a squeegee is used to spread the mixture into a thin pancake. Owing to the high heat, the crêpe cooks immediately. Once set, it is cut into squares, lifted off, and used to make rice noodle rolls. This process is easily adapted for the home kitchen. If wheat starch, a nonglutinous flour sold at most Chinese grocery stores, is unavailable, cornstarch may be substituted.*

1 Place the flour, wheat starch, and salt in a mixing bowl. Combine the oils and water, and lightly beat the liquid into the dry ingredients, whisking until smooth. Rest the batter in the refrigerator for 1 hour.

2 Fill a wok with water level with the bottom edge of a steamer tray and heat until just boiling.

3 Generously grease a 7-inch pie plate. Pour about ⅓ cup of the batter into the pie plate, tilting the pan so that the batter forms a thin pancake or crêpe. Place the pan in the steamer tray, cover, and steam for about 5 minutes over high heat. Remove, cool slightly, and using a spatula, lift an edge of the wrapper away from the dish. Carefully, pull the wrapper out of the pan and set aside on a tray or cookie sheet. Generously grease the pie plate and continue making wrappers, using up the batter. ***Makes about sixteen wrappers.*** Use as directed in making rice noodle rolls.

Rice Noodle Rolls

1 pound boneless chicken breast meat, skin removed

Chicken Marinade
1 tablespoon rice wine
1 teaspoon minced gingerroot
1 teaspoon sesame oil
½ teaspoon salt
¼ teaspoon freshly ground black pepper

4 tablespoons safflower or corn oil

8 dried Chinese black mushrooms, softened in hot water to cover, stems removed, and caps shredded
6 cups fresh bean sprouts, rinsed lightly and drained
2 cups scallion greens cut into ½-inch lengths
1 pound barbecued pork (page 40), cut into matchstick-size shreds

Sauce
1 tablespoon soy sauce
1 tablespoon rice wine
½ teaspoon salt
1 teaspoon sugar
1 teaspoon sesame oil
¼ teaspoon freshly ground black pepper
1 teaspoon cornstarch

1 recipe rice noodle wrappers (page 46)

¼ cup toasted sesame seeds
1 teaspoon sesame oil
1 tablespoon soy sauce

Rice noodle rolls are a Cantonese specialty offered at most dim sum parlors. The wrapper, which is ivory-colored and slippery-smooth, can be made at home (see previous recipe). Commercially made rice noodle wrappers are available at some Chinese grocery stores. Spring roll skins also may be used instead of rice noodle wrappers.

1 Remove any fat from the chicken meat. Holding a cleaver or knife parallel to the cutting surface, slice the chicken in half through the thickness. Cut the meat into matchstick-size shreds. Place in a bowl, add the **chicken marinade,** toss, and let marinate for 20 minutes. Prepare the sauce, and place it and the other prepared ingredients next to the stove.

2 Heat a wok, add the oil, and heat until very hot. Add the chicken shreds and stir-fry, over high heat, until they change color and separate. Remove with a handled strainer and drain. Remove all but 3 tablespoons of oil from the pan.

3 Reheat the oil until very hot. Add the black mushroom shreds and stir-fry for about 10 seconds, until fragrant. Add the bean sprouts and scallions. Stir-fry for another 30 seconds and add the barbecued pork, the chicken, and the **sauce.** Toss over high heat until the sauce thickens; then remove the mixture and spread out on a platter to cool.

4 Place a rice noodle wrapper on the counter with the shiny side down. Arrange a portion of the cooled filling in a line across the lower third of the wrapper. Starting from the edge closest to the filling, roll up the wrapper to enclose the filling and create a thin roll. Repeat for the remaining wrappers and filling. Arrange the rolls, seam side down, on a heat-proof pie plate that has been lightly greased with sesame oil. (You may stack the rolls.) Arrange the plate in a steamer tray and cover.

5 Fill a wok with water level with the bottom edge of the steamer tray and heat until boiling. Place the steamer tray containing the rice noodle rolls over the boiling water, cover, and steam for 5 minutes over high heat. Remove and sprinkle the top of the rolls with the sesame seeds, sesame oil, and soy sauce. Serve. ***Makes about sixteen rolls.***

SUMMER

· · · · · · · · · · · · · · ·

夏

The garlic

is ripe

and should be

picked

. . . .

THE DRAGON BOAT FESTIVAL

In the Orient as in the West, summer officially begins on the summer solstice, and it is the Dragon Boat Festival (otherwise known as the Festival of the Summer Solstice), celebrated on the fifth day of the fifth month of the lunar calendar, which most typifies summer. On the "double fifth," a carnival atmosphere prevails. The banks of rivers and lakes are usually lined with spectators who have gathered to watch brightly colored dragon boat races. And everyone eats *zong-zi*, the triangular rice dumplings wrapped in bamboo leaves that are traditionally prepared for this holiday.

The history of the Dragon Boat Festival can be traced to the beginnings of civilization in northern China. For the ancient farmers, the summer solstice, marking the turn of the year, was cause for celebration. Some scholars contend that since this festival occurs around the time when rain is needed for crops, the rice dumplings were offerings to the scaly dragon, who was — so the ancients believed — the bringer of rain. Dragon boat races, simulating dragon fights, were held to encourage real dragon fights in the heavens, which supposedly brought the heavy rains. (Today, in some parts of the Orient, the Dragon Boat Festival usually signals the *end* of the rainy season.)

In ancient China, the rice dumplings for this holiday were stuffed with cherries, mulberries, peaches, apricots, water chestnuts, and other seasonal fruits. Some families tied bunches of the dumplings together with long silk threads and hung them from children's backs. These "threads of prolonging life" were believed to ward off demons. Others exchanged cakes with the Five Poisonous Creatures (centipede, scorpion, snake, lizard, and toad) molded on top. The cakes were eaten in hopes that bites from these animals would be avoided. Calamus and mugwort leaves were posted over doorways and gates as a protection against other noxious insects.

Some time later, the Dragon Boat Festival and *zong-zi* became associated with yet another myth. During the Ch'ou dynasty (twelfth century B.C. to 221 B.C.), there was a famous poet named Ch'u Yuan, who was minister of the state of Ch'u, located in the middle of China. Ch'u Yuan was dearly loved by his constituents. One day he was unfairly accused by a superior and expelled from his office. Ch'u Yuan fled to Hunan province and committed suicide by throwing himself into the Mi Lo River. Once his death was discovered, people searched for his body in boats (hence another explanation for the dragon boats). Having searched in vain, they threw rice into the river to feed Ch'u Yuan's soul. To prevent fish from getting at the food, people began wrapping the rice in bamboo leaves. Later, the shape was adapted to the triangular dumpling we know today.

Zong-zi are made in all parts of China, but there are distinct regional variations. In central and southern China, sweet glutinous rice is used in the dumpling, whereas in the north, millet is more popular. In Beijing, *zong-zi* are triangular; in the south, they are often square. And since bamboo leaves for the wrapping are scarce in the north, lily leaves are often used there.

Almost all Chinese prepare both sweet and savory fillings: red bean paste and date paste are the most popular of the sweet variety; pork, chicken, black mushrooms, sausage, and dried shrimp are the usual ingredients for the savory renditions.

夏

MENU I

Poached Salmon Steaks in a Spicy West Lake Sauce

Steamed Chicken in Melon Soup

Chicken, Sausage, and Rice Wrapped in Lotus Leaves

Sweet Rice Dumplings

Poached Salmon Steaks in a Spicy West Lake Sauce

西湖魚

6 salmon steaks, about ¾ inch thick, each weighing about 6 ounces

Salmon Marinade
4 slices gingerroot, smashed lightly with the flat side of a cleaver
2 tablespoons rice wine
½ teaspoon salt

Fish Poaching Liquid
1 tablespoon safflower or corn oil
¼ cup rice wine
3 to 4 quarts boiling water

Fish Sauce
1 cup retained poaching liquid
2 tablespoons soy sauce
1½ tablespoons sugar
1½ tablespoons Chinese black vinegar
½ teaspoon freshly ground white pepper

2 tablespoons safflower or corn oil

Fish Seasonings
½ cup finely shredded scallions
¼ cup very finely shredded gingerroot
1 fresh red or green hot chili pepper, seeds removed and finely shredded

Thickener
1½ teaspoons cornstarch
2 tablespoons water

West Lake, situated near Hangzhou in eastern China, is renowned not only for its beautiful scenery but also as a culinary mecca. Foremost among the regional specialties is a classic dish known as West Lake fish, in which a whole carp is poached and then served masked in a spicy, tart sauce. In this recipe, the carp has been replaced by salmon steaks, producing a delicious variation. If salmon is unavailable, a meaty, firm-fleshed fish — such as haddock, pickerel, trout, or red snapper — will do nicely.

1 Lightly rinse the salmon steaks and drain thoroughly. Prepare the **salmon marinade** by lightly pinching the gingerroot slices in the rice wine repeatedly for several minutes to impart the flavor. Add the salt and pour the mixture over the fish steaks. Turn over lightly to coat, and let marinate for 20 minutes. Prepare the fish sauce, fish seasonings, and thickener.

2 Ready the ingredients of the **fish poaching liquid**, but do not combine them. Heat a large wok or a fish poacher, add the oil for the fish poaching liquid, and heat until hot. Add the rice wine and water. Cover and heat the liquid until boiling. Arrange the fish steaks in the poaching liquid (if they do not fit, poach them in two separate batches), adding the marinade. Heat the liquid until boiling again, then turn off the heat and cover. Let the steaks sit for 15 minutes, or until the fish flakes when prodded with a knife. If they are not completely cooked, turn on the heat to low and cook until done. Remove the fish steaks with a slotted spoon and arrange on a serving platter. Cover to keep warm. Add 1 cup of the poaching liquid, discarding the gingerroot slices, to the fish sauce.

3 Heat a wok, add the 2 tablespoons of oil, and heat until hot. Add the **fish seasonings** and stir-fry until fragrant, about 15 seconds. Add the **fish sauce** and heat until boiling. Slowly add the **thickener**, stirring constantly. When the sauce has thickened, slowly pour over the fish steaks. Serve immediately. *Serves six.*

Steamed Chicken in Melon Soup

香瓜盅

1 whole frying or broiling chicken, weighing about 2½ pounds
10 dried Chinese black mushrooms, softened in hot water and stems removed
6 paper-thin slices Chinese ham or prosciutto, weighing about ¼ pound

Soup Broth
4 cups boiling water
⅓ cup rice wine
1 teaspoon salt
4 scallions, smashed lightly with the flat side of a cleaver
4 slices gingerroot, smashed lightly with the flat side of a cleaver
1 large ripe muskmelon, Cranshaw, or cantaloupe, weighing 3 to 3½ pounds

The refined delicacy of eastern Chinese regional cooking shines through in this soup, which is said to have originated in the ancient city of Suzhou, famous for its stunning landscape, sophistication, and succulent watermelons. In the traditional recipe, a whole watermelon is hollowed out and used as a steaming vessel for the soup. This recipe has been adapted slightly to take advantage of the sweet cantaloupe and muskmelons available during the summer months.

1 Remove any fat from the cavity opening and around the neck of the chicken. Rinse lightly and drain. Using a heavy cleaver or knife, cut the chicken, through the bones, into 1½-inch square pieces. Heat 2 quarts of water until boiling and blanch the chicken pieces for one minute to clean them. Remove the pieces, rinse in cold water, and drain. Cut the mushroom caps in half and cut the ham or prosciutto slices into 1-inch squares.

2 Place the chicken pieces, black mushrooms, ham or prosciutto, and **soup broth** in a heat-proof pot or 2-quart soufflé dish. Cover tightly with plastic wrap and place in a steamer tray. Fill a wok with water level with the bottom edge of the steamer tray and heat until boiling. Place the steamer tray over the boiling water, cover, and steam for 1½ hours over high heat, replacing the water as necessary. Periodically skim off any grease from the surface of the chicken soup mixture.

3 Using a sharp knife, cut a thin wedge from the bottom of the melon so that it will stand upright. Cut off the top quarter of the melon, rinse, drain, and set aside. Scoop out and discard the seeds from inside the melon, leaving all but ½ inch of the flesh around the shell. Place the melon in a steamer and ladle as much of the chicken soup mixture into the melon as possible. Cover and steam for 12 to 15 minutes, or until the melon is soft but firm enough to hold its shape. Remove the melon to a large, shallow bowl and serve the soup from the melon. Refill the melon with the remaining soup and serve further helpings as desired. *Serves six.*

Chicken, Sausage, and Rice Wrapped in Lotus Leaves

糯
米
鷄
粉

3 cups uncooked glutinous
  (sweet) rice
1 pound boned chicken breast
  meat, skin removed

Chicken Marinade
2 tablespoons soy sauce
1 tablespoon rice wine
1 teaspoon sesame oil
1 teaspoon minced garlic
1 teaspoon minced gingerroot

6 dried lotus leaves (available
  at Chinese grocery stores)

Rice Flavorings
1 tablespoon rice wine
1 teaspoon salt
2 tablespoons soy sauce
1 tablespoon sesame oil
¼ cup safflower or corn oil
½ pound Chinese pork
  sausage, dried
8 dried Chinese black
  mushrooms, softened in hot
  water, stems removed and
  caps diced

Chicken Sauce
2 tablespoons soy sauce
1 tablespoon rice wine
¼ teaspoon freshly ground
  black pepper
¼ cup chicken broth or water
1½ teaspoons cornstarch

The arrival of the Dragon Boat Festival is always clearly proclaimed in the marketplaces in China. Bunches of triangular dumplings, zong-zi, *hang from every doorway. Almost every vendor insists that you sample his or her version of this holiday specialty, but there is danger in being too cooperative. According to an article in the* China Post, *a Taipei newspaper, eating too many sweet rice dumplings can be harmful to your health, since they clog up the digestive system. The article suggested restricting the intake of rice dumplings to no more than three per day. These delicious packages may be served as a staple, complementing other dishes, or as a filling snack or meal by themselves.*

1 Using your hand as a rake, rinse the glutinous rice in cold water until the water runs clear. Drain and place in cold water to cover. Soak for 1 hour. Line a steamer tray with wet cheesecloth and transfer the rice to the steamer tray, distributing it evenly. Cover and steam the rice for 20 minutes over high heat. Remove and keep covered.

2 Trim any fat or gristle from the chicken and cut the meat into 1-inch cubes. Place in a bowl, add the **chicken marinade**, toss lightly to coat, and let marinate for 20 minutes. Place the lotus leaves in hot water to cover for 1 hour. Remove and drain. Cut each leaf in half crosswise. Prepare the rice flavorings and chicken sauce.

3 Transfer the cooked rice to a mixing bowl and add the **rice flavorings**. Toss lightly to combine.

4 Heat a wok, add the safflower or corn oil, and heat until very hot. Add the chicken and stir-fry over high heat until the meat changes color. Remove and drain. Remove all but 2 tablespoons of oil from the pan and reheat. Add the Chinese sausage and cook, stirring occasionally, until golden brown. Add the black mushrooms, chicken, and **chicken sauce**. Stir-fry over high heat until the sauce has thickened. Remove and let cool.

5 Place two lotus leaf halves overlapping to form a circle. (The upper side of the leaf should be facing down.) Brush generously with sesame oil. Spoon some of the rice mixture into the center, and using a spoon, shape an indentation in the center. Fill with one-sixth of the chicken and sausage mixture. Cover with more of the rice mixture. Wrap the lotus leaves into a square package to enclose the filling and tie securely with twine. Repeat to make six packages. Arrange the packages in the bottom of a steamer tray. Cover.

6 Fill a wok with water level with the bottom edge of the steamer tray and heat until boiling. Place the steamer tray over the boiling water and steam for 25 minutes over high heat. Remove and cut open each package to serve. (The leaves are not eaten.) ***Serves six.***

. . . .

Sweet Rice Dumplings

Filling
½ pound dried red adzuki
  beans
¾ cup sugar
¾ cup unsalted butter or lard,
  cut into tablespoon-size
  pieces
1 tablespoon vanilla extract

3 cups glutinous (sweet) rice
30 dried bamboo leaves
  (available at Chinese grocery
  stores)
15 6-inch lengths of twine

Sweet rice dumplings stuffed with red bean paste are prepared and savored all over China. Their unique triangular shape is universally associated with the Dragon Boat Festival. All rice dumplings, sweet and savory alike, may be prepared in advance and then resteamed for 10 to 12 minutes before serving. They are also delicious served at room temperature, making them ideal for any picnic basket.

1 To begin the **filling:** Rinse the beans in cold water and place in a large bowl with water to cover. Discard any beans that rise to the surface. Let sit overnight in water to cover. (As the beans soften, you may have to add more water.) Drain the beans and place in a large pot with 3 cups of water. Heat until boiling, reduce the heat to medium, and cook uncovered for 1¼ hours, or until the beans are very tender. Drain the beans, discarding any water, and mash to a paste. (To do this, you may use a food processor fitted with the steel blade.)

2 Transfer the bean paste to a saucepan and cook, stirring constantly, for about 10 minutes, until thick. Add the sugar and the butter or lard. Cook, stirring constantly, over low heat, until the mixture is very thick and comes away from the sides of the pan. Remove the pan from the heat and add the vanilla extract. Let the mixture cool. There will be about 3 cups.

3 Using your hand as a rake, rinse the glutinous rice in cold water until the water runs clear. Drain the rice, place in cold water to cover, and soak for 1 hour. Drain thoroughly. Place the bamboo leaves in cold water to cover and soak for 30 minutes. Drain thoroughly.

4 Place two bamboo leaves together, facing in opposite directions. (The stems should be at opposite ends.) Fold over the leaves to make a cone shape — as you would fold paper to make a cone for piping icing. Place a heaping tablespoon of rice in the base of the cone. Using a spoon, make a slight indentation in the center of the rice. Place 2 heaping tablespoons of the red bean filling in the indentation and cover with more rice, so that the filling is completely enclosed. Fold over the ends of the bamboo leaves and wrap under and around the cone, to make a neat package. Wrap the twine around the package to secure the leaves. Repeat for the remaining leaves and filling to make fifteen packages. Tie one end of all the strings together so that the packages are attached at one end.

5 Fill a stockpot with water and heat until boiling. Add the rice dumplings and cook for 1½ hours, covered, over medium heat. Remove the packages and cut the twine. Serve immediately. Each diner unwraps the bamboo leaves and eats the rice and red bean filling. *Makes about fifteen dumplings.*

夏

MENU II

Tea-Smoked Chicken with a Red Pepper Dressing

Seafood Rice Salad

Melon Balls and Loquats in a Candied Ginger Syrup

Tea-Smoked Chicken with Red Pepper Dressing

2 whole chicken breasts (with bone in), weighing about 1½ pounds apiece

Chicken Marinade
2 tablespoons rice wine
1 teaspoon salt
3 scallions, smashed lightly with the flat side of a cleaver
2 slices gingerroot, smashed lightly with the flat side of a cleaver

Tea-Smoking Mixture
4 tablespoons loose black tea
2 tablespoons light brown sugar
3 tablespoons aniseed

1 tablespoon safflower or corn oil
6 cups iceberg lettuce, cut into strips about 1 inch wide
1 tablespoon rice wine
½ cup sesame oil
½ cup minced scallion greens
3 medium red peppers, cores removed, seeded, and finely diced
4 to 5 tablespoons red wine vinegar, or to taste
1 teaspoon salt
½ teaspoon freshly ground black pepper
⅓ cup chopped fresh tarragon

Tea-smoking originated in western China as a means of preserving and flavoring food. Unlike the smoking method used in this country, in which food is cooked while being smoked, Chinese smoking merely colors and flavors. In this recipe, the pale cooked chicken breast becomes a rich mahogany brown and a subtle smoky-anise flavor is imparted to the meat. The contrast of the chicken with the tart red pepper dressing and the sweet stir-fried lettuce in the base makes this dish nothing short of superb.

1 Remove any fat from the chicken breasts. Run the **chicken marinade** over the breasts. Let sit for 3 to 4 hours, or overnight in the refrigerator. Transfer the chicken breasts to a heat-proof plate and set in a steamer tray. Cover.

2 Fill a wok with 4 to 5 inches of water level with the bottom edge of the steamer tray and heat until boiling. Place the steamer tray containing the chicken breasts over the boiling water and steam for 20 minutes, until the chicken is just cooked. Remove and set aside.

3 Empty the wok and line it with heavy-duty aluminum foil. Cover the inside of the lid with foil as well. Mix the ingredients of the **tea-smoking mixture** and place in the bottom of the wok. Balance a smoking rack or four crisscrossed chopsticks over the smoking mixture and arrange the chicken breasts, skin side up, on top. Cover and turn the heat to high. Cook for about 15 minutes from the time a smoky smell is apparent. Turn off the heat and let stand, covered, for 10 minutes. Remove the chicken breasts and cool slightly. With the heel of your hand, press down on the central cartilage of the breastbone, turn the breast skin side down, and remove the breastbone. Using a sharp knife, cut the breasts lengthwise in half and crosswise into pieces about 1 inch thick.

4 Heat a wok or skillet until very hot. Add the tablespoon of safflower or corn oil and heat until smoking. Add the lettuce and the rice wine. Toss lightly over high heat, stirring constantly, for 1 to 2

minutes, until the lettuce is just wilted. Remove and arrange the lettuce on a serving platter. Place the cut chicken breasts on top, arranging them in an attractive pattern and keeping intact the shape of each chicken breast half.

5 Heat a wok and add the sesame oil. Heat until just smoking. Add the scallions and the red peppers. Stir-fry briefly over high heat until fragrant, about 10 seconds. Add the vinegar, salt, and pepper, and cook for about 1½ minutes, stirring occasionally. Add the tarragon, toss lightly, and season to taste. Remove the dressing from the heat and pour over the chicken pieces. Serve immediately. ***Serves six.***

. . . .

Seafood Rice Salad

4 cups cooked long-grain rice
1 ripe avocado, peeled and
　cut into ¼-inch cubes
2 tomatoes, peeled, seeded,
　and cut into ¼-inch cubes
¼ pound snow peas, ends
　trimmed and veiny strings
　removed, blanched briefly
½ pound lightly poached
　medium shrimp, peeled and
　deveined
½ pound lightly poached
　scallops

Sesame Vinaigrette
¼ cup soy sauce
½ teaspoon salt
1 tablespoon sugar
2 tablespoons sesame oil
3 tablespoons Chinese rice
　vinegar
1 tablespoon rice wine

½ cup minced scallion greens

This unusual rice salad is delicious as a side dish with meat and vegetable entrées, or it may be served by itself, as a light meal. Other garnishes than the seafood and vegetables in this recipe may be substituted, depending on the tastes of the cook.

1 In a large bowl, combine the rice, avocado, tomatoes, snow peas, shrimp, and scallops. Toss to blend.

2 Prepare the **sesame vinaigrette**, add it to the rice mixture, and toss lightly. Sprinkle the top with the minced scallions. Serve at room temperature, or chill before serving. ***Serves six.***

Melon Balls and Loquats in a Candied Ginger Syrup

4 cups combined honeydew, cantaloupe, and Cranshaw melon balls

2 15-ounce cans loquats in syrup

¼ cup finely shredded stem ginger preserved in syrup, drained

3 tablespoons stem ginger syrup

This simple fruit dish provides a refreshing conclusion to any meal — whatever the season. Any fresh or poached fruit — such as strawberries and peaches — would be excellent in this dish. Similarly, lychees or arbutus packed in syrup may be substituted for the loquats.

Place the melon balls, loquats, shredded stem ginger, and stem ginger syrup in a large mixing bowl. Toss to coat, and chill for at least 1 hour before serving. ***Serves six.***

CHINESE BARBECUE

夏

In most countries of the world, barbecue is a cooking method associated with the balmy days of summer. Chinese barbecued dishes are enjoyed not only during the summer season but throughout the year. The Barbecue Chi Restaurant, a hundred-year-old eatery situated in Beijing that specializes in Mongolian barbecued dishes, is one of the few restaurants in the city that prospers year round, even during the brutal heat of Beijing's summer. (Its lakeside location probably has as much to do with its popularity as the menu.)

In China, barbecue, or *kao*, is not just cooking food directly over charcoal or fire. (The classic recipes for Peking duck and Cantonese barbecued pork probably best illustrate this method.) It also refers to a technique akin to searing, as in Mongolian barbecue, when the food is placed in a heavy pan with holes and "scorched" over high heat. Both types of barbecue have a long history in the Chinese kitchen.

According to legend, it was a Chinese man by the name of Sui Ren (who later became known as Firewood Man) who first invented and used fire for cooking. And reliable archeological evidence confirms that Peking Man, who lived during the Pleistocene epoch from 460,000 to 230,000 years ago, regularly cooked all types of game meats over an open fire. As civilization in China progressed, the Han Chinese (who were the ethnic majority) were slower to accept this method of cooking. In fact, they considered it barbaric. But their views may have been influenced by their disdain for the nomads of Manchuria and Outer Mongolia, who came to specialize in barbecued meat dishes.

Some believe that the classic Mongolian barbecue originated with horsemen who would return from a day of hunting on the steppes with freshly slaughtered animals. They would cut up the meat and combine it with wild garlic, onions, and herbs. Then, placing their iron shields over the fire and using them as cooking vessels, they would toss the meat mixture on the hot surface, until it was done.

Later, these barbecued, or "scorched," meat dishes were introduced to Peking as a simple street food. Vendors in the marketplace would push a wheeled cart containing a portable coal-burning stove. Thin slices of lamb and beef were brushed with sauces and flavorings, and seared in a large heated pan. The cooked meat was then stuffed into a rough steamed bun and eaten like a sandwich.

Under the reign of the Mongolian emperor Sung Chi in the sixteenth century, barbecued meats were officially added to the Imperial Palace menus for visiting dignitaries who longed for food from their native lands. Early barbecued meat dishes were made from cooked beef and lamb, sprinkled with water, and eaten with leeks and scallions. Barbecued raw meats came into vogue a number of years later. The dish that came to be known as Mongolian barbecue was further refined by Peking chefs, and in time, even the local gentry relished it.

For the refined version of Mongolian barbecue, the meat was cut into paper-thin slices. (Some chefs became famous for the speed and agility with which they wielded their slicing knives.) The barbecue stove, which was a large open brazier, was fueled by charcoal from such hardwoods as willow and cypress. Both were believed to produce the most fragrant smoke. Once cooked to a turn, the meat was stuffed in flaky sesame rolls (*shao bing*). Skewered meats were later introduced to China from the Near East, and they, too, became popular in the north.

Today, skewered meats and barbecued dishes are still popular in China. Grilled and barbecued dishes are delicious all year long, but they are especially fitting in the warmer months, when they can be enjoyed on a picnic.

MENU I

Hacked Chicken Salad with Noodles in a
Spicy Peanut Dressing

Mongolian Barbecue

Steamed Lotus Buns

Almond Curd with Assorted Fruits

Hacked Chicken Salad with Noodles in a Spicy Peanut Dressing

棒
棒
鷄

½ pound thin egg noodles, such as vermicelli or spaghettini
1 tablespoon safflower or corn oil
1 tablespoon sesame oil
3 cups cooked chicken meat, skin removed, cut or torn into very thin julienne strips
2 cups shredded carrots
2 cups shredded celery
2 cups peeled, seeded, and shredded cucumbers

Spicy Peanut Dressing
3 cloves garlic, peeled
3 scallion stalks, white part only, cut into 1-inch lengths
1 ½-inch-thick slice gingerroot
3 tablespoons chunky peanut butter
¼ cup soy sauce, or to taste
¼ cup sesame oil
3 tablespoons rice wine
2 tablespoons Chinese black vinegar
1½ tablespoons sugar
1½ teaspoons chili paste or chili paste with garlic
⅓ cup chicken broth

1 tablespoon minced scallion greens

Ideally, any barbecued meal should begin with a cold platter, which keeps the diners occupied while the coals are being readied and the other food is cooking. This cold noodle salad, which hails from Sichuan province, is one of my favorite dishes. As well as being an excellent appetizer, it stands beautifully on its own as a meal in itself. For those interested in an equally delicious variation, Chinese sesame paste may be substituted for the peanut butter in the spicy dressing.

1 Heat 2 quarts of water and the safflower or corn oil until boiling. Add the noodles and cook until just tender. Remove, drain, and lightly rinse the noodles in a colander. Drain thoroughly and toss the noodles with the sesame oil. Place the noodles in a deep dish or on a platter. Arrange the chicken, carrot, celery, and cucumber shreds individually in attractive rows or piles over the noodles.

2 Prepare the **spicy peanut dressing**: In a food processor fitted with the steel blade, finely mince the garlic, scallions, and gingerroot. Add the peanut butter and pulse, blending the ingredients. Add the remaining ingredients in the order listed and process until the mixture is smooth and evenly blended. It should be the consistency of slightly thickened heavy cream. If it is too thick, add a little water. If it is too thin, add a tablespoon of peanut butter. Before serving, pour the sauce over the salad and sprinkle the minced scallion greens on top. Alternatively, you may serve the dressing on the side so that each diner may add his or her own. Serve at room temperature or slightly chilled. *Serves six.*

Mongolian Barbecue

蒙古烤肉

2½ to 3 pounds sirloin roast
  or eye-of-the-round roast

Meat Marinade
½ cup soy sauce
¼ cup rice wine
¼ cup sweet bean sauce or
  hoisin sauce
2 tablespoons minced garlic
3 tablespoons sugar
¼ cup water

Sesame oil or peanut oil
3 cups finely shredded leeks
  or scallion greens
4 cups fresh bean sprouts,
  rinsed lightly and drained

When I was living in Taipei, a trip to a Mongolian barbecue restaurant was a very special event. Since most of these eateries charge one price for "all you can eat," my fellow classmates and I would repeatedly return to the line for seconds and thirds. The meats and vegetables were displayed in refrigerated cases and each customer would pick and choose the makings for his dish, loading everything (ingredients and seasonings) into a deep bowl. The bowls would then be handed to chefs cooking at huge charcoal braziers. Tossing the ingredients with their 36-inch chopsticks over a red-hot grill, they would instantly ready them for eating. Mongolian barbecue can be re-created at home. Ghengis Khan grills are available at some gourmet shops and Oriental grocery stores.

1 Remove any fat or gristle from the meat and partially freeze the meat (for 20 minutes) to facilitate cutting. Cut the meat, across the grain, into paper-thin slices that are about 2 inches square. Place the beef slices in a bowl, add the **meat marinade,** toss lightly to coat, and let marinate for at least 4 hours, or overnight.

2 Prepare the charcoal and wait until the fire has reduced to low, red coals, or use an electric hot plate heated to the maximum setting and place it in the center of the table. Place a Ghengis Khan grill or a well-seasoned cast-iron skillet over the fire or burner and heat until hot. (A drop of water sprinkled on the surface should evaporate immediately.) Brush the surface with sesame oil or peanut oil and place some of the meat slices on the grill in one layer. Cook the meat on both sides until golden. Add some leeks or scallions and bean sprouts. Toss lightly with chopsticks until the vegetables are just cooked. Remove and serve the mixture in steamed lotus buns (page 68) or Mandarin pancakes (page 40). Continue preparing the beef and vegetables in the same manner. (If the cooking is being done at the table, the diners can help themselves.)
Serves six.

Steamed Lotus Buns

荷
葉
夾

3 cups all-purpose flour
2 tablespoons sugar
1½ teaspoons active dry yeast
1 cup lukewarm water
1 tablespoon safflower or corn
  oil
1 teaspoon baking powder
½ cup sesame oil

Like a hot dog and bun, Mongolian barbecue is meant to be stuffed into a roll, whether it's a flaky sesame shao bing or a steamed lotus bun. Lotus buns are excellent not only with barbecued meat; they may be served in place of rice with any stir-fried meat, poultry, or vegetable dish. Another advantage is that they may be prepared in advance and resteamed for 10 minutes before serving.

1 Place the flour in a large bowl. Add the sugar and yeast to the water and stir to dissolve. Let the mixture stand for 10 minutes until it foams to a head, then add it to the flour along with the safflower or corn oil. Mix to a rough dough. Turn out onto a lightly floured surface and knead for about 10 minutes, until smooth and homogeneous. (If the mixture is dry, add a little more water.) Place the dough in a lightly oiled bowl and cover with a damp towel. Let rise for 3½ to 4 hours, or until tripled in bulk.

2 Punch down the dough and turn out onto a lightly oiled surface. Make an indentation in the center with your fist and place the baking powder in it. Gather up the edges to seal and enclose the baking powder. Knead the dough lightly to incorporate the baking powder evenly. Let the dough rest briefly.

3 Form the dough into a long snakelike roll about 1½ inches in diameter, and cut it into twenty-four pieces. Using your fingers or a rolling pin, roll out each piece to a 3-inch circle. Brush the surface of one circle liberally with sesame oil. Fold it over to form a half-moon shape. Using a sharp knife, lightly score the top surface lengthwise and crosswise. With your fingers, push in the rounded edge at two points to make the shape resemble a lotus leaf. Continue with the remaining circles and arrange the shaped buns about ½ inch apart on steamer trays that have been lined with parchment paper or wet cheesecloth. Let the buns rise for 15 minutes. Steam over high heat for about 12 minutes, until springy to the touch. Remove and serve. To reheat, steam the buns for 10 minutes over high heat. ***Makes twenty-four buns.***

Almond Curd with Assorted Fruits

杏仁豆腐

2½ tablespoons unflavored
  gelatin
3 cups warm water
¼ cup sugar
½ cup sweetened condensed
  milk
1 tablespoon almond extract
2 cups ripe watermelon cut
  into diamond-shaped 1-inch
  pieces
2 cups ripe cantaloupe or
  muskmelon cut into
  diamond-shaped 1-inch
  pieces
3 tablespoons Grand Marnier
  or kirsch

Almond curd is a refreshing dessert that originated in Sichuan province, where the climate is hot and muggy and peppers are a standard seasoning in many dishes. It is especially soothing after the spicy chicken appetizer and barbecued meat slices in this menu, but it would go well with any meal. For those wishing to experiment, any seasonal fruit would be delicious with the almond curd.

1 Place an 8- or 9-inch square or round cake pan in the freezer to chill. In a small saucepan, soften the gelatin in ½ cup of the water. Heat the mixture very slowly, stirring constantly to dissolve the gelatin. Remove from the heat as soon as it is dissolved. Place the sugar, remaining 2½ cups of water, condensed milk, and almond extract in a mixing bowl and stir to dissolve the sugar. Add the dissolved gelatin and mix again. Pour the mixture into the chilled pan and let chill in the refrigerator for about 4 hours, or until firm.

2 While the almond curd is being chilled, place the watermelon and cantaloupe or muskmelon in a mixing bowl. Add the liqueur and toss to coat. Refrigerate for 1 hour, tossing occasionally. Cut the almond curd into 1-inch diamond-shaped pieces. To serve, place a tablespoon or two of crushed ice in each dessert bowl. Spoon some of the almond curd on top and surround with the melon pieces and liquid. *Serves six.*

MENU II

Sweet-and-Sour Cucumber Salad

Spicy Lamb Kebabs

Grilled Fish Steaks with Three Sauces

Three-Treasure Rice Noodles

Sweet-and-Sour Cucumber Salad

糖
醋
黄
瓜

2 pounds gherkin or Kirby
  cucumbers, or 3 gourmet
  seedless cucumbers
2 tablespoons salt

Seasonings
2 tablespoons soy sauce
¼ cup sugar
¼ cup clear rice vinegar
2 tablespoons sesame oil

In China, dishes like this cucumber salad are placed on restaurant tables for diners to nibble on while studying the menu. Their primary function is to "amuse" the mouth and stomach while the other food is being prepared, but they are equally good as a vegetable side dish or pickle. Like other pickled vegetable dishes, these cucumbers may be prepared in advance and chilled. Their flavor will only intensify and improve with age.

1 Rinse the cucumbers and drain thoroughly. Trim the ends and cut lengthwise into halves. Using a spoon, scoop out the seeds. Cut the halves lengthwise again into halves. Roll-cut the strips into 1½-inch pieces and place in a bowl. Add the salt, toss lightly, and let stand at room temperature for 1 hour. Drain off any liquid, rinse lightly under cold running water, and pat dry. Place the pieces in a bowl.

2 Combine the **seasonings,** stirring until the sugar dissolves. Add the mixture to the cucumber pieces and toss lightly to coat. Chill for at least 1 hour before serving. *Serves six.*

夏

Spicy Lamb Kebabs

2½ pounds boned leg of
  lamb, shank portion

Lamb Marinade
½ cup sweet bean sauce or
  hoisin sauce
3 tablespoons soy sauce
¼ cup rice wine
2 tablespoons sugar
2 tablespoons minced garlic
1 tablespoon crushed dried
  chili pepper
1 tablespoon safflower or corn
  oil

1 pound small white onions,
  parboiled and peeled
1 pound fresh button
  mushrooms, rinsed,
  drained, and stems trimmed
3 large green peppers, seeded
  and cut into 2-inch squares

*The delectable flavor of grilled lamb is here beautifully
complemented by the rich marinade with a base of sweet
bean sauce. At first glance, this dish might be considered
a classic recipe, but the addition of the skewered pearl
onions, mushrooms, and peppers raises it above classic
status. Pork, beef, or chicken may be substituted for the
lamb to create an excellent variation.*

1 Remove any fat or gristle from the lamb. Separate
the muscles of the meat and cut it into cubes about
1½ inches square. Place the **lamb marinade** ingredients in a large bowl and stir to combine well. Add
the lamb pieces, toss to coat, cover, and let marinate in the refrigerator for 8 hours or overnight.
Drain off the marinade and reserve.

2 Thread the lamb cubes, green pepper squares,
white onions, and mushrooms onto skewers, alter-
nating items as you do so. Brush some of the marinade over the meat and vegetables.

3 Arrange the skewers about 3 inches from the
source of heat (either the broiler or a charcoal grill)
and cook for 15 to 20 minutes, turning several times
and basting with the marinade. Remove the skewered meat and vegetables, arrange on a serving
platter, and serve with three-treasure rice noodles
(page 75) or steamed lotus buns (page 68). *Serves
six.*

Grilled Fish Steaks with Three Sauces

3 fresh swordfish or halibut
   steaks, about 1 inch thick
   and weighing a little over a
   pound apiece

Fish Marinade
2 tablespoons rice wine
2 slices gingerroot, smashed
   lightly with the flat side of a
   cleaver
3 scallions, smashed lightly
   with the flat side of a
   cleaver
1 teaspoon salt
2 tablespoons sesame oil

Black Bean Sauce
2 tablespoons fermented black
   beans, rinsed and drained
1 tablespoon minced garlic
½ cup chicken broth
1 tablespoon soy sauce
2 tablespoons rice wine
1 teaspoon sugar
1½ teaspoons cornstarch

Spicy Hot-and-Sour Sauce
2 tablespoons minced garlic
2 teaspoons minced
   gingerroot
3 tablespoons minced
   scallions
1 teaspoon chili paste
½ cup chicken broth or water
3 tablespoons soy sauce
2 tablespoons rice wine
1 tablespoon sugar
2 teaspoons Chinese black
   vinegar
1 teaspoon sesame oil
¼ teaspoon freshly ground
   black pepper
1 teaspoon cornstarch

Green Coriander Sauce
1 tablespoon minced
   gingerroot
½ cup chicken broth
1 teaspoon salt
¼ teaspoon freshly ground
   white pepper
½ teaspoon sugar

Swordfish is the perfect food for grilling. Its firm, meaty texture and fresh flavor are greatly enhanced when it is roasted over coals. The flavors of the black bean, spicy Sichuan, and fresh coriander sauces make this dish truly remarkable. Be sure to let the coals get red hot before grilling, and do not overcook the fish.

1 Rinse the fish steaks lightly and drain. Pat dry and cut each one in half crosswise. Place in a deep dish or bowl. Prepare the **fish marinade** by combining the ingredients and lightly pinching the gingerroot and scallions in the rice wine repeatedly for several minutes to impart the flavor. Add the marinade to the fish steaks and turn the steaks so that they are coated. Cover with plastic wrap and let stand at room temperature for 30 minutes.

2 Ready the sauce mixtures for cooking: For the **black bean sauce,** mince the black beans and place with the garlic in a dish near the stove. Combine the remaining ingredients and place near the stove. For the **spicy hot-and-sour sauce,** combine the minced garlic, gingerroot, and scallions. Add the chili paste, and place near the stove. Combine the remaining ingredients and place near the stove. For the **green coriander sauce,** place the minced gingerroot near the stove. Combine the remaining ingredients and place near the stove.

3 Ready charcoals in an outdoor grill or preheat the broiler. Arrange the fish steaks 3 inches from the source of heat, and grill or broil them, basting occasionally and turning once, for 7 to 9 minutes on each side, or until the fish flakes when prodded with a fork.

4 While the fish is cooking, heat a wok, add 2 tablespoons of oil, and add the black beans and garlic. Stir-fry over high heat for about 10 seconds and add the remaining **black bean sauce** mixture. Cook until thickened, about 1 minute, stirring constantly. Transfer to a serving bowl. Clean out the pan and reheat. Add two more tablespoons of oil and heat until hot. Add the minced garlic, ginger-

1 teaspoon sesame oil
1 teaspoon cornstarch
3 tablespoons minced fresh
  coriander (Chinese parsley)

6 tablespoons safflower or
  corn oil

root, scallions, and chili paste. Stir-fry until fragrant, about 10 seconds, and add the remaining **spicy hot-and-sour sauce** mixture. Cook until thickened, about 1 minute, stirring constantly, and remove to a serving dish. Clean out the pan and reheat. Add the remaining oil and heat until hot. Add the gingerroot and stir-fry until fragrant, about 10 seconds. Add the remaining **green coriander sauce** mixture and cook until thickened, about 1 minute, stirring constantly. Remove to a serving bowl and serve the three sauces with the fish. (The diner may choose among the sauces, or put a little bit on different sections of the fish steak.) **Serves six.**

· ·

Three-Treasure Rice Noodles

½ pound rice noodles (*mi fen*)

Minced Seasonings
1 tablespoon minced garlic
1 tablespoon minced
  gingerroot
8 fresh shiitake mushrooms,
  rinsed, drained, and cut
  into thin julienne strips (if
  unavailable, substitute
  dried; soften in hot water,
  remove the stems, and use
  the caps.)
3 cups shredded leeks or
  1-inch-long scallion pieces
2 cups shredded carrots
3 tablespoons safflower or
  corn oil

Sauce
3½ tablespoons soy sauce
2 tablespoons rice wine
½ teaspoon salt
1 teaspoon sugar
1 teaspoon sesame oil
1½ cups chicken broth

For special meals, my Chinese surrogate mother would often prepare staple dishes other than rice. Noodles were a natural choice, and she favored thin rice noodles for their delicacy and versatility. Meats and vegetables would be shredded and used as a garnish. The noodles, she insisted, must be tossed gently, so that they remain whole. This dish is my adapted version of her stir-fried noodle recipe.

1 Place the rice noodles in hot water to cover for 10 minutes. Remove and drain. Place the minced seasonings, the shredded mushrooms, leeks, and carrots, and the prepared sauce near the stove.

2 Heat a wok, add the safflower or corn oil, and heat until very hot. Add the **minced seasonings** and stir-fry for about 10 seconds, until fragrant. Add the shredded mushrooms, leeks, and carrots. Stir-fry over high heat for about 1½ minutes, adding a tablespoon or two of the sauce if the mixture is very dry. Add the **sauce** and heat until boiling. Add the rice noodles and cook for about 5 minutes, until the sauce has evaporated and the noodles are tender. Transfer to a platter and serve. **Serves six.**

夏

CHINESE SALADS

In the Orient, as in the West, summertime is the peak season for vegetables. The shelves of open-air markets are overflowing with firm, ripe produce — evidence of the balmy days of summer.

There are tender hearts of baby cabbage; the highly prized hollow-stalked "empty heart vegetable"; spinach; kale; and rape. Bamboo shoots — both the larger, more mature varieties, and the delicate, thin baby shoots — are everywhere, not to mention the numerous gourds and squashes.

In China, fresh vegetables are prized. Cooking methods such as stir-frying, steaming, and blanching are favored, since they preserve the vegetables' crisp textures, vibrant colors, and fresh flavors. Vegetables are also used in multilayered salads with assorted meats and seafood and tossed in a light, pungent dressing. And many are transformed into fragrant pickles through preserving techniques that evolved with the ancient Chinese.

Chinese pickles are varied and versatile. They may be divided into groups according to their preparation method and culinary use. First, there are the non-homemade pickles that are used as pungent seasonings. Notable examples from this category are Sichuan preserved mustard greens, fermented or salted black beans, "red-in-snow," and dried, salted turnip.

The second type of Chinese pickle is similar to common Western varieties. These pickles generally are prepared in the home and served as a piquant side dish or a spicy vegetable entrée. They call for the use of a brine or pickling marinade and require a steeping period — though not as lengthy as pickles from the first category. Some of the most popular examples from this group are *pao cai* (a pickled cabbage dish believed to be the inspiration for sauerkraut), sweet-and-sour cucumbers, and pickled gingerroot.

To most Westerners, the third category of Chinese pickles may resemble a cooked vegetable side dish. Many of these, such as eggplant fingers with spicy sesame sauce and saucy green beans, are ready to be eaten immediately after preparation, but like most pickles, their flavor improves with age. Some are served as side dishes or vegetable entrées, and others are served as *amuse-gueules*, small-bite appetizers, like those from the previous category. Their role is to combat any hunger pangs while awaiting the arrival of the meal. These pickles are especially handy for entertaining.

Vegetables also play a major role in Chinese layered salads. Like French composed salads, they may be prepared completely in advance, and they are excellent appetizers. They are ideal for warm-weather picnics or buffets but work beautifully any time of the year, and they are appropriately served at room temperature or chilled.

Most Chinese layered salads follow the same general formula:

Textural Base

The base serves as a foil and provides a textural contrast to the other ingredients. Noodles such as bean threads, vermicelli, rice sticks, or homemade seasoned pasta may be used.

Vegetable Layer

Vegetables enhance and accentuate the freshness of the dish and provide a contrasting crisp texture. Most vegetables are blanched in boiling water and then refreshed in ice water. This intensifies their color and flavor yet keeps them crisp.

Meat or Seafood Layer

For the third layer, the Chinese use cooked beef, pork, chicken, duck, or seafood. Marinating the meat or seafood before cooking enhances the flavor and increases the tenderness. The most popular cooking methods for these ingredients are stir-frying, poaching, steaming, braising, and barbecuing.

Finally, the assembled salad is topped with a spicy dressing, such as a Chinese vinaigrette, a light mustard dressing, or a spicy sesame or peanut sauce. Oriental sesame oil often is used for a base, and Japanese or Chinese vinegar frequently gives the sauce its tart edge.

CHINESE SALADS

Pickled Gingerroot

Hot-and-Sour Cabbage

Peanut Salad

Drunken Mushrooms

Spicy Pickled Cucumbers

Celery Hearts and Peppercorn Dressing

Carrot Salad with Fresh Coriander

Eggplant Fingers in a Spicy Sesame Sauce

Bell Peppers and Snow Peas in a Spicy Garlic Dressing

Saucy Green Beans

Silver Pin Noodles

Chicken Noodle Salad with Spicy Chili Oil Dressing

Shrimp with Snow Peas in a Light Mustard Dressing

Peking Three-Treasure Layered Salad

Ginger Noodles with Mussels and Asparagus

Pickled Gingerroot

½ pound fresh gingerroot,
  preferably spring ginger
  with pink stems
2 teaspoons salt

Marinade
1 cup clear rice vinegar
¼ cup sugar
½ cup water

In the late summer, when young, pink-tipped gingerroot is available at American Chinese markets, customers are often seen carting it away by the barrel. They most certainly are buying it in such vast quantities for pickling. Sweet-and-sour pickled gingerroot is a favored side dish in China, especially among the Cantonese. In the Orient, young ginger shoots are available all summer; in the United States they appear a little later. If mature gingerroot — with a thicker skin — is the only kind available, it may be used in this recipe, but be sure to peel away the tough outer skin before pickling.

1 If the gingerroot is young, with pink stems and paperlike skin, scrub with a vegetable brush and drain thoroughly. If the piece is more mature, remove the thick skin, using a vegetable peeler. Rub the surface of the gingerroot with the salt and let stand for 2 hours at room temperature. Drain the gingerroot, rinse it, pat dry, and place in a pickling jar or bowl.

2 Combine the **marinade** ingredients in a saucepan. Heat the marinade until boiling and pour it over the gingerroot. Let cool, uncovered, to room temperature. Cover tightly and refrigerate for 24 hours before serving. Using a sharp knife, cut the gingerroot into paper-thin slices and serve as a pickle. The gingerroot will keep indefinitely in the marinade in the refrigerator. *Serves six.*

Hot-and-Sour Cabbage

酸
辣
白
菜

1 large head Chinese cabbage
  (Napa)
1½ teaspoons salt
¼ cup sesame oil
10 thin slices gingerroot
3 to 4 dried red chili peppers,
  cut into ¼-inch pieces and
  seeds removed
1 teaspoon Sichuan
  peppercorns

The peak season for Chinese cabbage is the fall, but most Chinese markets carry an ample supply of this versatile vegetable year round. And a Chinese cabbage pickle, particularly this one, is ideally suited for warm-weather eating. The oval-leafed Napa is recommended for this recipe, but celery cabbage or bok choy, thinly sliced, will also work nicely.

1 Rinse the cabbage leaves lightly and drain thoroughly. Cut away and discard the stem portion of

Seasonings
2½ tablespoons clear rice
vinegar
2 tablespoons sugar
1 tablespoon soy sauce

each leaf. Cut the leaves into 2-inch squares. Place the pieces in a bowl, add the salt, toss lightly, and let stand for 20 minutes. Pour off any water that has accumulated and drain the cabbage pieces on paper towels. Place the cabbage in a mixing bowl.

2 Heat a wok or a heavy skillet with a lid, add the sesame oil, and heat until just smoking. Add the gingerroot, chili peppers, and peppercorns. Cover and remove from the heat. Let the mixture stand for about 20 minutes, or until it reaches room temperature. Strain out the flavorings, reserving the oil. Mix the oil with the **seasonings**, stirring until the sugar dissolves. Add the mixture to the cabbage and toss lightly to coat. Chill for several hours before serving. *Serves six.*

Peanut Salad

涼
拌
花
生

1½ pounds raw peanuts, in
their skins
6 cups water
1 tablespoon safflower or corn
oil
2 fresh red chili peppers,
seeded and minced

Spicy Vinaigrette
¼ cup soy sauce
½ teaspoon salt
1 tablespoon sugar
2 tablespoons sesame oil
2 tablespoons clear rice
vinegar
2 tablespoons rice wine

1 cup chopped coriander
(Chinese parsley)

Small dishes of fried peanuts are often served to customers in restaurants as they ponder the menu. Some restaurants even go to the trouble of preparing unusual salads with peanuts — like this one. The crunchy peanuts are an excellent foil for the delicious coriander dressing. Serve this dish as an appetizer, or as an unusual side dish or pickle with the entrées.

1 Place the peanuts in the water in a wok or heavy saucepan and heat until boiling. Reduce the heat to medium and cook for 15 minutes, or until the peanuts are still just a tiny bit chewy. (Their skins will loosen but not fall off.) Remove, drain, and discard the water. Place the peanuts in a mixing bowl.

2 While the peanuts are cooking, combine the ingredients of the spicy vinaigrette and place near the stove. Heat another wok or saucepan and add the safflower or corn oil. Heat until hot and add the chili peppers. Stir-fry for about 10 seconds, until fragrant, and add the **spicy vinaigrette**. Heat until the mixture begins to boil; then continue cooking for about 2 minutes. Remove and add to the peanuts. Toss lightly to coat. Let sit for at least 1 hour, turning constantly. Add the coriander and transfer to a serving dish. Serve at room temperature. *Serves six.*

Drunken Mushrooms

Drunken Marinade

1 cup good-quality rice wine, or ½ cup Scotch

1½ cups chicken broth (increase to 2 cups if using Scotch)

1 teaspoon salt

6 slices gingerroot, lightly smashed with the flat side of a cleaver

6 scallions, lightly smashed with the flat side of a cleaver

4 cloves garlic, lightly smashed with the flat side of a cleaver

1 pound fresh button mushrooms, ends trimmed and lightly rinsed

2 15-ounce cans straw mushrooms, drained, plunged into boiling water for 1 minute (to remove the tinny flavor), and drained again

2 tablespoons freshly squeezed lemon juice

In eastern China, where the renowned Shaohsing rice wine is made, there is a group of dishes that are termed "drunken." In this particular process, various types of meat, poultry, and seafood are barely cooked and then marinated in a strong rice-wine mixture. The finished dishes are served, in their fragrant marinade, as appetizers or snacks. In this recipe, fresh button mushrooms and canned straw mushrooms are cooked in a seasoned marinade, then served as a delicious pickled salad or vegetable side dish.

1 Place the **drunken marinade** ingredients in a non-aluminum pot and heat until boiling. Boil 10 minutes, to marry the flavors. Toss the mushrooms in the lemon juice and add them to the drunken marinade. Reheat until boiling and cook for about 2 minutes. Turn off the heat and let cool to room temperature. Serve at room temperature or chilled. The mushrooms will keep for several days refrigerated in the marinade. *Serves six.*

Spicy Pickled Cucumbers

2 pounds gherkin or Kirby cucumbers, or 3 gourmet seedless cucumbers, rinsed and drained

1 tablespoon salt

Spicy Dressing

2 tablespoons sesame oil

2 fresh hot red or green chili peppers (if unavailable, substitute dried; cut lengthwise into strips, removing the seeds)

4 slices gingerroot, smashed lightly with the flat side of a cleaver

This pickled cucumber dish reminds me of lunches of a favorite northern-style haunt from my student days in Taipei. We would often order a plate of crusty-brown pan-fried dumplings and a small bowl of this cucumber salad. The two dishes made an inexpensive, filling — and delicious — lunch or dinner. Other vegetables — such as cabbage, carrots, and daikon radishes — may be substituted for the cucumbers.

1 Trim the ends of the cucumbers and slice lengthwise in half. Scoop out the seeds and cut each cucumber lengthwise into strips about 1 inch wide. Slicing on the diagonal, roll-cut the cucumbers into 1-inch-square pieces. Place in a mixing bowl, add

¼ cup clear rice vinegar
¼ cup sugar
1 tablespoon soy sauce

the salt, and toss lightly to coat. Let stand for 1 hour. Rinse lightly, drain, and pat dry.

2 To make the **spicy dressing**: Heat a wok and add the sesame oil. Heat until very hot and add the chili peppers. Toss lightly in the hot oil for 15 seconds and add the gingerroot. Stir-fry for 5 seconds and add the cucumbers. Toss lightly and add the rice vinegar, sugar, and soy sauce. Stir-fry for about 1 minute and remove to a serving dish. Let stand about 20 minutes before serving, tossing occassionally. Serve at room temperature or chilled. *Serves six.*

Celery Hearts with Peppercorn Dressing

2 pounds celery hearts

Spicy Peppercorn Dressing
1 teaspoon freshly ground white pepper
¼ cup soy sauce
2 tablespoons sesame oil
2 tablespoons minced scallions
1 tablespoon minced gingerroot
1 tablespoon Chinese black vinegar
2 teaspoons sugar

1 tablespoon minced scallion greens (for garnish)

In the western provinces of Sichuan and Hunan, peppers and peppercorns figure prominently in the seasoning of many dishes. The Sichuanese chefs claim that rather than detracting from the natural taste of the ingredients, these strong flavorings accentuate and complement. Such is the case in this dish. The spicy peppercorn sauce subtly underlines the fresh crispness of the celery slices.

1 Rinse the celery hearts and peel away the tough skin, if any. Trim the ends and cut away any leaves. Cut the celery stalks into 3-inch lengths and then cut crosswise into thin slices about ⅛ inch thick. Heat 2 quarts of water until boiling and drop the celery slices into the boiling water for 30 seconds. Remove and immediately immerse in cold water. Drain thoroughly and pat dry. Place the slices in a large bowl.

2 To make the **spicy peppercorn dressing**: Heat a dry wok until hot and add the white pepper. Stirring constantly, cook over medium heat for about 1 minute, until fragrant. Transfer to a bowl and add the remaining dressing ingredients. Mix to blend and then add to the celery slices. Toss to coat. Transfer the slices to a serving platter and sprinkle the minced scallions on top. Serve at room temperature. *Serves six.*

Carrot Salad with Fresh Coriander

1 pound carrots, peeled, ends trimmed, and cut into matchstick-size shreds
½ cup coarsely chopped fresh coriander (Chinese parsley)

Dressing
⅓ cup light soy sauce (if unavailable, use medium-grade, all-purpose soy sauce)
½ teaspoon salt
1 tablespoon sugar
3 tablespoons clear rice vinegar
1 tablespoon rice wine
2 tablespoons sesame oil

Fresh coriander, or Chinese parsley, is a popular seasoning in the Orient. It is often used in soups, but it is found most frequently on cold platters. Paired with the sweet carrots and tart dressing, the coriander provides a colorful and flavorful addition to this simple salad. For those who are not particularly fond of the taste, the coriander may be omitted and replaced by fresh parsley.

1 Place the carrot shreds and the chopped coriander in a large mixing bowl.

2 Combine the **dressing** ingredients and stir until the sugar dissolves. Add the dressing to the carrots and coriander. Toss lightly to coat and chill for 1 hour before serving. Transfer to a platter or bowl and serve. *Serves six.*

Eggplant Fingers in a Spicy Sesame Sauce

芝
蔴
茄
子

2 pounds Chinese eggplant or young Italian eggplant

Spicy Sesame Sauce
¼ cup soy sauce
¼ cup sesame oil
3 tablespoons rice wine
2 tablespoons Chinese sesame paste
2 tablespoons Chinese black vinegar
1½ tablespoons sugar
2 tablespoons minced scallions
1 tablespoon minced garlic
1 tablespoon minced gingerroot
1 teaspoon chili paste

2 tablespoons roasted sesame seeds

Chinese eggplant, with its long, thin body and deep purple color, could easily be considered a delicacy when compared to the large, seedy specimens found in American supermarkets. It is worth the trek to the nearest Chinese grocery store, but if time or availability is a problem, the larger Western eggplant may be substituted. (In this case, peel the eggplant, cut it into strips as directed in the recipe, and steam for 20 minutes, or until tender.)

1 Trim the ends of the eggplants and cut them in half lengthwise. Cut the halves lengthwise into strips about ½ inch wide and 3 to 4 inches long. Arrange the pieces in two 10-inch quiche pans or pie plates. Place the pans in the bottom of two 12-inch steamer trays. Stack the trays and cover.

2 Fill a wok with water level with the bottom edge of the steamer and heat until boiling. Place the steamer trays over the boiling water and steam for 15 minutes, or until the eggplant pieces are tender when pierced with a knife. Reverse the order of the steamer trays midway through the steaming period. Let the eggplant cool slightly and transfer to a serving dish.

3 Combine the ingredients of the **spicy sesame sauce** and stir until smooth. Before serving, pour this mixture over the steamed eggplant. Sprinkle the top with sesame seeds. Serve at room temperature. *Serves six.*

....

Bell Peppers and Snow Peas in a Spicy Garlic Dressing

4 medium-sized red bell peppers, rinsed, cored, and seeded
½ pound fresh snow peas, ends snapped and veiny strings removed
1 tablespoon safflower or corn oil
1 tablespoon sesame oil
1½ tablespoons rice wine

Spicy Garlic Dressing
3 tablespoons soy sauce
1 tablespoon minced garlic, chopped to a smooth paste
1½ teaspoons sugar
2 teaspoons sesame oil
1 teaspoon chili paste (optional)

2 tablespoons chopped scallion greens

This simple salad dish is not only delicious but versatile as well. It may be served warm as a vegetable side dish or cold as a salad-pickle or appetizer. You may further embellish the dish by tossing pieces of cooked or smoked chicken and turkey in the warm, garlicky dressing.

1 Cut the peppers into matchstick-size shreds. Rinse the snow peas and drain thoroughly. Combine the ingredients of the spicy garlic dressing.

2 Heat a wok and add the safflower or corn oil and the sesame oil. Heat until nearly smoking and add the peppers and snow peas. Toss lightly over high heat, stirring constantly, and add the rice wine. Continue cooking for about 1 minute, then add the **spicy garlic dressing**. Toss lightly over high heat and cook for about 2 minutes, or until the sauce has reduced slightly and the snow peas and peppers are still crisp but cooked. Transfer to a serving platter and sprinkle the scallion greens on top. Serve warm or at room temperature. *Serves six.*

Saucy Green Beans

2 pounds yard-long string beans
2 tablespoons safflower or corn oil
1 cup minced leeks or scallions

Sauce
¼ cup soy sauce
1½ tablespoons sugar
3 tablespoons rice wine
½ cup water

1 teaspoon sesame oil

This dish was inspired by a green bean dish that my mother made every year at Thanksgiving. I would often snack on the cold leftovers the next day, and it is this memory that inspired my Chinese rendition of that family classic. If yard-long string beans are unavailable, substitute Western green beans.

1 Trim the ends of the string beans and cut them into pieces about 3 inches long. Combine the sauce ingredients.

2 Heat a wok or a heavy skillet and add the safflower or corn oil. Heat the oil until very hot and add the leeks. Stir-fry for about 1 minute over high heat and add the string beans. Toss lightly over high heat for about 1 minute, adding a little rice wine if the mixture is too dry. Add the **sauce** and heat until boiling, stirring constantly. Turn the heat to low, cover, and cook for about 12 minutes, or until the beans are tender. Uncover and turn the heat to high. Cook until the sauce has reduced to a glaze and add the sesame oil. Toss lightly and transfer to a serving platter. Serve hot, at room temperature, or cold. ***Serves six.***

Silver Pin Noodles

銀
針
粉

Noodle Dough
¾ cup wheat starch
¼ cup tapioca starch
2 teaspoons sesame oil
2 tablespoons ginger wine
    (2 tablespoons rice wine
    infused with the juice of 2
    slices of gingerroot)
½ cup hot water

½ pound small raw shrimp,
    peeled

Shrimp Marinade
1 tablespoon rice wine
½ teaspoon salt
½ teaspoon sesame oil

1½ cups barbecued pork
    (page 40), cut into
    matchstick-size shreds
6 dried Chinese black
    mushrooms, softened in hot
    water for 20 minutes, stems
    removed, and caps
    shredded finely
¼ pound snow peas, ends
    snapped and veiny strings
    removed
2 cups fresh bean sprouts,
    rinsed lightly and drained
2 eggs, lightly beaten
¼ cup safflower or corn oil

Dressing
3 tablespoons light soy sauce
½ teaspoon salt
2 tablespoons Chinese rice
    wine
2 teaspoons sugar
1 tablespoon sesame oil

In most Cantonese dim sum restaurants, "silver pin" noodles are a staple. They are often seen displayed on carts, along with savory pastries, topped with inverted glass bowls. The layers of barbecued pork, bean sprouts, snow peas, and shredded egg sheets make a colorful contrast to the oval white noodles. Serve this dish with others as an appetizer or salad-staple, or by itself as a filling snack or a light lunch.

1 Place the wheat starch and tapioca starch in a mixing bowl, and stir to combine. Add the sesame oil, ginger wine, and boiling water, and mix with a wooden spoon to form a rough dough. Turn the dough out onto a counter and knead lightly for about 2 minutes. Using the palms of your hands, form a long snakelike roll. Cut it into about fifty pieces. Roll each piece into a 3-inch "pin," tapered at the ends and thicker in the middle. Line a bamboo steamer with parchment paper and lightly brush it with oil. Place the noodles in the steamer tray and cover. Steam for 10 to 15 minutes over vigorously boiling water. Remove and arrange in a deep serving dish. Arrange the barbecued pork shreds in a circular pile on top.

2 Score each shrimp along the length of the back and remove the vein. The scoring will allow the shrimp to "butterfly" when cooked. Rinse the shrimp and drain thoroughly. Place them in a linen dishtowel and squeeze out as much moisture as possible. Place the shrimp in a bowl, add the **shrimp marinade**, toss lightly, and let stand for 20 minutes. Assemble the other ingredients and prepare the dressing.

3 Wipe the inside of a 10-inch nonstick skillet or a well-seasoned wok with a paper towel soaked with some of the safflower or corn oil. Heat the pan until a little water sprinkled onto the surface evaporates immediately. Remove from the heat, add one third of the beaten eggs, and tilt the pan to form a thin, circular pancake. Place the pan back over the heat and cook until set. Flip the egg sheet over and set it aside to cool. Make two more egg sheets in the same manner and cut all of them into match-stick-size shreds. Arrange in a circular strip around the barbecued pork.

4 Heat a wok, adding the remaining safflower or corn oil, and heat until hot. Drain the shrimp and add to the hot oil, stir-frying until they change color and curl. Remove with a handled strainer and drain. Arrange the cooked shrimp in a circle in the center of the barbecued pork. Reheat the pan and the oil. Add the black mushrooms and stir-fry for 10 seconds. Add the snow peas and bean sprouts. Toss lightly over high heat for about 1 minute and add the **dressing**. Cook until heated through and the liquid begins to boil. Remove the bean sprouts, snow peas, and black mushrooms with a handled strainer and arrange around the egg sheets. Pour the heated dressing over all. Serve warm, cold, or at room temperature. *Serves six.*

Chicken Noodle Salad with Spicy Chili Oil Dressing

1 tablespoon safflower or corn oil

½ pound thin egg noodle clusters or vermicelli

1 teaspoon sesame oil

2 cups carrots, peeled, ends trimmed, and cut into julienne strips

2 cups cucumbers, peeled, seeded, ends trimmed, and cut into julienne strips

2 cups fresh bean sprouts, rinsed lightly and drained

2 cups scallion greens, cut into 1-inch lengths

2 cups cooked chicken, cut into julienne strips

Spicy Chili Oil Dressing

2 tablespoons sesame oil

2 tablespoons safflower or corn oil

4 dried red chili peppers, cut into ¼-inch-square pieces, seeds removed

6 slices gingerroot, smashed lightly with the flat side of a cleaver

6 scallions, smashed lightly with the flat side of a cleaver

¼ cup soy sauce

2 tablespoons rice wine

1½ tablespoons sugar

3 tablespoons Chinese black vinegar

Sichuan province, in southwestern China, is known for its spicy home-style fare. This fragrant noodle dish admirably demonstrates the delights of this particular cuisine. Serve these noodles with other entrées as a flavorful staple, or as a meal in itself for lunch or dinner. This salad is also perfect for picnics.

1 In a large pot, bring 2 quarts of water and the safflower or corn oil to a boil. Add the noodles and cook until just tender. (Do not overcook.) Remove and drain in a colander. Lightly rinse the noodles under cold running water. Drain thoroughly and toss with the teaspoon of sesame oil.

2 Arrange the noodles in the bottom of a deep round dish. Arrange the carrots, cucumbers, bean sprouts, and scallions in concentric circles over the noodles, leaving a space in the center. Place the chicken in the center.

3 Prepare the **spicy chili oil dressing**: Heat the safflower or corn oil and sesame oil until smoking in a wok or saucepan with a lid. Add the chili peppers, gingerroot, and scallions. Cover and remove from the heat. Let cool, covered, to room temperature. Strain the oil, discarding the seasonings. Mix the seasoned oil with the remaining ingredients, stirring to dissolve the sugar. Just before serving, pour the dressing over the salad, toss lightly to combine the ingredients and to coat them. Serve at room temperature or cold. Alternatively, you may serve the dressing separately. ***Serves six.***

Shrimp with Snow Peas in a Light Mustard Dressing

1½ pounds medium raw
  shrimp, peeled

Shrimp Marinade
2 tablespoons rice wine
3 slices gingerroot, smashed
  lightly with the flat side of a
  cleaver
¼ teaspoon salt

1 ounce bean threads
  (cellophane noodles),
  softened in warm water to
  cover for 10 minutes

Bean Thread Dressing
1 teaspoon sesame oil
2 tablespoons chicken broth

½ pound fresh snow peas,
  ends snapped and veiny
  strings removed

Mustard Dressing
1 tablespoon mustard powder
2 tablespoons hot water
½ cup duck (or plum) sauce
3 tablespoons clear rice
  vinegar
2 tablespoons sesame oil
1 tablespoon soy sauce
1 teaspoon salt
1 tablespoon sugar
2 tablespoons chopped
  scallion greens

Although mustard powder is considered a powerful sea-soning, when it is used in a light sauce, its spicy flavor serves to accentuate the fresh, sweet taste of other ingredients — particularly seafood and vegetables, as in this dish. Freshly poached scallops, in place of the shrimp, are also excellent in this layered salad.

1 Score each shrimp along the length of the back and remove the vein. The scoring will allow the shrimp to "butterfly" when cooked. Rinse the shrimp lightly under cold running water and drain thoroughly. Place the shrimp in a linen dishtowel, and squeeze out as much moisture as possible. Place the shrimp in a bowl. To make the **shrimp marinade**, pinch the gingerroot in the rice wine repeatedly for several minutes to impart the flavor, then add the salt. Add the marinade to the shrimp, toss lightly to coat, and let marinate for 20 minutes at room temperature. Discard the gingerroot slices. Heat 1 quart water in a saucepan or wok until boiling. Add the shrimp, reduce the heat to medium, and cook for 1½ minutes, or until just cooked. Remove and drain. Set the shrimp aside.

2 Drain the bean threads and cut them into 3-inch lengths. In a wok or saucepan, heat 1 quart water until boiling. Add the snow peas and remove immediately with a handled strainer. Refresh in cold water and drain thoroughly. Reheat the water until boiling and drop the bean threads into the water. Cook for about 1 minute, and remove to a colander. Rinse with cold water, drain, and toss lightly with the **bean thread dressing**. Arrange the bean threads on a plate, arrange the snow peas on top, and place the shrimp on top of the snow peas. Combine the ingredients of the **mustard dressing**. Before serving, pour the dressing over the shrimp and snow peas. Sprinkle the minced scallions on top. Lightly toss the ingredients so that all are coated with the dressing. Serve at room temperature or chilled. *Serves six.*

Peking Three-Treasure Layered Salad

2 pounds center-cut pork loin

Pork Marinade
1 tablespoon sweet bean
  sauce (if unavailable,
  substitute hoisin sauce)
2 tablespoons soy sauce
1 tablespoon rice wine
1 teaspoon sesame oil
1 teaspoon sugar
2 teaspoons minced
  gingerroot
1 teaspoon minced garlic

1 pound yard-long string
  beans (if unavailable,
  substitute Western string
  beans)
1 teaspoon salt
2 ounces bean threads
  (cellophane noodles),
  softened in warm water to
  cover for 10 minutes

Bean Thread Seasonings
1 teaspoon sesame oil
2 tablespoons chicken broth

Dressing
2 tablespoons sesame oil
2 or 3 dried red chili peppers,
  seeds removed, minced
2 tablespoons minced
  scallions
¼ cup soy sauce
1 teaspoon salt, or to taste
1 tablespoon sugar
2 tablespoons clear rice
  vinegar
2 tablespoons rice wine

This is one of the most classic presentations of the Chinese layered salad concept. Although this dish traditionally is made with pork, beef or chicken easily could be substituted. If bean threads are unavailable, use thin rice vermicelli, or omit the noodles altogether.

1 Remove any fat or gristle from the pork loin and discard. Cut the meat, lengthwise, into strips that are 2 to 3 inches thick. Place the pork strips in a bowl. Combine the **pork marinade** ingredients, and add the marinade to the bowl containing the pork loin. Toss lightly to coat, cover with plastic wrap, and let stand for at least 4 hours at room temperature, or overnight in the refrigerator.

2 Preheat the oven to 375 degrees. Arrange the pork strips on a rack in a roasting pan and bake for 45 minutes, or until the inside is cooked and the outside is brown. Remove, let cool to room temperature, and cut, across the grain, into thin slices, about ¼ inch thick. Set aside.

3 Cut off the ends of the green beans and cut the beans into 3-inch lengths. Heat 2 quarts of water with the teaspoon of salt until boiling, and add the green beans. Cook for 3 to 5 minutes, or until just tender (if you are using Western string beans, you will need to cook them a little longer). Remove and immediately immerse in cold water until cool.

4 Drain the bean threads and, using kitchen scissors, cut them into 3-inch lengths. Toss lightly with the **bean thread seasonings** and arrange the seasoned bean threads on a platter, making a slight indentation in the center. Arrange the green beans on top, once again making a slight indentation in the center. Arrange the sliced pork loin in the center.

5 Prepare the **dressing**: Heat a wok or a saucepan, add the sesame oil, and heat until nearly smoking. Add the minced peppers and scallions. Cook for 10 seconds, stirring constantly until fragrant. Add the remaining ingredients and heat until boiling. Cook for about 1 minute over high heat and remove. Pour the dressing over the salad and serve warm or at room temperature. *Serves six.*

Ginger Noodles with Mussels and Asparagus

Ginger Noodles
2 whole eggs, at room temperature
1 egg yolk, at room temperature
2½ tablespoons finely minced gingerroot
½ teaspoon sesame oil
1 teaspoon salt
1¾ to 2 cups all-purpose flour

3 pounds mussels

Mussel Cooking Mixture
½ cup water
½ cup rice wine
3 scallions, smashed lightly with the flat side of a cleaver
6 peppercorns

1½ pounds fresh asparagus
2 cloves garlic
½ cup safflower or corn oil
Juice of ½ lemon
1 teaspoon salt

Thanks to the food processor and pasta machine, fresh, seasoned pasta can be prepared quickly in the home kitchen. The gingery noodles in this dish have an incredibly delicate flavor. Cooked until just tender in the sesame-flavored water, they become a delicious foil for the poached mussels and asparagus. Other seafoods, such as shrimp, oysters, and scallops, also would do nicely in this dish.

1 Prepare the **ginger noodles**: In a food processor fitted with the steel blade, combine the eggs, egg yolk, gingerroot, sesame oil, and salt. Pulse, turning the machine on and off, until well blended. Add the flour and pulse again for about 15 seconds, or until the mixture forms small beads. Remove the dough and press it together into a ball. Knead it lightly to form a smooth and homogeneous dough (about 1 minute), cover with plastic wrap, and let rest for 30 minutes at room temperature.

2 Divide the dough in half and dust each half with flour. Set a pasta machine at the widest setting (number 1) and roll the dough through the machine. Fold the dough in thirds, folding the top and bottom inward, dust lightly with flour, and roll the dough through the machine. Repeat this process one more time, flouring the dough lightly. Change the machine to the next highest setting and roll through the machine again. Dust again lightly and move the machine up a notch. Roll and dust one more time and lay the dough strips out on a lightly floured tray. Let dry for 30 minutes. Cut the dough strips into ¼-inch-wide fettucini noodles and set aside.

3 Clean the mussels, rinsing in several changes of cold water. Drain and set aside. Place the **mussel cooking mixture** in a saucepan or wok, and heat until boiling. Lower the heat and let simmer for about 5 minutes. Add the mussels and cover. Cook for 3 to 5 minutes, shaking the pot, until the mussels open. Remove the mussels, discarding any that didn't open, and remove the meat from the shells. Set aside. Turn up the heat under the cooking mixture and cook, uncovered, until the liquid is reduced to about ⅓ cup. Strain out the seasonings, set aside, and cover.

4 Break each asparagus at the point where it begins to get tough, and roll-cut the asparagus into 1½-inch lengths. Heat 1 quart water until boiling and cook the asparagus for about 5 minutes, or until tender. Remove and refresh in cold water. Drain.

5 In a food processor fitted with the steel blade, purée the garlic cloves. Slowly add the olive oil and process until the mixture is slightly thick. Slowly add the reduced cooking liquid to make a creamy dressing. Add the lemon juice and salt and taste for seasoning. Set aside.

6 Bring 4 to 6 quarts water and a tablespoon of sesame oil to a boil in a large pot. Add the noodles, stirring once, and cook for 3 to 5 minutes, until just tender. Remove and drain in a colander. Arrange the noodles in a deep bowl, top with the mussels and asparagus, add the dressing, and toss lightly to coat. Serve warm or at room temperature. *Serves six.*

FALL

· · · · · · · · · · · · · · · · ·

秋

秋

If white clouds

are abundant

there will be

a good harvest

for late crops

. . . .

THE FESTIVAL OF THE HARVEST MOON

As the days grow shorter and the balmy breezes of summer become brisk with the first chill of fall, the moon begins to reach a luminous fullness. At this time, the Chinese begin their preparations for the Festival of the Harvest Moon, which takes place on the fifteenth day of the eighth month of the lunar calendar. For the Chinese, this holiday officially marks the arrival of autumn.

The ancient Chinese believed that this is the time of the year when the female principle, signifying darkness and cold, begins to take the upper hand in nature. The moon, which is considered a female deity, was believed to consist of "yin" fluid or water. On the evening of the Moon Festival, the moon is at its brightest, and for one night only — so the Chinese say — it is perfectly round.

In ancient China, since this festival was dedicated to a female deity, it was the responsibility of the women in the household to honor the moon and orchestrate the festivities. Five plates were set out on an altar stacked with apples, peaches, pomegranates, grapes, and melon. The round shape of the fruits resembled the moon and symbolized the family unit. A tablet inscribed with the design of a rabbit, known as the Moon Hare, was also placed on the altar.

Around midnight, when the moon was nearing its fullest stage, the ancient ritual would begin: A pair of candles was lit and incense sticks were burned in the family urn. A poster showing the Moon Hare standing under the sacred cassia tree and pounding the pill of immortality in his mortar was first displayed, then removed and burned. The festival that followed this rite lasted for three days.

Nowadays, in modern China, the holiday is celebrated by moon gazing and by sampling moon cakes, a traditional delicacy since ancient times. Moon cakes are eaten with as much enthusiasm today as in the past.

For weeks before the holiday, bakeries are brimming with countless varieties of moon cakes —

sweet and savory alike. The cakes are usually circular, or take the form of a rabbit, fish, or pagoda. Since sweet moon cakes are often cloying and rich with pork lard, many contain a salty duck egg in the center for contrast. Sweet fillings consist of lotus seeds, candied fruits, and nuts. Savory moon cakes are stuffed with pork, dried shrimp, and assorted vegetables, but there are numerous variations on both sweet and savory themes.

Moon cakes have earned a special place in the hearts of the Chinese because they were used by the enslaved Han Chinese during the Yüan dynasty (1271–1368) to hide messages for a planned overthrow of their Mongolian oppressors. The rebellion was successful, marking the beginning of the Ming dynasty (1368–1644), and since that time, moon cakes have been a special favorite of many Chinese.

Moon cakes are not an inexpensive delicacy, owing to their sumptuous fillings, and many Chinese set aside money throughout the year to pay for the generous supply that is traditionally sent to relatives and friends for the holiday. Some resourceful recipients recycle the cakes they receive by changing the names on the box and sending them on to their family and friends without even breaking open the seal.

MENU I

Spicy Spareribs Steamed in Winter Squash

Triple-Shred Chicken Soup

Savory Moon Cakes

Sweet Moon Cakes

Spicy Spareribs Steamed in Winter Squash

粉
蒸
排
骨

3 pounds country-style
spareribs

Sparerib Marinade
4 tablespoons sweet bean
sauce or hoisin sauce
3 tablespoons soy sauce
2 tablespoons rice wine
1½ teaspoons sesame oil
1 tablespoon sugar
2 teaspoons minced dried chili
peppers
2 tablespoons minced
scallions
1 tablespoon minced garlic
1 tablespoon minced
gingerroot

Spicy Rice Powder
1½ cups glutinous (sweet) rice
1 teaspoon five-spice powder

1 acorn or butternut squash,
weighing about 3 pounds,
cut in half and seeds
removed
2 tablespoons minced scallion
greens

*In western China, where this classic recipe originated, a
seasoned rice powder is frequently used as a coating for
steamed pork, chicken, and duck. Once cooked, the rice
soaks up the juices from the fragrant sparerib marinade,
creating a delicious coating. For a simpler version of this
recipe, the steps for making seasoned rice coating may be
omitted and glutinous rice (which has been rinsed,
soaked, drained, and flavored with five-spice powder) may
be used instead.*

1 Direct the butcher to cut the spareribs crosswise
in thirds so that they measure about 2 to 2½ inches
in length. Trim off any excess fat and place the ribs
in a bowl. Combine the ingredients of the **sparerib
marinade** and add it to the ribs. Toss lightly and let
marinate for at least 3 hours at room temperature or
overnight in the refrigerator.

2 To make the **spicy rice powder**: Rinse the glutinous rice until the water runs clear and place in a
bowl with cold water to cover. Let soak for 1 hour.
Drain thoroughly in a colander and place in a dry,
heated wok (with no oil). Fry the rice over medium-
low heat, stirring constantly until completely dry
and slightly golden. Remove and let cool briefly;
then pulverize to a coarse powder in a blender or a
food processor fitted with the steel blade. Remove
and mix with the five-spice powder. Add the spicy
rice powder to the spareribs and mix to coat them.
Arrange the squash halves in a heat-proof pie plate
or quiche pan and spoon the spareribs on top. If
there are extra spareribs, place them in a separate
heat-proof dish and set aside.

3 Fill a wok with water level with the bottom edge
of a steamer tray and heat until boiling. Place the
spareribs and squash in a steamer tray and cover.
Place the steamer tray over the boiling water and
steam for 40 to 45 minutes, or until the spareribs
are cooked and the squash is very tender when
pierced with a sharp knife. If there are extra spareribs to be steamed, steam them for 35 minutes in
another steamer tray. Remove the spareribs and
sprinkle with the minced scallion greens. Serve immediately. Scoop out and serve the squash meat
with the seasoned spareribs. *Serves six.*

Triple-Shred Chicken Soup

三
絲
鷄
湯

1½ pounds boneless chicken breast meat, skin removed

Chicken Marinade
1 tablespoon rice wine
1 teaspoon salt
½ teaspoon sesame oil

2 squares bean curd, measuring about 3 inches by 3 inches
1 cup matchstick-size shreds of Chinese ham or prosciutto

Soup Mixture
4 cups chicken broth
2 tablespoons rice wine
1 teaspoon salt

Thickener
1½ tablespoons cornstarch
3 tablespoons water

2 tablespoons finely shredded gingerroot
2 tablespoons coarsely chopped coriander (Chinese parsley)
1½ teaspoons sesame oil

This soup was inspired by one of the master chefs I studied with in Taipei, whose specialty was Shanghai cuisine. The delicacy and refinement of eastern regional cooking was always clearly apparent in his food. This dish, with its exquisite seasoning and colorful appearance, honors those traditions. Customarily, the Chinese serve soup toward the end of a meal, but for those who prefer the Western custom, it may be served at the beginning.

1 Holding a cleaver or a sharp knife parallel to the cutting surface, cut the chicken breast meat into thin slices. Cut the slices, with the grain, into matchstick-size shreds. Place the shreds in a bowl, add the **chicken marinade,** toss lightly to coat, and let marinate for 20 minutes. Cut the bean curd into thin, matchstick-size shreds. Heat 1 quart of water until boiling and drop the bean curd shreds into the water, cooking for about 1 minute. Remove and drain thoroughly. Prepare the soup mixture and the thickener.

2 Place the **soup mixture** in a large pot and heat until boiling. Add the chicken shreds and stir to separate. With a spoon, skim away any impurities from the surface. Add the Chinese ham or prosciutto, the bean curd shreds, and the **thickener,** stirring constantly. Cook the mixture over medium heat for 2 minutes. Add the gingerroot, coriander, and sesame oil. Mix to blend. Pour into a soup tureen and serve. *Serves six.*

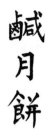

Savory Moon Cakes

Skin
1½ cups all-purpose flour
1½ cups cake flour
1 teaspoon salt
⅓ cup lard, chilled and cut
    into tablespoon-size pieces
⅓ cup unsalted butter, chilled
    and cut into tablespoon-size
    pieces
⅓ cup cold water
1 large egg, lightly beaten

Filling
8 cups shredded daikon
    radish
1¼ teaspoons salt
1 tablespoon safflower or corn
    oil
1 cup chopped scallions
1½ cups minced Chinese ham
    or prosciutto

Filling Seasoning
2 tablespoons rice wine
½ teaspoon freshly ground
    black pepper
2 teaspoons sesame oil

Savory mooncakes are not as universally known as their sweet counterparts, but they are no less delicious. Cooks from the city of Suzhou, located due west of Shanghai, are renowned for their savory moon cake variations. In this recipe, a delectable filling of daikon radish, ham, and scallions is baked in a flaky pastry skin. Unlike sweet moon cakes, which are traditionally formed in a mold, savory moon cakes are shaped by hand.

1 To prepare the **skin**: In a mixing bowl, combine the flours and salt. Add the lard and butter and, using a pastry blender or two knives, cut the shortening into the flour until the mixture resembles cornmeal. Combine the water and egg, add this to the flour-butter mixture, and mix to form a rough dough. Turn the dough out onto a lightly floured surface and gather the dough, pressing it into a ball. Do not overwork; it should still be a little rough. Wrap it in plastic wrap and chill for 1 hour.

2 To begin preparing the **filling**: Place the shredded radish in a bowl, add the salt, toss lightly, and let stand for 20 minutes. Squeeze out any water that has accumulated and set the radish aside. Combine the filling seasoning ingredients and place near the stove with the remaining filling ingredients.

3 Heat a wok, add the safflower or corn oil, and heat until hot. Add the scallions and stir-fry for about 10 seconds, until fragrant. Add the shredded radish and the minced ham or prosciutto. Stir-fry for about 1 minute, until the radish is slightly cooked, and add the **filling seasoning.** Toss lightly for another minute and remove. Spread the mixture out on a tray and refrigerate until cool.

4 Preheat the oven to 425 degrees. On a lightly floured surface, roll out the dough to a thickness of about ¼ inch. Using a 4-inch circular cutter, cut out circles. Gather the scraps together into a ball and chill for 15 minutes. Roll out the dough again and cut more circles until all the dough has been used. Pinch the edges of the circles lightly so that they are reduced to a thickness of about ⅛ inch.

秋

5 Place a heaping tablespoon of the radish filling in the center of a dough circle. Gather up the edges in the center to enclose the filling and pinch to seal, forming a ball. Lightly flatten each cake into a round approximately 3 inches wide. Arrange the cakes on an ungreased cookie sheet about 1 inch apart. Bake in the preheated oven for 35 to 40 minutes, until golden brown and crisp. Remove, cool, and serve warm or at room temperature. *Makes eighteen to twenty moon cakes.*

Sweet Moon Cakes

甜
月
餅

Filling
½ cup chopped dates
1 cup chopped dried apricots
   (softened in hot water for 1
   hour before chopping)
1 cup sweetened flaked
   coconut
1 cup raisins
1½ cups coarsely chopped
   walnuts

Crust
4 cups all-purpose flour
1 tablespoon baking powder
1 teaspoon salt
3 large eggs
¾ cup sugar
¾ cup unsalted butter, melted
   and cooled slightly
1 teaspoon vanilla extract
2 tablespoons water

Glaze
1 egg, lightly beaten
2 tablespoons water

During the Harvest Moon Festival, bakery shelves all over the Far East are loaded with countless versions of this holiday cake. I have adapted the traditional moon cake recipe, substituting butter for lard. This recipe, I find, is more appealing to Western palates. Moon cake molds are sold at some gourmet cookware stores, but the cakes can also be shaped by hand. To finish, merely draw or stamp a simple decoration on top. Serve these baked cakes as a dessert or as a teatime snack.

1 To make the **filling**: Combine the ingredients, mix well, and divide into twenty-four equal portions.

2 To make the **crust**: Sift together the flour, baking powder, and salt. Using a large whisk or an electric mixer, beat the eggs with the sugar for about 10 minutes, until a ribbon is formed. Add the melted butter, the vanilla extract, the water, and the dry ingredients and stir until a rough dough is formed. Use your hands to press the dough into a ball. Form the dough into a long snakelike roll about 1¼ inches thick. Cut it into twenty-four pieces.

3 Preheat the oven to 375 degrees. Using your hands, press each dough section into a 3-inch circle, with the edges pinched thinner than the center. Place a portion of the filling in the center, gather up the edges of the dough to meet in the center, and pinch to seal. Roll the cake into a ball and flatten it to a 3-inch round. Carve a decorative design on top, or press the cake, joined edges up, into a lightly floured moon cake mold. Invert the molded cake onto a cookie sheet. Repeat for the remaining dough and filling. Arrange the cakes about 1 inch apart on an ungreased cookie sheet. Prepare the **glaze** and brush the surface of each cake lightly with it. Bake the cakes for about 30 minutes, until golden brown. Remove, cool, and serve. ***Makes twenty-four moon cakes.***

秋

MENU II

Chinese Black Mushroom Bisque

Star Anise Beef Served over Fresh Fennel

Spiced Pears

Chinese Black Mushroom Bisque

1 pound fresh mushrooms
1 tablespoon lemon juice or
  vinegar
⅓ ounce (or 10 to 12) dried
  Chinese black mushrooms
½ cup hot water
6 tablespoons butter
2 teaspoons minced garlic
2 tablespoons minced shallots
1½ slices white bread, crusts
  removed
4 cups chicken broth
1 cup heavy cream
2 teaspoons salt
½ teaspoon freshly ground
  black pepper
¼ cup dry sherry
2 tablespoons minced fresh
  parsley

This soup features the flavors of both fresh and dried mushrooms. Dried black mushrooms vary in quality, flavor, and price. Ideally, mushrooms with the thickest caps and the most pungent taste should be used in this dish. The soup may be prepared in advance up to the final step. Before serving, it may be reheated, and the cream, sherry, and parsley may be added at the last minute.

1 Rinse the fresh mushrooms quickly in a bowl of cold water to which the lemon juice or vinegar has been added. Drain them thoroughly and slice thinly. Soak the black mushrooms in the hot water for 20 minutes. Drain, reserving the liquid. Remove the stems and shred the caps.

2 In a heavy saucepan, heat the butter until the foam begins to subside and add the garlic and shallots. Sauté briskly over medium-high heat and add all the mushrooms. Cook the mushrooms for about 5 minutes, stirring constantly.

3 Place the bread in a bowl with chicken broth to cover and let stand until the bread is soaked through. Squeeze out all the chicken broth and add the soaked bread to the mushrooms. Sauté this mixture until the bread is evenly distributed among the mushrooms. In a blender or a food processor fitted with the steel blade, purée the mixture to a smooth paste. Return this mixture to the pan and add the chicken broth and mushroom-soaking liquid. Cook, uncovered, over medium heat for 15 minutes. Add the cream (being sure the soup is not boiling, or it will curdle), salt, pepper, and dry sherry. Heat until piping hot and garnish with the minced parsley. Ladle into cups and serve.
Serves six.

Star Anise Beef Served over Fresh Fennel

3 pounds London broil or pot
   roast
2 tablespoons safflower or
   corn oil

Star Anise Braising Mixture
2 cups water or chicken broth
½ cup soy sauce
½ cup rice wine
2 tablespoons sugar
2 whole star anise
2 pieces dried orange peel,
   about 2 inches long
1 cinnamon stick
3 scallions, smashed with the
   flat side of a cleaver
3 slices gingerroot, smashed
   with the flat side of a
   cleaver

2 pounds fennel bulbs with
   stalks (if unavailable,
   substitute celery hearts and
   reduce the cooking time to 1
   minute)
1 teaspoon sesame oil

Dressing
4 tablespoons soy sauce
1½ tablespoons rice wine
1½ tablespoons Chinese black
   vinegar
1½ tablespoons sugar
2 teaspoons sesame oil
2 tablespoons minced
   scallions
2 teaspoons minced garlic
2 teaspoons minced
   gingerroot

1 tablespoon minced fresh
   coriander (optional)

Red-cooking is a braising method that has been used by the Chinese since ancient times. The cooking liquid's soy sauce base not only flavors and colors the meat but helps to preserve it. The dish, with its crunchy fennel or celery underlayer and spicy dressing, is ideal for fall moon-gazing outings as well as for summer picnics.

1 Trim the beef of excess fat and gristle. Cut the meat, lengthwise and with the grain, into long strips about 3 inches wide and 2 inches thick. Heat a heavy skillet and add the safflower or corn oil. Heat until very hot, about 375 degrees. Add several strips of beef and briefly sear over high heat until all sides are golden brown. Remove, reheat the oil, and sear the remaining strips of beef. Discard the oil.

2 Place the ingredients of the **star anise braising mixture** in a large saucepan or a wok and heat until boiling. Add the strips of beef and return the liquid to the boil. Reduce the heat to low, partially cover the pot, and cook for 1½ hours, or until tender. Set aside to cool.

3 Rinse the fennel and remove the ends and any sprigs. Cut each bulb crosswise in half, without removing the core, and cut the fennel into thin slices or strips. Bring 2 quarts of water to the boil, add the fennel, and cook for 3 to 5 minutes, or until just tender. Remove and rinse under cold running water. Drain thoroughly and add the sesame oil. Toss lightly to coat, and arrange on a serving platter. Cutting across the grain, thinly slice the beef. Arrange it on top of the fennel slices. Prepare the **dressing** and pour it over the beef. If using the coriander, sprinkle it on top. Toss to coat the ingredients with the dressing. Serve at room temperature or cold. ***Serves six.***

Spiced Pears

2 pounds slightly underripe
Bosc or Anjou pears
6 whole star anise
4 cinnamon sticks
4 slices fresh gingerroot
½ cup white vinegar
1½ cups water
3 cups sugar

Most Chinese meals end with the serving of fruit. This dish offers a departure from the usual selection of sliced oranges or watermelon. In this recipe, pears are pickled in a spicy marinade redolent with cinnamon. Since they keep indefinitely, I usually make a large batch, storing a supply to use throughout the year. These pears may be served reheated until warm, at room temperature, or chilled.

1 Peel, halve, and core the pears. Heat 2 quarts of water until boiling. Add the pears and poach for 5 minutes. Remove and drain.

2 Tie the star anise, cinnamon, and gingerroot in a square of cheesecloth. Combine the vinegar, water, and sugar in a heavy pot. Add the spice bag and boil for 20 minutes, stirring until all the sugar has dissolved. Add the pears and poach for another 5 minutes, or until tender. Let stand until cool.

3 Remove the spice bag. Using a slotted spoon, fill hot sterile jars with the pears. Reheat the syrup until boiling and pour it over the pears, filling the jars to the top. Seal and store for at least a week before serving. ***Serves six.***

CHRYSANTHEMUM FESTIVAL IN CRAB SEASON

"The blooming of the chrysanthemum marks the golden wedding of the spring, the reminiscence in November of nuptials in May. When these flowers are gone, there are no others left in the world."
— *an ancient Chinese saying*

For the Chinese, the chrysanthemum flower, with its sunburst of brightly colored petals, typifies the fullness of the year. In the ninth month of the lunar calendar (in the heart of the fall season), the Chinese pay homage to their beloved chrysanthemum. They eat chrysanthemum-shaped "flower cakes," stuffed with dried fruits and nuts; they drink teas and wine infused with dried chrysanthemums; and they serve delicate soups garnished with a sprinkling of fresh chrysanthemum petals.

The chrysanthemum has long been credited with magical properties because of its resemblance in shape to the sun. Dried chrysanthemum petals were believed to be particularly good for the eyes and were used in many Chinese herbal remedies.

In ancient China, the holiday was marked by chrysanthemum-viewing parties. Poets and scholars would take leisurely strolls through gardens filled with chrysanthemums in full bloom, stopping to recite newly composed odes to the flower and sip chrysanthemum wine, which was believed to ensure longevity.

The ninth month is also the time for the Festival of the Double Yang, a holiday whose origin is connected with the yang, or male, element of the universe, which is symbolized by the number nine. Activities for this day, which is also known as "the mounting of the heights," include trips to the countryside for picnics and feasting on wheat cakes, or *deng gao.*

Another notable event connected with the ninth month is the official opening of crab season, and many Chinese anticipate the availability of this delicacy with a fervor bordering on obsession. "Before crabs are in season," wrote Li Yu, a prominent seventeenth-century poet and dramatist, "I always saved up money to await their arrival. My family used to tease me about my obsession with crab, saying crabs are my life. So, I called the money saved for buying crabs 'life-buying money.' From the first day crabs appear in the market to the day when they disappear, I never go without them at meals."

Crabs are relished all over China in myriad dishes, but it is the sweet meat of the river crab that is most treasured. The dishes vary according to the region and the tastes of the cook. There are delicate steamed crabs with a ginger-vinegar dipping sauce, a dish that is served throughout the country; steeped or preserved crabs in wine lees, or sediment, prepared by chefs in eastern China; and the classic Cantonese specialty, stir-fried crabmeat with egg white over fried rice noodles. Crab roe is also highly prized for its distinctive taste and is used to flavor steamed dumplings or to garnish stir-fried vegetables.

MENU I

Steamed Crabs with a Ginger Dipping Sauce

Shrimp Fu Rong

Chrysanthemum Fire Pot

Stir-Fried Cabbage with Crabmeat

Steamed Crabs with a Ginger Dipping Sauce

清蒸蟹

6 medium-sized live blue crabs, weighing approximately 5 to 7 ounces apiece — preferably females (look on the underside of the crab; the tail should be an oval shape)

Crab Marinade
3 tablespoons rice wine
4 scallions, smashed lightly with the flat side of a cleaver
4 slices gingerroot, smashed lightly with the flat side of a cleaver

Ginger Dipping Sauce
½ cup light soy sauce
2½ tablespoons clear rice vinegar or Chinese black vinegar
1 tablespoon sesame oil
1 tablespoon sugar
1½ tablespoons very finely shredded or grated gingerroot

In China, the arrival of fresh river crabs in the market-place is cause for celebration. The crabs' diet usually consists of ripening rice, and as a result, the meat is plump and sweet. Many Chinese believe that the only way to eat this delicacy is steamed and served with a dipping sauce of vinegar and shredded ginger, as in this recipe. In the United States, fresh blue or stone crabs are best for this dish; ideally, they should be alive and kicking until they are ready to be cooked.

1 Blanch the crabs for about 1 minute in boiling water, remove, and rinse briefly in cold water. Remove the upper shell from each crab, and reserve the roe that may be attached to it. Remove and discard the spongy tissue from inside the top of the crab. Twist off and discard the apron from the underside of the crab. Rinse the bodies lightly and drain well. Cut off the last two hairy joints of the legs on each side of the crab, and separate the crab claws from the main body. Holding a very sharp cleaver parallel to the cutting surface, cut the crab in half crosswise through the thickness, exposing the meat contained in the body. Using the blunt edge of the cleaver, tap the claws so that the shells crack. (This will facilitate removal of the meat later.) Place the prepared crabs on a heat-proof plate or plates. Prepare the **crab marinade** by combining the ingredients and pinching the scallions and gingerroot repeatedly for several minutes in the rice wine to impart the flavor. Pour the marinade over the crab pieces and let marinate for 20 to 30 minutes. Place the crab, still on the plates, in a steamer tray or trays, stacking the layers one on top of another if necessary, and cover.

2 Prepare the **ginger dipping sauce** by combining the ingredients, stirring until the sugar dissolves. Transfer the sauce to individual serving bowls.

3 Fill a wok with water level with the bottom edge of the steamer tray and heat until boiling. Place the steamer over the boiling water and steam the crabs for 15 to 20 minutes, reversing the order of layers once. Remove the crabs and discard the seasonings. Serve the steamed crabs with the dipping sauce. *Serves six.*

Shrimp Fu Rong

蝦
肉
芙
蓉

½ pound medium raw
  shrimp, peeled

Shrimp Marinade
1 tablespoon rice wine
2 slices gingerroot, smashed
  lightly with the flat side of a
  cleaver

Egg Mixture
6 large eggs, lightly beaten
1 teaspoon salt
¼ teaspoon freshly ground
  white pepper
1½ teaspoons sesame oil
2 tablespoons minced
  scallions
1 tablespoon minced
  gingerroot

¼ cup safflower or corn oil
1 tablespoon minced scallion
  greens

*Years ago, Cantonese master chefs created a number of fu
rong dishes, named after the hibiscus flower, which were
made with whole eggs or egg whites and garnished with
shrimp or crabmeat. Since these dishes rarely resemble the
flower in appearance, one can only assume that the similarity was between the coloring of the flower and the food.
This simple platter, with its delicately scrambled eggs and
shrimp garnish, is just such a dish.*

1 Score each shrimp along the length of the back
and remove the vein; the scoring will allow the
shrimp to "butterfly" when it is cooked. Rinse all
the shrimp and drain thoroughly. Place the shrimp
in a linen dishtowel and squeeze out as much moisture as possible. Place the shrimp in a bowl. Prepare the **shrimp marinade** by pinching the gingerroot slices in the rice wine repeatedly for several
minutes to impart the flavor. Add the marinade to
the shrimp, toss lightly, and let stand for 30 minutes. Drain the shrimp and discard the gingerroot
slices. Combine the ingredients of the egg mixture
and beat lightly.

2 Heat a wok or a heavy skillet and add two tablespoons of the oil. Heat until very hot, add the
shrimp, and stir-fry for several minutes until the
shrimp change color and curl up. Remove and
drain. Remove the oil from the pan and discard.

3 Reheat the pan and add the remaining oil. Heat
until hot and add the **egg mixture** and the cooked
shrimp. Stir-fry over medium heat until the eggs
are just set (they should not be overcooked). Transfer the mixture to a serving platter. Sprinkle the
minced scallion greens on top and serve. *Serves six.*

Chrysanthemum Fire Pot

菊
花
火
鍋

1 pound boneless chicken
   breast meat
1 pound firm-fleshed fish
   fillets, such as haddock,
   pickerel, or lake trout, skin
   removed
½ pound medium raw
   shrimp, peeled and
   deveined
1 pint freshly shucked oysters

Marinade
¼ cup rice wine
4 slices gingerroot, smashed
   lightly with the flat side of a
   cleaver
1 teaspoon salt
1½ teaspoons sesame oil

2 squares bean curd,
   measuring about 3 inches
   square and 1 inch thick, cut
   into ¼-inch dice
2 ounces bean threads
   (cellophane noodles),
   softened in hot water for 10
   minutes, drained, and cut
   into 3-inch lengths
2 large chrysanthemums,
   lightly rinsed, petals only
   (use flowers picked fresh
   from the garden, since
   many florists spray their
   chrysanthemums with
   chemicals)
½ pound fresh spinach,
   trimmed and cleaned
2 tablespoons safflower or
   corn oil
2 whole cloves garlic,
   smashed lightly with the flat
   side of a cleaver
6 cups Chinese cabbage
   (Napa), cut into 2-inch
   squares

Soup Base
8 cups Chinese chicken broth
   (page 194)
¼ cup rice wine
1 teaspoon salt

This classic dish from Canton incorporates pieces of chicken, seafood, and vegetables to be cooked, fondue-style, in a fragrant, boiling broth. The raw, sliced ingredients are often arranged on a platter in a flower shape, and fresh chrysanthemum petals are sprinkled decoratively on top. This soup pot is a meal in itself, or it may be served with other dishes, as in this holiday menu. Mongolian fire pots are sold at most well-equipped gourmet cookware shops and at some Chinese grocery stores. If a fire pot is unavailable, you may improvise, using an electric deep-fryer or wok placed in the center of the table.

1 Holding the cleaver at a 45-degree angle to the cutting board, cut the chicken breast, across the grain, into paper-thin slices. (You may partially freeze the meat to facilitate cutting.) Repeat this same procedure for the fish fillets. "Butterfly" the shrimp, leaving the halves connected along the back. Prepare the **marinade** by combining the ingredients and repeatedly pinching the gingerroot in the rice wine for several minutes to impart its flavor. Discard the gingerroot and place the chicken, fish, shrimp, and oysters in separate bowls. Add a little of the marinade to each, and toss lightly to coat. Let marinate for 20 minutes. On a large serving platter, arrange the chicken, in overlapping slices, around the edge, followed (in separate rows, working toward the center) by the fish, shrimp, oysters, bean curd, and bean threads. Arrange the chrysanthemum petals in the center and place the spinach on the side in a bowl.

2 Combine the ingredients for the **soup base** and place near the stove. Heat a wok, add the oil, and heat until smoking. Add the garlic and cabbage. Toss quickly over high heat, turning constantly to prevent burning. Add several tablespoons of the soup base and cook for about 2 minutes, until the cabbage just begins to wilt. Add the remaining soup base and heat until boiling. Lower the heat to medium-low and simmer for 30 minutes. Transfer the mixture to a Mongolian fire pot that has been prepared for the table with red-hot charcoal briquettes, or an electric skillet or wok with the setting

Dipping Sauce
1 cup soy sauce
¼ cup rice wine
¼ cup clear rice vinegar or
  Chinese black vinegar
2 tablespoons sugar
2 tablespoons minced
  gingerroot
2 tablespoons minced
  scallions
1 tablespoon minced garlic

on high. (If using briquettes, make certain the area is well ventilated.)

3 Arrange the fire pot or wok in the center of the table with the platter of the main ingredients and the bowl of spinach next to it. Portion the **dipping sauce** into individual serving bowls and place next to the diners' empty bowls. Once the broth starts to boil, each diner takes a slice of chicken or a bit of seafood or vegetable and holds it in the boiling stock to cook. (The host or hostess may place a group of the ingredients in the stock and let the diners take them out themselves.) The cooked food is then dipped in the dipping sauce before eating. The chicken, seafood, spinach, and chrysanthemum petals will cook in 1 minute or less. The bean curd and bean threads will take about 10 minutes. Once the diner has eaten his fill of the chicken and seafood, the broth (which has been flavored by all the ingredients) is eaten with the bean curd and bean threads. *Serves six.*

Stir-Fried Cabbage with Crabmeat

蟹
肉
白
菜

10 to 12 hearts of baby
  Chinese cabbage, about 2
  pounds (or bok choy)
2 tablespoons safflower or
  corn oil

Minced Seasonings
2 tablespoons minced
  scallions
1 tablespoon minced
  gingerroot

6 to 8 ounces shredded
  crabmeat, picked over to
  remove any cartilage or
  shell
2 tablespoons rice wine

Sauce
⅓ cup chicken broth
¾ teaspoon salt
1 teaspoon sesame oil
1 teaspoon cornstarch

1 egg white, lightly beaten
  until frothy

In eastern China, where this dish originated and where ingredients are generally of a very high quality, seasonings are used to accentuate the natural flavors of the foods. Vegetables, like the baby hearts of cabbage used in this recipe, are paired with delicate foods like crabmeat or shrimp to bring out their natural sweetness. Baby cabbage hearts are suggested for this dish, but bok choy, cut into smaller pieces, may be substituted.

1 Remove any wilted outer leaves from the hearts of baby cabbage. Trim off the remaining leaf tips, leaving about 1 inch on the end. If the cabbage hearts are large, cut them in half lengthwise. (If you are using the bok choy, cut away the ends of the leaves and roll-cut the stalks into 1½-inch lengths about 1 inch thick.) Heat 2 quarts of water until boiling, add the cabbage, and cook for 10 to 12 minutes, or until just tender. Remove and plunge immediately into cold water. Drain thoroughly. Prepare the minced seasonings and the sauce, and place them near the stove.

2 Heat a wok until very hot. Add the oil and heat until hot. Add the **minced seasonings** and stir-fry for about 10 seconds, until fragrant. Add the crabmeat and continue stir-frying over very high heat for about 1 minute. Add the rice wine and cook for 10 seconds. Add the **sauce** and heat, stirring constantly, until it begins to thicken. Add the cabbage hearts and slowly, in a thin stream, add the egg white. Stir the mixture once or twice and remove to a serving platter. Serve immediately. *Serves six.*

MENU II

Shrimp Salad with Fresh Coriander

Grilled Fish Steaks with Sweet Bean Sauce

Chrysanthemum Rice

Pine Nut Puffs

Shrimp Salad with Fresh Coriander

1 pound medium shrimp,
  lightly poached

Coriander Dressing
⅓ cup light soy sauce (if
  unavailable, use medium-
  grade)
½ teaspoon salt
1½ tablespoons sugar
 3 tablespoons sesame oil
3½ tablespoons clear rice
  vinegar
2 tablespoons rice wine
2 teaspoons finely minced or
  grated gingerroot
¼ cup chopped fresh
  coriander (Chinese parsley)

3 large eggs, lightly beaten
¼ teaspoon salt
1 tablespoon safflower or
  corn oil
6 cups fresh bean sprouts

Although this dish is not a classic recipe, it follows the same formula as that of any Chinese layered salad. The textured base (in this case shredded egg sheets), is covered by a layer of crisp vegetables and followed by a topping of cooked seafood and a light but pungent dressing. For optimal flavor, let the shrimp marinate in the spicy dressing overnight.

1 Remove the shells and devein the shrimp. Combine the ingredients of the coriander dressing. Place the shrimp in a bowl, add the **coriander dressing,** toss lightly to coat, cover, and refrigerate for at least 3 hours or, preferably, overnight, turning occasionally. Drain the shrimp, reserving the dressing.

2 Lightly beat the eggs, adding the salt. Rub a non-stick frying pan or a well-seasoned wok with an oil-soaked paper towel. Heat the pan until a few drops of water sprinkled on the surface evaporate immediately. Add a third of the egg mixture and tilt the pan so that a thin pancake is formed. Cook until the pancake is light golden; then flip it over. Cook for a few more seconds and remove. Prepare two more egg sheets in the same manner. Cut the egg sheets into very thin julienne strips. Lightly rinse the bean sprouts in cold water and drain thoroughly.

3 Arrange the bean sprouts in the bottom of a wide, deep serving dish. Arrange the shredded egg sheets in a circular strip on top of the bean sprouts. Arrange the shrimp in the center.

4 Before serving, pour the reserved coriander dressing over the salad, toss well to coat the ingredients with the dressing thoroughly, and serve. **Serves six.**

Grilled Fish Steaks with Sweet Bean Sauce

2½ to 3 pounds halibut, swordfish, or tuna steaks, about ¾ inch thick

Ginger-Scallion Oil
6 scallions, split lengthwise and smashed lightly with the flat side of a cleaver
8 slices gingerroot, smashed lightly with the flat side of a cleaver
¼ cup sesame oil
¼ cup safflower or corn oil

Sweet Bean Sauce
1 cup sweet bean sauce (or use hoisin sauce, if necessary)
2 tablespoons soy sauce
3 tablespoons rice wine
2 tablespoons sugar
2 tablespoons water

6 tablespoons finely minced scallion greens

The presentation of this dish might be compared more closely to that of a nouvelle French recipe than a Chinese one. The grilled fish steaks, which have been basted with a fragrant ginger-scallion oil while cooking, are cut into individual portions and served in a pool of pungent sweet bean sauce. The sauce is on the bottom so that the delicate flavor of the fish will not be overpowered.

1 Lightly rinse the fish steaks and pat dry. Cut them into serving-size pieces, and arrange on a tray. Prepare the **ginger-scallion oil** by first combining the scallions and gingerroot. Then heat a wok or a heavy saucepan and add the two oils. Heat the oil until smoking and add the scallions and gingerroot. Cover and remove from the heat. Let stand until completely cool; then strain out the seasonings and discard them.

2 Pour the seasoned oil over the fish and turn the fish steaks so that they are completely coated. Cover with plastic wrap and let marinate for at least 3 hours, at room temperature, turning occasionally.

3 Prepare the **sweet bean sauce**: Place the ingredients in a saucepan or wok, heat until boiling, and cook, stirring constantly, until slightly thickened. Keep warm until the fish is cooked.

4 Arrange the fish steaks over a medium-hot charcoal fire. (Alternatively, you may place them on a broiler pan about 3 inches from the source of heat.) Grill or broil the fish steaks for 8 to 9 minutes on each side, or until the meat flakes, basting with the ginger-scallion oil. Spoon one or two tablespoons of the sweet bean sauce onto each serving plate. Place a grilled fish steak on top. Sprinkle each fish steak lightly with a tablespoon of the minced scallion greens. Serve the fish immediately. Any remaining sauce may be served on the side. *Serves six.*

Chrysanthemum Rice

6 cups cold cooked long-grain rice
2 cups cooked diced shrimp
1½ cups fresh peas, cooked for 1 minute in boiling water (or thawed frozen peas)
1 cup scallion greens, cut into ¼-inch lengths
3 large eggs, lightly beaten
3 tablespoons safflower or corn oil

Rice Sauce
1½ teaspoons salt
¼ teaspoon freshly ground white pepper
2½ tablespoons rice wine
1 teaspoon sesame oil
2 tablespoons chicken broth

This delicately seasoned fried rice dish complements the grilled fish nicely. The secret to this fried rice, as with any, is to make certain that the rice is cold before stir-frying. Notice, too, that no soy sauce is used in the dish, so that the vibrant colors of the rice and its garnishes are highlighted.

1 Place the rice, shrimp, peas, scallions, eggs, and rice sauce near the stove.

2 Heat a wok, add the safflower or corn oil, and heat until hot. Add the eggs and stir-fry over high heat, using a spatula to break them up, until hard-cooked and scrambled. Add the scallions and stir-fry for about 1 minute; then add the shrimp and peas. Stir-fry briefly to heat through; then add the rice. Stir-fry vigorously to break up the rice and mix the ingredients well. Add the **rice sauce** and quickly toss the mixture together to coat evenly. Transfer the rice to a platter and serve immediately. *Serves six.*

Pine Nut Puffs

2¼ cups all-purpose flour
1 teaspoon baking powder
½ teaspoon salt
4 tablespoons lard or unsalted
   butter, at room temperature
¾ cup sugar
2 eggs, lightly beaten
2 tablespoons minced
   blanched orange peel
1 cup untoasted pine nuts,
   crushed coarsely
4 cups safflower or corn oil

Like other Chinese sweets, this dish might be considered a snack more than a dessert, but the buttery orange-flavored "puffs" end any meal beautifully. These deep-fried pastries are also especially delicious served with tea. When deep-frying, make certain that the oil is not too hot; otherwise, the pine nut coating will darken and burn before the cookie is completely cooked.

1 Sift together the flour, baking powder, and salt. Cream the lard or butter and the sugar for about 5 minutes, until smooth and lemon-colored. Add the eggs and mix to blend. Add the orange peel, and slowly mix in the dry ingredients. Mix to a rough dough and turn out onto a lightly floured surface. Briefly knead to a smooth consistency and form the dough into a long snakelike roll. Cut the roll into twenty pieces.

2 Form each piece into a cigar-shaped roll about ½ inch thick and 2 inches long, rounding the ends, and roll it in the pine nuts so that the outside is completely coated.

3 Heat a wok or deep skillet and add the oil. Heat the oil to 325 degrees. Add half the rolls and deep-fry over medium heat, stirring constantly until the rolls begin to expand and crack. Turn the heat to high and continue frying until golden brown. Remove with a handled strainer, and drain on absorbent paper. Reheat the oil, and deep-fry the remaining rolls in the same manner. Arrange the fried rolls on a platter and serve immediately. *Makes about twenty puffs.*

FINGER FOODS

Finger foods figure prominently in the Chinese diet. First and foremost among them are the delectable "dot the heart" snacks known as *dim sum,* which are served at Chinese tea parlors. *Dim sum* finger foods are numerous and varied. Some of the most popular are sweet and savory dumplings and turnovers, steamed breads, cakes, and selected pastries.

In China, lively teahouses are filled to capacity until early afternoon with businessmen negotiating major deals; friends exchanging the latest gossip; and gatherings of large family clans, enjoying one another's company. Everyone meets to sip tea and feast on assorted *dim sum.* In this country, most sizable Chinatowns have one or two *dim sum* parlors. The menu is much the same as in the Far East. Carts loaded with a variety of dishes, hot and steaming from the kitchen, are wheeled around to the tables periodically. To order, customers need only point to the foods that they find appealing.

A number of these same finger foods are served at banquets. In this role, they become "wine-accompanying" foods, or appetizers, and they are served with the endless toasts that are a part of any multi-course banquet. These dishes are also enjoyed in the late afternoon or evening by those who have persistent in-between-meal or nocturnal hunger cravings.

And finger food treats greet a diner as he is seated in any Chinese restaurant in the Orient. Usually they are placed strategically on the table, close to the fingertips of the customer. They may be as simple as a small dish of garlic peanuts or a sweet-and-sour cucumber salad. Like olives or cheese and crackers, these foods are designed to soothe gnawing hunger pangs. They may be daintily nibbled on (or hungrily wolfed down) while the customer consults the menu and mentally plans the meal.

In this country, finger foods are as much a part of the daily and yearly social ritual as in the Far East. But they are never more popular than in the fall

秋

and winter months, when the cooler weather fore-
tells the coming of the holidays and suggests a time
for entertaining friends and relatives with lively
conversation, drink, and a selection of unusual appetizers or finger foods.

秋

CHINESE FINGER FOODS

Fried Peanuts with Whole Garlic Cloves

Honey-Coated Crispy Pine Nuts

Crispy Scallion-Ham Pancakes

Vegetable Sticks with a Spicy Peanut Dip

Barbecued Spareribs in Hoisin Sauce

Skewered Scallops and Shrimp in a Plum-Mustard Dressing

Cantonese-Style Chicken Wings

Cooked Shrimp with Two Dipping Sauces

Deep-Fried Chicken Wontons

Stuffed Bell Peppers with Ground Meat and Black Beans

Loquats and Lychees Stuffed with Duck in a Fresh Orange Sauce

Steamed Open-Faced Dumplings (Shao Mai)

Skewered Chicken with Almond Coating

Country Terrine with Black Beans

Steamed Scallop Rolls with Fresh Lemon Sauce

Deep-Fried Shrimp Fingers

Steamed Juicy Buns

Deep-Fried Crab Toasts

Savory Baked Turnovers with a Ground Meat and Black Bean Filling

Flaky Turnovers with a Dried Mushroom Duxelle Filling

Fried Peanuts with Whole Garlic Cloves

蒜炸花生

1 pound raw peanuts, skins
  removed
10 garlic cloves, peeled and
  cut lengthwise into ⅛-inch-
  thick slices
½ cup safflower or corn oil

Diners never go hungry for long in any restaurant in the Orient. Inevitably, upon being seated, they will find a small dish of nuts or pickled vegetables magically appearing on the table, to be nibbled on while looking over the menu. This simple peanut dish is such an amuse-gueule *— delicious morsels that most certainly will amuse the mouth.*

1 Place the peanuts and the garlic in a bowl with 2 tablespoons of the oil. Toss to coat and let stand for 1 to 2 hours, tossing occasionally.

2 Heat a wok until hot and add the remaining oil. Heat the oil to 325 degrees. Add the peanuts and garlic cloves and deep-fry, stirring constantly, until golden brown. Remove with a slotted spoon and let drain for a minute in a handled strainer. Drain until cool on absorbent paper. Transfer to a serving dish and serve. (The garlic is not generally eaten, but is served as a garnish.) *Serves six.*

. . . .

Note
You may reduce the amount of oil to 2 tablespoons and follow step 1 of the recipe. Then preheat the oven to 275 degrees and place the peanuts on a cookie sheet. Roast the peanuts in the oven, tossing periodically, to make certain they cook evenly. Bake until golden brown, about 15 minutes, and cool on absorbent paper. Serve.

Honey-Coated Crispy Pine Nuts

蜜汁松子

2 cups water
¼ cup honey
1 pound raw pine nuts
3 cups safflower or corn oil

Like cashews, pine nuts are often first cooked in a mixture of water and honey, and then deep-fried to a deep mahogany brown. They make the perfect accompaniment to any type of drink. The honey accentuates the buttery flavor of the crisp nuts.

1 Place the water and honey in a saucepan, stirring to dissolve the honey. Add the pine nuts and heat the mixture until boiling. Reduce the heat to medium and cook uncovered for 15 minutes, skimming the surface to remove any impurities. Using a handled strainer or a slotted spoon, remove the pine nuts and drain thoroughly. Place on a tray covered with paper towels and let air-dry for 1 hour, turning occasionally.

2 Heat a wok, add the oil, and heat to 300 degrees. Add the pine nuts and turn up the heat. Deep-fry until a deep mahogany brown, turning the pine nuts constantly so that they cook evenly. Remove the pine nuts with a handled strainer and let drain briefly. Spread them out on a tray lined with brown paper to drain further. Let cool completely and transfer to a serving dish. *Serves six.*

Crispy Scallion-Ham Pancakes

1 cup all-purpose flour
1 cup cake flour
½ teaspoon salt
1 cup boiling water
¼ cup sesame oil
½ cup finely minced scallion greens
½ cup finely minced Chinese ham or prosciutto
½ cup safflower or corn oil

Scallion pancakes are standard in the repertory of traditional northern Chinese staples, and there are a number of variations on this one theme. Some cooks like to make small, thin, crispy pancakes, while others prefer thick ones that are crisp but have a soft center. In this recipe, I opt for the latter, adding a sprinkling of Chinese ham or prosciutto and cutting the fried cakes into wedge-shaped pieces for serving.

1 In a large mixing bowl, combine the two flours with the salt, mixing with a wooden spoon. Add the boiling water and mix to a rough dough. Turn the dough out onto a lightly floured surface and knead for 5 minutes, until smooth and elastic. (If the dough is very wet, add a little more flour as you are kneading. If it is dry, add a little cold water.) The dough should be soft and pliable, but not sticky. Dust lightly with flour, cover with a cloth, and let rest for 25 minutes.

2 On a lightly floured surface, divide the dough into four pieces. Lightly flatten a piece with your fingers into a 2- to 3-inch circle. (Cover the other pieces with a cloth to prevent them from drying out.) Using a rolling pin, roll out the dough to a ¼-inch-thick circle. Brush the surface liberally with sesame oil and sprinkle with minced scallions and Chinese ham or prosciutto.

3 Starting at the edge nearest you, roll up the dough, jellyroll-style, to enclose the filling. Pinch the two ends to prevent the filling from oozing out.

Arrange the roll so that the seam is on top, lightly flatten the roll, and starting at one of the pinched ends, roll it up from end to end, pinching the end to prevent it from unraveling. (It should have a rounded, snail-like shape.) Repeat for the remaining pieces and let them rest for 20 minutes, covered with a damp cloth.

4 Arrange one roll so that it lies flat on a lightly floured surface, and using a rolling pin, roll it out to a 6-inch circle. Repeat for the other rolls. Let them rest for 15 minutes.

5 Heat a heavy skillet and add the oil. Heat to 375 degrees and add one of the pancakes. Lightly press the center so that the whole pancake will cook evenly, and fry for 3 to 5 minutes, until a deep golden brown. Turn over and fry on the other side, pressing down at the center to cook evenly. Cook until golden brown and crisp. Remove with a slotted spoon and drain for about 1 minute in a handled strainer. Drain until cool on absorbent paper. Continue frying the remaining pancakes until crisp and golden brown, keeping the others warm in a preheated 200-degree oven. Remove and cut each pancake into six pieces. Transfer to a platter and serve. ***Makes four 6-inch cakes.***

Vegetable Sticks with a Spicy Peanut Dip

¼ pound snow peas
3 red bell peppers, cored and
seeded
3 thick carrots, peeled and
ends trimmed
1 cucumber, peeled, ends
trimmed, and seeds
removed

Spicy Peanut Dip
1 cup smooth peanut butter
3 tablespoons soy sauce
1½ tablespoons sugar
2 tablespoons rice wine
1½ tablespoons Chinese black
vinegar
¼ cup sesame oil
1 tablespoon minced garlic
1 tablespoon minced
gingerroot
1 teaspoon chili paste, or to
taste
3 tablespoons chicken broth
or water

1 tablespoon minced scallion
greens

*Traditionally, vegetables are not eaten raw in the Orient;
they are blanched or stir-fried before serving. But in this
country, raw vegetables, or crudités, are a popular hors
d'oeuvre. In this dish, the crunchy vegetable sticks are a
superb foil for the spicy peanut dip. The vegetables may
be blanched in boiling water for 15 seconds, and then refreshed in cold water to remove the raw taste and liven
the colors. Also, other vegetables can be substituted for
those listed in the recipe.*

1 Snap the ends of the snow peas and remove the
veiny strings from the sides. Rinse lightly and pat
dry. Cut the peppers lengthwise into strips that are
about 1½ inches wide. Cut the carrots and cucumbers into sticks measuring about 3 inches in length
and ½ inch thick. Arrange the vegetables in alter-
nating piles on a circular platter, leaving a space in
the center for the peanut dip.

2 In a blender or a food processor fitted with the
steel blade, combine the ingredients of the **spicy
peanut dip,** blending until smooth. If the sauce is
too thick, add more chicken broth or water. Transfer to a serving dish, sprinkle the top with the scallions, and place in the center of the platter of vegetables. Serve. ***Serves six.***

Barbecued Spareribs in Hoisin Sauce

3 pounds spareribs

Sparerib Marinade
¼ cup hoisin sauce
3 tablespoons soy sauce
3 tablespoons rice wine
3 tablespoons sugar
2 tablespoons ketchup
2 tablespoons minced garlic

*No selection of Chinese finger foods would be complete
without a recipe for tender barbecued spareribs. In addition to their exquisite flavor, one of their chief advantages
is that they may be prepared in advance and reheated before serving. For a spicy rendition of this dish, add a bit
of chili paste to the marinating mixture.*

1 Direct the butcher to cut the slab of spareribs
crosswise in half or in thirds so that the ribs measure about 3 inches in length. Using a sharp knife,
separate the ribs, cutting between the bones.

2 In a large pot, bring about 2 quarts of water to
the boil. Add the spareribs, and return to the boil.
Reduce the heat to medium and cook for about 20

minutes. Remove the spareribs, drain, rinse lightly, and drain thoroughly. Place the ribs in a bowl.

3 Combine the **sparerib marinade** ingredients. Add the marinade to the ribs and toss lightly to coat. Cover with plastic wrap and let marinate for at least 4 hours or, if possible, overnight in the refrigerator.

4 Preheat the oven to 350 degrees. Arrange the spareribs on a cookie sheet or in a pan and spoon the marinade over them. Bake 30 to 45 minutes, until golden brown and crisp. Transfer to a serving platter and serve with plum sauce and mustard. *Serves six.*

Skewered Scallops and Shrimp in a Plum-Mustard Dressing

1 pound fresh sea scallops
1 pound medium raw shrimp, peeled and deveined
⅓ pound Chinese ham or prosciutto
¼ pound thinly sliced bacon

Mustard Dressing
1 tablespoon mustard powder
2 tablespoons hot water
½ cup plum (or duck) sauce
3 tablespoons clear rice vinegar
1 tablespoon sesame oil
1 tablespoon soy sauce
1 teaspoon salt
1 tablespoon sugar

10 10-inch bamboo skewers soaked in cold water to cover for 1 hour

Skewers or barbecued meat and seafood are popular hors d'oeuvres at any gathering, whatever the season. In this dish, the smoky slices of bacon and Chinese ham or prosciutto contrast beautifully with the fresh, sweet flavor of the seafood. Make certain to soak the bamboo skewers in cold water to prevent them from burning while the food is being grilled.

1 Lightly rinse the scallops and shrimp and drain thoroughly. Cut the Chinese ham and bacon slices crosswise in half, so that they are about 3 inches long.

2 Combine the ingredients of the **mustard dressing.** Toss the scallops and shrimp separately in some of the mustard dressing to coat. Pour the rest of the mustard dressing into a bowl for serving. Wrap the scallops in the Chinese ham pieces and the shrimp in the bacon slices. Separately thread the scallops and shrimp onto the bamboo skewers.

3 Broil the scallops and shrimp or grill over a charcoal fire for 8 to 10 minutes on each side, or until cooked. Remove and serve hot with the remaining dressing for dipping. Serve as an hors d'oeuvre or a light seafood entrée with other dishes. ***Serves six.***

Cantonese-Style Chicken Wings

廣
東
鷄
翼

18 chicken wings, preferably
  "drumettes" only

Marinade
2½ tablespoons soy sauce
1½ tablespoons rice wine
1 teaspoon sugar
1 teaspoon sesame oil
1½ tablespoons minced garlic
1½ tablespoons minced
  gingerroot

1 egg, lightly beaten
1 cup cornstarch
4 to 6 cups safflower or corn
  oil
3 tablespoons minced scallion
  greens (optional)

My father is especially fond of the deep-fried chicken wing appetizers served in most Chinese restaurants. In fact, it is not unusual for him to place a double order and make a meal of them. I too must admit to being a fan, but this recipe is dedicated to my father: may they taste the same as they do in his favorite restaurant! To ensure that the wings will be crisp, make certain that the oil is very hot before deep-frying. For extra-crispy wings, reheat in a 375-degree oven for 10 minutes before serving.

1 If using the whole wings, cut each one in half at the elbow joint. Set aside the wing tips. (You may marinate and deep-fry them as well.) Using a sharp knife or a cleaver, cut through the skin, meat, and tendons at the larger end of one drumette, cutting all the way around the bone. With the tip of your knife, scrape and push the meat and skin toward the opposite end of the bone. Using your hands and the tip of the knife, push the meat and skin inside out so that it is bunched up at that end of the bone. Prepare all the drumettes in the same manner, and place them in a bowl.

2 Combine the **marinade** ingredients and add the marinade to the drumettes. Toss lightly to coat and cover with plastic wrap. Let marinate for at least 1 hour at room temperature, or, if possible, overnight in the refrigerator. Add the egg and toss lightly to coat. Dredge the drumettes in the cornstarch, coating thoroughly. Lightly press the cornstarch to make it adhere to the chicken. Arrange the drumettes on a tray and let air-dry for 1 hour, turning once.

3 Heat a wok, add the oil, and heat to 375 degrees. Add 7 or 8 of the drumettes and deep-fry, turning carefully, until golden brown and crisp. Remove and drain for about 1 minute in a handled strainer. Drain on absorbent paper until cool. Reheat the oil and deep-fry the remaining drumettes in batches. Drain and serve with plum sauce and hot mustard. To reheat, bake for 5 to 10 minutes in a preheated 450-degree oven. *Serves six.*

秋

Cooked Shrimp with Two Dipping Sauces

1½ pounds medium raw
shrimp, peeled and
deveined

Shrimp Marinade
4 scallions, smashed lightly
with the flat side of a
cleaver
4 slices gingerroot, smashed
lightly with the flat side of a
cleaver
1½ tablespoons rice wine
½ teaspoon salt

Mustard Dipping Sauce
1 tablespoon mustard powder
2 tablespoons hot water
1 tablespoon rice wine
½ teaspoon salt
¼ teaspoon sugar
1 teaspoon soy sauce
1½ teaspoons sesame oil

Sweet-and-Sour Chili Sauce
½ cup ketchup
1½ tablespoons sugar
1½ tablespoons clear rice
vinegar
1 teaspoon soy sauce
½ teaspoon salt
1 teaspoon chili paste
1 teaspoon minced gingerroot

*In China, shrimp is relished for its simple, sweet flavor.
In fact, many Chinese prefer fresh shrimp to be steamed
and served unadorned, with a dipping sauce on the side.
In this recipe, I have coupled two dipping sauces — a
pungent mustard-based mixture, and a tart and spicy
sweet-and-sour chili sauce. I like to offer a choice of
sauces, but you could easily serve the delicate shrimp
with only one of them. Either way, this dish makes an
excellent hors d'oeuvre, first course, or entrée.*

1 Holding a cleaver or a sharp knife parallel to the
cutting surface, score each shrimp along the back;
the scoring will allow the shrimp to "butterfly"
when cooked. Place the shrimp in a bowl, and add
the **shrimp marinade.** Toss lightly to coat and let
marinate for at least 30 minutes, but longer if possible.

2 While the shrimp are marinating, prepare the
dipping sauces. To make the **mustard dipping
sauce,** mix the mustard powder with the hot water
to form a smooth paste. Add the remaining ingredients, blending until smooth. Transfer the sauce to a
serving dish. To make the **sweet-and-sour chili
sauce,** combine the ingredients and blend until
evenly mixed. Transfer the sauce to a serving dish.

3 In a wok or heavy saucepan, bring 2 quarts of
water to the boil and add the shrimp and marinade.
Cook for about 3 minutes, or until the shrimp curl
and change color. Remove with a slotted spoon,
discarding the liquid and seasonings, and arrange
on a serving platter. Serve at room temperature or
cold, with the two dipping sauces. *Serves six.*

Deep-Fried Chicken Wontons

1½ pounds boneless chicken
  breast, skin removed
½ cup finely chopped celery
½ cup finely chopped water
  chestnuts, blanched for
  about 10 seconds in boiling
  water, drained thoroughly,
  and patted dry on paper
  towels

Wonton Seasonings
1½ tablespoons soy sauce
2 teaspoons rice wine
½ teaspoon salt
1½ teaspoons sesame oil
¼ teaspoon freshly ground
  black pepper
1 teaspoon five-spice powder
2 teaspoons minced
  gingerroot
1½ tablespoons cornstarch

30 wonton wrappers
6 cups safflower or corn oil

Dipping Sauce
½ cup soy sauce
2 tablespoons Chinese black
  vinegar
1 tablespoon finely shredded
  gingerroot
2 teaspoons sugar

Wontons have long been a favorite among Chinese and Westerners alike. Traditionally, they are stuffed with a combination of pork and shrimp, but I often prefer to use chicken meat, chopped water chestnuts, celery, and a sprinkling of five-spice powder. The flavors and textures combine to create a unique and pleasing variation on a classic theme.

1 In a food processor fitted with the steel blade, chop the chicken to a coarse paste. Add the **wonton seasonings,** except the cornstarch, and process to a smooth paste. Transfer the mixture to a bowl and add the cornstarch, stirring vigorously in one direction. The mixture should be a stiff paste.

2 Place a teaspoon of the chicken mixture in the center of a wonton wrapper. Fold the wrapper in half to form a triangle. With the top of the triangle pointing up, grasp the wonton in both hands and use your thumbs to bend the wrapper slightly, molding it around the filling. Dab a finger in a little water and moisten the two ends. Fold one end over the other and press firmly to secure together. Repeat for the remaining wontons, placing the folded wontons on a tray that has been dusted with cornstarch. Combine the **dipping sauce** ingredients and stir until the sugar dissolves. Transfer the sauce to a serving bowl.

3 Heat a wok, add the oil, and heat to 375 degrees. Add about ten of the wontons and deep-fry, stirring constantly, until crisp and golden brown. Remove and drain for about 1 minute in a handled strainer. Then drain on absorbent paper until cool. Deep-fry the remaining wontons, drain, and serve with the dipping sauce. *Makes thirty wontons.*

Stuffed Bell Peppers with Ground Meat and Black Beans

1 pound ground pork butt or shoulder (or use ground chuck, if preferred)

Meat Seasonings
2 tablespoons fermented black beans, rinsed, drained, and coarsely chopped
1 tablespoon minced garlic
2 tablespoons minced scallions
2 teaspoons minced gingerroot
1½ tablespoons soy sauce
2 tablespoons rice wine
2 teaspoons sesame oil
1 tablespoon sugar
1½ tablespoons cornstarch

6 medium-sized red bell peppers, cored and seeded
2 tablespoons cornstarch
48 coriander (Chinese parsley) leaves

Most Cantonese dim sum parlors include among their specialties steamed peppers stuffed with fish paste. When they are prepared properly, the flavor is superb. Inspired by this dish and the classic recipe for braised peppers in black bean sauce, I created this recipe. The peppers, with their spicy filling, are perfect for eating with your fingers.

1 Lightly chop the ground meat until fluffy. Place the meat in a mixing bowl, and add the **meat seasonings.** Stir vigorously in one direction to combine evenly. Lightly throw the mixture against the inside of the bowl.

2 Cut each pepper into eight pieces. Lightly dust the inside of each pepper wedge with cornstarch and stuff a heaping tablespoon of the ground meat mixture into the wedge, shaping it to conform to the pepper shape, smoothing and rounding off the top. Spread a coriander leaf across the top of the filling. (Alternatively, you may omit the coriander and sprinkle the cooked stuffed pepper wedges with finely shredded carrots.) Arrange the stuffed pepper wedges, stuffing side up, in a steamer tray that has been lined with parchment paper, wax paper, or cheesecloth that has been moistened with water. Cover. (If there is an overflow, arrange the rest in a second steamer.)

3 Fill a wok with water level with the bottom edge of the steamer tray and heat until boiling. Place the steamer(s) over the boiling water and steam for 15 to 20 minutes, or until the meat is cooked. (If there are two steamer layers, reverse them after 10 minutes.) Remove the peppers, arrange on a platter, and serve. *Serves six.*

Loquats and Lychees Stuffed with Duck in a Fresh Orange Sauce

Duck Filling

1 whole duck, about 5 pounds, boned and skin removed (reserve about 2 tablespoons of fat)

4 strips dried tangerine or orange peel about 2 inches long, softened in hot water for 20 minutes and drained

1 tablespoon minced gingerroot

1½ tablespoons soy sauce

2 tablespoons rice wine

1½ teaspoons sesame oil

½ teaspoon freshly ground black pepper

1½ tablespoons cornstarch

2 15-ounce cans loquats

1 20-ounce can lychees

Fresh Orange Sauce

¼ cup fresh orange juice

¼ cup chicken broth

½ tablespoon sugar

1 teaspoon salt

1 teaspoon sesame oil

1 teaspoon cornstarch

Most Chinese chefs, like the French, are fond of pairing the rich flavor of duck meat with that of tart fruits. With this affinity in mind, I was inspired to create the following dish in which a mousseline of duck meat is stuffed into loquats and lychees, steamed, and served with a fresh orange sauce. The sauce may be poured lightly over the stuffed fruit, or served in a small bowl, on the side, for dipping.

1 Using a sharp knife, scrape out the largest tendons in the duck leg meat and discard. Cut the meat, and the reserved fat, into 1½-inch squares. Cut the tangerine peel into ½-inch squares. Turn on a food processor fitted with the steel blade; with the motor running, drop the tangerine peel through the feed tube and mince finely. Add the gingerroot and process until minced. Place the duck meat and fat in the work bowl and process until chopped to a paste. Remove the mixture and add the remaining ingredients of the **duck filling.** The mixture should be thick and pasty.

2 Stuff the duck mixture into a pastry bag, without a tip. Drain the loquats and lychees of their syrup. Pipe a generous amount of the duck mixture into each loquat and lychee. Arrange the stuffed fruits in a steamer lined with parchment paper, wax paper, or cheesecloth that has been moistened with water. (You may need more than one steamer. If so, stack the layers.) Cover. Combine the **fresh orange sauce** ingredients in a saucepan.

3 Fill a wok with water level with the bottom edge of the steamer tray and heat until boiling. Place the steamer layer(s) over the boiling water and steam for 20 minutes over high heat. (Reverse the steamer layers midway through steaming.) Heat the orange sauce until thickened, stirring constantly to prevent lumps. Transfer to a serving bowl. Remove the stuffed lychees and loquats and arrange on a platter. Serve with the fresh orange sauce. *Serves six.*

Steamed Open-Faced Dumplings (Shao Mai)

燒

賣

1 pound ground pork

⅓ pound medium raw shrimp, peeled and deveined

½ cup chopped water chestnuts, blanched briefly in boiling water, immersed in cold water, and drained thoroughly

6 dried Chinese black mushrooms, softened in hot water for 20 minutes, stems removed, and caps finely chopped

Dumpling Seasonings

2 teaspoons soy sauce

1 tablespoon rice wine

1 teaspoon salt

2 teaspoons sesame oil

½ teaspoon sugar

¼ teaspoon freshly ground black pepper

1 tablespoon minced scallions

2 teaspoons minced gingerroot

1 egg white, lightly beaten

1½ tablespoons cornstarch

30 dumpling skins (*goyoza*)

½ cup grated carrot

In eastern and southern China, dumplings are more delicate than their northern counterparts. The skin, which is usually made with flour, egg, and water, is much thinner. In the filling, the ever-present ground pork is garnished with shrimp, black mushrooms, and occasionally shark's fin. Even the shape is more elaborate and refined. Shao mai, as illustrated in this recipe, are a perfect example of the delicacy and refinement of southeastern Chinese steamed dumplings.

1 Lightly chop the ground pork until fluffy. Place in a mixing bowl. Place the shrimp in a linen dishtowel and squeeze out as much moisture as possible. Mince the shrimp to a coarse paste and add to the ground meat with the water chestnuts, the black mushrooms, and the **dumpling seasonings.** Stir vigorously in one direction to combine evenly.

2 Place a heaping tablespoon of the filling in the middle of one dumpling skin and gather up the edges of the skin around the filling. (Keep the remaining skins covered with a damp cloth to keep them from drying out.) Holding the dumpling between your fingers, lightly squeeze it in the center to form a type of "waist." Push up the filling from the bottom of the dumpling to create a flat surface. Smooth the top surface with the underside of a spoon dipped in water. Make the remaining dumplings in the same manner. Arrange the shaped dumplings about ¼ inch apart in steamer trays that have been lined with wet cheesecloth or lightly oiled parchment.

3 Fill a wok with water level with the bottom edge of a steamer tray and heat until boiling. Stack the steamer trays, cover, and place over the boiling water. Steam the dumplings for 15 minutes over high heat, reversing the trays after 8 minutes. Remove and sprinkle the tops with the grated carrot. Serve with soy sauce for dipping. ***Makes thirty dumplings.***

Skewered Chicken with Almond Coating

2 pounds boneless chicken
  breast meat, skin removed

Chicken Marinade
2 tablespoons soy sauce
2 tablespoons rice wine
1 teaspoon sesame oil
½ teaspoon freshly ground
  white pepper
1 teaspoon five-spice powder
1½ tablespoons minced
  gingerroot
2 tablespoons minced
  scallions
1 teaspoon minced garlic

6 10-inch bamboo skewers,
  soaked in cold water to
  cover for 1 hour
½ cup all-purpose flour
2 eggs, lightly beaten
1 cup slivered or sliced
  almonds
4 cups safflower or corn oil

Cantonese master chefs have long been partial to the marriage of meat and nuts, coating both pork and chicken with walnuts, cashews, pine nuts, and almonds. In this dish, nuggets of chicken that have been marinated in a pungent dressing are coated with slivered almonds and deep-fried. Chopped walnuts or cashews may be used in place of the almonds. Serve the deep-fried, skewered chicken with a soy sauce–vinegar dipping sauce, adding a dash of chili paste if desired.

1 Trim the chicken meat of any fat or gristle. Cut into 1½-inch squares and place in a mixing bowl. Add the **chicken marinade,** toss lightly to coat, and let sit for at least 3 hours at room temperature, or overnight in the refrigerator.

2 Thread the chicken meat onto the bamboo skewers, taking care not to push the pieces too closely together. Place the flour, eggs, and almonds in separate pie plates or deep dishes.

3 Dip the skewered chicken in the flour, then the eggs (letting the excess drain off), and then the almonds, coating well. Place the skewers of chicken on a tray that has been lightly dusted with cornstarch or flour. Let air-dry for 1 hour, turning once.

4 Heat a wok, add the safflower or corn oil, and heat to 350 degrees. Add several of the skewers of chicken and deep-fry, turning constantly, for about 5 minutes, or until the chicken is cooked and the outside is golden brown. Remove with a slotted spoon and drain. Drain until cool on absorbent paper. Meanwhile, reheat the oil and deep-fry the remaining chicken. Remove and drain. Serve the chicken with one of the dipping sauces from the pan-fried meat dumplings (page 157). *Serves six.*

Country Terrine with Black Beans

1 slice of cooked ham,
  weighing ½ pound
¼ cup rice wine
¼ cup Scotch
2 pounds ground pork butt or
  shoulder (should be fatty)
1 tablespoon safflower or corn
  oil
1 tablespoon minced garlic
½ cup fermented black beans,
  rinsed lightly and drained
2 eggs, lightly beaten
1 teaspoon five-spice powder
½ teaspoon salt
½ teaspoon freshly ground
  black pepper
½ pound thinly sliced fatback
  or bacon

From the very first days of my culinary training in France, I noticed similarities in French and Chinese cooking philosophies and methods. Certain ingredients were even similar. When I first tasted a fresh black truffle, I was immediately reminded of the pungent flavor of fermented black beans. That memory inspired the creation of this recipe. Like any terrine, the flavor of this one improves if it is made several days before serving.

1 Cut the ham slice lengthwise into long strips about ½ inch wide and ½ inch thick. Place in a bowl, add the rice wine and Scotch, and toss lightly to coat. Let marinate at room temperature for 1 hour. Remove the ham slices, reserving the marinade.

2 Place the ground meat in a large mixing bowl, add the reserved ham marinade, and stir to combine.

3 Heat a wok or skillet, add the safflower or corn oil, and heat until hot. Add the garlic and black beans. Sauté lightly for about 30 seconds and remove from the heat. Let the mixture cool to room temperature and add to the ground pork. Add the eggs, five-spice powder, salt, and pepper. Stir vigorously in one direction. Preheat the oven to 350 degrees.

4 If using the fatback, rinse it and drain. If using the bacon, blanch it by dipping it briefly into boiling water and refreshing in cold water. Pat dry. Line a 1½-quart terrine mold with the sliced fatback or bacon, leaving a slight overhang down the sides of the terrine mold. Firmly pack the terrine mold with half the pork mixture and spread out evenly. Arrange the ham strips lengthwise on top of the layer of ground pork and spread the remaining pork mixture over the top. Pack down evenly with a spatula and fold up the overhang of fatback or bacon to cover the top of the terrine. Cover tightly with aluminum foil. If the terrine has a lid, place it on top.

5 Set the mold in a large square pan containing about an inch of water and bake for about 1 hour and 20 minutes, or until a skewer inserted into the center of the terrine for 1 minute is hot to the touch when withdrawn. Remove from the oven and place a weight or heavy pan on top of the terrine to set the shape. Let stand at room temperature for six hours, or overnight. Refrigerate for at least one day before serving. Using a sharp knife, trim away the bacon or fatback. Cut into slices and serve with Chinese pickles. *Serves six.*

. . . .

Steamed Scallop Rolls with Fresh Lemon Sauce

½ pound fresh snow peas, ends snapped and veiny strings removed

Scallop Mixture
1⅓ pounds sea scallops, rinsed and patted dry
1 tablespoon minced gingerroot
1 tablespoon minced scallions
1 tablespoon rice wine
1 teaspoon salt
¼ teaspoon freshly ground white pepper
1 teaspoon sesame oil
½ egg white, lightly beaten
1 tablespoon cornstarch
⅓ pound medium raw shrimp, peeled, deveined, and finely diced

Fresh Lemon Sauce
2 tablespoons freshly squeezed lemon juice
6 tablespoons chicken broth
1 tablespoon sugar
1 teaspoon salt
1 teaspoon sesame oil
1 teaspoon cornstarch

Dried scallops have long played a vital role in classic Chinese cuisine as a delicacy and a pungent seasoning. In Taiwan and Hong Kong, fresh scallops recently have begun to appear in several dishes, but they are still somewhat rare. Fortunately, in this country scallops are plentiful and easily obtainable. Although bay and Cape scallops tend to be sweeter, sea scallops are recommended for these scallop rolls. Their firm, meaty texture works best in a mousseline mixture.

1 Lightly rinse the snow peas and pat dry. Using a sharp knife, split open one long side of each snow pea. Dice ⅓ pound of the scallops and set aside. To prepare the **scallop mixture,** in a food processor fitted with the steel blade, purée the remaining scallops. Add the gingerroot, scallions, rice wine, salt, pepper, sesame oil, and egg white. Process, turning the machine on and off several times, to blend the ingredients. Transfer the mixture to a bowl and add the cornstarch, mixing vigorously by hand or with a spatula, in one direction. The mixture should be stiff and pasty. Fold in the diced shrimp and scallops, and chill for 1 hour. Combine the fresh lemon sauce ingredients in a saucepan and place near the stove.

2 Using a spoon or a pastry tube without a tip, spoon or pipe the scallop mixture into the snow peas. Arrange the stuffed snow peas in steamer trays that have been lined with parchment paper or wax paper and lightly brushed with sesame oil. Stack the steamer trays and cover.

3 Fill a wok with water level with the bottom of one steamer tray and heat until boiling. Place the steamer trays containing the stuffed snow peas over the boiling water and steam for 5 to 7 minutes, reversing the trays midway through the steaming time. When done, the scallop mixture should be firm to the touch. Steam longer if necessary. Transfer the stuffed snow peas to a platter and cover to keep warm. Heat the **fresh lemon sauce,** stirring constantly. When thickened, spoon over the stuffed snow peas, or serve as a dipping sauce on the side. *Serves six.*

. . . .

Note
You may substitute 7 medium-sized red or green peppers for the snow peas, cutting 3-inch rounds in the seeded peppers. Spread the scallop mixture on top, smoothing with a knife, and steam for 10 minutes.

. . . .

Deep-Fried Shrimp Fingers

1 pound medium raw shrimp, peeled and deveined
½ cup chopped water chestnuts, blanched briefly in boiling water, immersed in cold water, and drained thoroughly
½ cup grated carrot
6 dried Chinese black mushrooms, softened in hot water to cover, stems removed, and caps shredded

Shrimp Seasonings
2 tablespoons rice wine
1 teaspoon salt
¼ teaspoon freshly ground black pepper
1 teaspoon sesame oil
3 tablespoons minced scallions
1 tablespoon minced gingerroot
1 egg white, lightly beaten
1½ tablespoons cornstarch

Shrimp paste, redolent with ginger and scallions, is a popular ingredient in numerous dim sum *dishes. To make shrimp toast, it is spread on slices of bread and deep-fried. In another dish, it is stuffed into dried mushrooms and steamed. Shaped into balls and coated with bread cubes, it forms the base for "hundred-corner" shrimp balls. In this dish, a strip of the paste is garnished with shredded carrots and black mushrooms, and wrapped in a wonton skin. Deep-fried until golden brown, the resulting "fingers" are superb when served with plum sauce and hot mustard.*

1 Rinse the shrimp and drain thoroughly. Place in a linen dishtowel and squeeze out as much moisture as possible. Using the same method, squeeze out any excess moisture in the water chestnuts. In a food processor fitted with the steel blade, chop the shrimp to a paste. Transfer the shrimp to a large mixing bowl, and add the water chestnuts, carrots, black mushrooms, and **shrimp seasonings,** except for the cornstarch. Stir vigorously in one direction to combine evenly. Add the cornstarch and continue mixing to combine.

秋

35 to 40 wonton skins
1 egg yolk
4 cups safflower or corn oil

2 Place a tablespoon of the shrimp paste on one wonton skin (keep the remaining skins covered with a damp cloth) and shape it into an even strip in the center of the skin. (Alternatively, you may fill a pastry tube without a tip with the shrimp mixture and pipe a strip lengthwise in the center of the wonton skin.) Using your finger, rub a little egg yolk along one edge of the wonton skin. Fold in the opposite edge, then fold over the edge with the yolk. Do not fold too tightly, or the wonton skin will split open while deep-frying. Press lightly to form a thin roll and to seal. Repeat for the remaining filling and skins. Place the finished skin on a tray that has been lightly dusted with cornstarch.

3 Heat a wok, add the oil, and heat to 350 degrees. Add a batch of the shrimp rolls and deep-fry for 3 to 4 minutes, turning constantly until golden brown and crisp. Remove with a slotted spoon and drain on absorbent paper; keep warm in a low oven. Meanwhile, reheat the oil and continue frying the remaining rolls. Remove and drain. Serve piping hot with plum sauce and hot mustard. ***Serves six.***

. . . .

Note

For an alternative method of preparing the shrimp fingers: Do not add the carrots and black mushrooms to the shrimp filling. After piping or placing a tablespoon of the shrimp mixture on the wonton skin, sprinkle a line of shredded carrots and black mushrooms in the center. Fold over the skin to enclose, and deep-fry as directed.

秋

Steamed Juicy Buns

小籠包

Savory Aspic
1 raw chicken carcass or backs
   and necks, cut into 1½-inch
   pieces
1¼ cups water
¼ cup soy sauce
1½ tablespoons sugar
1½ tablespoons rice wine
1 strip dried tangerine or
   orange peel, about 1½
   inches long and 1 inch wide

Yeast Dough
2 tablespoons sugar
1 cup warm water
1½ teaspoons active dry yeast
3 cups all-purpose flour
1 tablespoon safflower or corn
   oil

½ pound ground pork
2 tablespoons rice wine
1 tablespoon soy sauce
2 teaspoons sesame oil
1 tablespoon minced scallions
1½ teaspoons minced
   gingerroot

Steamed savory buns are a classic dim sum *or snack, and most regions of China offer their own individual versions. In eastern China, these meat-filled pastries are also stuffed with a spoonful of fragrant, rich aspic. The aspic dissolves when the buns are steamed, so that a bite of the filling is accompanied by a burst of fragrant juice — hence the name. These buns may be cooked in advance, and then resteamed for 10 minutes before serving.*

1 To make the **savory aspic**: Combine all the ingredients in a heavy saucepan and heat until boiling. Reduce the heat to very low and simmer, uncovered, for 2 hours. Strain the broth through a fine-meshed strainer or a double layer of cheesecloth, and return to the saucepan. Reduce the broth to ½ cup. Cool completely and measure 1 teaspoon of aspic into individual ice tray molds. Freeze for about 2 hours, until firm.

2 To make the **yeast dough**: Dissolve the sugar in the warm water. Add the yeast, stir, and set aside for about 5 minutes, until foamy. Place the flour in a mixing bowl. Add the oil and yeast mixture. Stir with a wooden spoon to form a rough dough. Turn out onto a lightly floured surface and knead until smooth and elastic, about 5 minutes. If the dough is sticky, sprinkle in a little flour as you knead. Shape the dough into a ball, place in a lightly oiled bowl, cover with a damp cloth, and let rise in a warm place, free from drafts, for 3 hours or until tripled in bulk.

3 Lightly chop the ground pork until fluffy. Place in a bowl with the rice wine, soy sauce, sesame oil, scallions, and gingerroot. Stir in one direction to combine evenly. Separate the mixture into twenty-four portions, and roll them into balls.

4 Punch down the dough and turn out onto a counter. Cut it in half and form each half into a long snakelike roll about 1 inch thick. Cut each half into twelve pieces. Flatten a piece of dough into a 3-inch circle, pinching to make the edges thinner than the center. Place one piece of frozen aspic in the center of the dough and a ball of ground pork on top. Working quickly, and using your index finger and thumb, gather up the dough edge into small pleats meeting at the center so that the filling is completely enclosed. (The finished bun should look almost like an igloo.) Repeat for the remaining dough and filling. Arrange the buns, about 1 inch apart, in two steamer trays lined with wet cheesecloth or lightly oiled parchment paper.

5 Fill a wok with water level with the bottom edge of a steamer tray and heat until boiling. Place one steamer tray over the boiling water and cover. Steam for 12 to 15 minutes over high heat. Steam the remaining buns in the same manner. Serve hot. To reheat, steam the buns for 10 minutes. *Makes twenty-four buns.*

. . . .

Deep-Fried Crab Toasts

½ pound lump crabmeat, picked over to remove any cartilage
¾ pound medium raw shrimp, peeled
½ cup chopped fresh water chestnuts, cooked for about 1 minute in boiling water, refreshed in cold water, and drained

Seasonings
2 teaspoons minced gingerroot
1 tablespoon rice wine
1 teaspoon salt
1 egg white, lightly beaten
1½ teaspoons sesame oil
2 tablespoons cornstarch

10 slices sandwich bread, crusts removed
3 tablespoons sesame seeds (optional)
6 cups safflower or corn oil

For the Chinese, there is no better accompaniment to drinks than a crisp, deep-fried savory morsel of food. After tasting a crabmeat toast dipped in plum sauce with a tiny bit of hot mustard, anyone would have to agree.

1 Using your fingers or a fork, shred the crabmeat into small pieces. In a food processor fitted with the steel blade, process the shrimp to a coarse paste. Add the **seasonings,** except for the cornstarch, and process to a fine paste. Transfer the mixture to a mixing bowl and add the cornstarch, crabmeat, and water chestnuts, beating vigorously in one direction. The mixture should be a stiff paste.

2 Spread the mixture rather thickly on the slices of bread. Using a spatula dipped in a little water, smooth the top of the crab paste. Sprinkle sesame seeds over the top and press lightly so they will stick to the paste. Cut each slice diagonally in half and then into quarters with a sharp knife.

3 Heat a wok, add the oil, and heat to 350 degrees. Add six or seven of the crabmeat triangles and deep-fry, turning constantly until they are golden brown. Remove with a slotted spoon and drain briefly in a handled strainer. Transfer to a paper towel and drain. Deep-fry the remaining triangles, remove, and drain. Serve with plum sauce and hot mustard for dipping. *Serves six.*

Savory Baked Turnovers with a Ground Meat and Black Bean Filling

1 pound ground pork or beef
2 teaspoons soy sauce
1 teaspoon rice wine
1 teaspoon sesame oil
1 cup coarsely chopped water
  chestnuts, blanched in
  boiling water for 15 seconds

Minced Seasonings
2 tablespoons fermented black
  beans
2 tablespoons minced
  scallions
1 tablespoon minced
  gingerroot
1 tablespoon minced garlic

Sauce
¼ cup soy sauce
2 tablespoons rice wine
1 tablespoon sugar
¾ cup chicken broth or water
2 teaspoons cornstarch

3 tablespoons safflower or
  corn oil
2 cups all-purpose flour
1 teaspoon salt
⅔ cup unsalted butter
⅓ cup ice water

Egg Wash
1 egg, lightly beaten
1 tablespoon water
½ teaspoon salt

Since most Chinese kitchens do not have an oven, home-baked goods are a rare commodity. There are many bakeries, however, which offer sweet and savory snacks with a wide variety of fillings. Turnovers are not only a popular bakery item, they are also found in dim sum *parlors and teashops. Lard is traditionally used in Chinese pastry crusts, but since I was trained by a French pastry chef, I prefer the flavor of butter to lard. The recipe has been adapted accordingly.*

1 To prepare the filling, place the ground meat in a bowl, and add the soy sauce, rice wine, and sesame oil. Toss lightly to blend. Assemble the minced seasonings and the sauce, and place near the stove.

2 Heat a wok, add 1 tablespoon of the safflower or corn oil, and heat until very hot. Add the ground meat and cook over high heat, stirring constantly to break it up. Cook until it changes color. Remove the meat and drain.

3 Reheat the wok, add the remaining oil, and heat until very hot. Add the **minced seasonings** and stir-fry for about 10 seconds, until fragrant. Add the water chestnuts and stir-fry until heated through. Add the **sauce** and cook, stirring constantly, until thickened. Add the cooked meat, toss lightly to coat with the sauce, and transfer to a platter. Refrigerate until cool.

4 Combine the flour and salt in a mixing bowl. Using a pastry blender or two knives, cut the butter into the flour until the mixture is the consistency of cornmeal. Add the water, and mix lightly until the dough comes together. (It may still be a little rough, but should be somewhat homogeneous.) Form the dough into a ball, sprinkle lightly with flour, and wrap in plastic wrap. Refrigerate for 30 minutes.

5 Preheat the oven to 425 degrees. On a lightly floured surface, roll out the dough to a large rectangle about ⅙ inch thick. Using a 3-inch round cutter, cut out circles. Gather the scraps into a ball and chill briefly. Roll out again and cut more circles.

Gather up the scraps, press together, chill, and roll out once more.

6 Place a tablespoon of the pork filling in the center of a dough circle and fold into a half-moon shape. Bring the two outer edges together and pinch to seal and enclose the filling. Press the edge and crimp by hand, or with the tines of a fork, to form a scalloped pattern. Place the finished turnovers on an ungreased baking sheet and brush the surface with the **egg wash.** Bake for 20 minutes, or until golden brown. Transfer to a cooling rack. Serve warm or at room temperature. ***Makes about thirty turnovers.***

Flaky Turnovers with a Dried Mushroom Duxelle Filling

Filling
1 pound fresh mushrooms
⅔ ounce (15 to 20) dried
  Chinese black mushrooms
2 tablespoons safflower or
  corn oil
2 teaspoons minced garlic
2 cups minced garlic chives
2 cups minced leeks
3 tablespoons Madeira
½ teaspoon five-spice powder
2 tablespoons bread crumbs

Pastry Crust
2 cups all-purpose flour
1 teaspoon salt
⅔ cup unsalted butter
⅓ cup ice water

Egg Wash
1 egg, lightly beaten
1 tablespoon water

Turnovers are always a popular hors d'oeuvre or first course. The advantage for the cook is that they may be made completely in advance and reheated. And since they consist of a filling contained in a pastry, guests usually find them easy to eat. The filling in these turnovers combines both fresh and dried mushrooms, producing an unusual and pleasing contrast in flavor.

1 Clean the fresh mushrooms, rinsing lightly in cold water and draining thoroughly. Trim the stem ends and chop the mushrooms coarsely. Soften the dried mushrooms in hot water to cover for 10 to 15 minutes. Remove, drain, and remove and discard the stems. Chop the caps. Place the mushrooms and other filling ingredients near the stove.

2 Heat a wok or a skillet and add the safflower or corn oil. Add the black mushrooms and garlic. Toss briefly over high heat for about 10 seconds, until fragrant. Add the fresh mushrooms and stir-fry, over medium heat, until they render liquid and the liquid evaporates. Add the garlic chives and leeks, and continue stir-frying for several minutes, adding the Madeira. (If the pan is very dry, add a tablespoon or two of butter.) Remove from the heat, cool slightly, and add the five-spice powder and bread crumbs. Chill.

3 To prepare the **pastry crust,** combine the flour and salt in a bowl. Using a pastry blender or two knives, cut the butter into the flour until the mixture is the consistency of cornmeal. Add the water and mix lightly until the dough is smooth and homogeneous. Do not overwork the dough. (Alternatively, you may prepare the dough in a food processor fitted with the steel blade, blending the ingredients in the same order as when doing it by hand. Once again, do not overwork the dough.) Form the dough into a ball and wrap it in plastic wrap. Refrigerate for 20 minutes.

4 Preheat the oven to 400 degrees. Roll out the dough to a large rectangle about ⅙ inch thick. Using a 3-inch round cookie cutter, cut out circles.

Gather the scraps together into a ball and chill. Roll out the dough again and cut more circles. You should have approximately thirty circles. If not, roll out the dough once more and cut more circles.

5 Place a teaspoon of the filling in the center of one dough circle and fold it into a half-moon shape. Pinch the two edges together to enclose the filling. Seal the edge tightly by scalloping by hand into a decorative pattern or crimping with a fork. Place the finished turnovers on a baking sheet and brush with the egg wash. Bake for 20 minutes, or until golden brown. Briefly cool the turnovers on a rack, and serve while still warm. *Makes about thirty turnovers.*

WINTER

· · · · · · · · · · · · · · · ·

冬

The Emperor

makes a sacrifice

at the Temple

of Heaven

. . . .

冬

CHINESE NEW YEAR

For the Chinese, the New Year is unlike any other holiday. Of all the festivals celebrated throughout the year, the first day of the first month of the lunar calendar is the most significant.

In the home, the Chinese New Year celebration embodies reunion; relatives from all over the world gather to eat, drink, rejoice in one another's company, and honor their ancestors. In the marketplace, the holiday marks the time for a clean slate — all accounts are settled and outstanding debts are paid. Chinese New Year also heralds the coming of spring (even though in a large part of China conditions are anything but springlike). It is a time when the opposing ruling forces of the universe — the yin and the yang — fuse once again in a renewal of their natural harmony. And at no other point in the year is there more cause for jubilant celebration.

According to legend, the New Year's festival originated when an offended household deity returned to heaven and demanded that the Jade Emperor destroy the earth. The other gods heard of the demand and joined in to defend mankind, urging the Emperor to visit and decide for himself. Forewarned of his impending arrival, the people on earth halted their daily routines, tidied up their affairs — both at home and at work — and presented lavish food and drink offerings to the gods as atonement. The Supreme Rulers, impressed by the sumptuous display, relented and called off the destruction of the world.

Many of these ancient rituals are observed in much the same way today. Preparations for the holiday begin a month prior to the festival. Houses are cleaned from top to bottom; all business affairs are tidied up and accounts are settled; and offerings are made to the gods of the household. The kitchen god, whose majestic presence graces the walls of many Chinese kitchens, is paid special attention. His mouth is smeared with honey and sweet things are presented in his honor so that when his image is burned and he returns to heaven to give his annual accounting of the household, only sweet remarks concerning his patrons will emerge from his lips. A new image of the god is posted on New Year's Eve and a bowl of freshly made rice ("New Year rice") studded with assorted dried nuts is placed in front as an offering. Gifts — most frequently consisting of food — are exchanged among relatives, friends, and business acquaintances.

The kitchen is particularly busy as the family prepares for the holiday feasting. In ancient China, a pig was always slaughtered in anticipation of the New Year's celebration; freshly made links of fragrant Chinese sausage were hung from the rafters to mature and dry out before cooking. Even today, Chinese sausage still remains a favored New Year specialty. Savory and sweet puddings (called *gao* and signifying "high honors") made of sweet rice, turnips, taro, or sweet red bean paste are steamed and set aside for holiday eating, when they will be cut into slices and pan-fried until golden brown. Dumplings, with fillings consisting of meat and vegetables — or just vegetables, since many families observed the practice of not eating any meat on New Year's Day — are folded, arranged on endless trays, and set to chill in the cool winter air. Some cooks like to enclose a coin or some lucky token inside the filling, imparting a wish for prosperity and good luck for the recipient. On New Year's Day and the following days, these same dumplings will be boiled, steamed, deep-fried, or pan-fried (to resemble golden ingots).

On New Year's Eve, the whole family gathers for a multicourse banquet. Platters usually are exceptionally impressive in appearance and cost, in honor of the great occasion. The menu includes the most sumptuous and expensive ingredients available, including shark's fin, bird's nest, and sea cucumbers. Foods that either resemble or symbolize auspicious things are also served. There are delicately thin fried spring rolls with an appearance said to be similar to bricks of gold; clams, which indicate a receptivity to good fortune; vegetables carved in the shape of coins and cooked with dried scallops; and lotus root, through the holes of which "good luck will hopefully pass in the coming year."

In many parts of China, a whole fish is served, since it symbolizes bounty and the Chinese name for fish sounds like the word for "surplus." In the areas of China where fish is scarce, a whole fish sculpted out of wood is placed on the table, signifying a wish for prosperity.

As the feasting progresses, red envelopes (*hong bao*) containing money are passed out to children and servants, and firecrackers are set off to scare away the evil spirits and honor the benevolent gods.

Sleep is discouraged on New Year's Eve as the entire family stays up to usher in the holiday. Gambling, eating, gossiping, and setting off firecrackers are the traditional activities. At dawn the door is opened and the master of the house utters a blessing of prosperity on the dwelling for the coming year. The day is spent with relatives, eating and talking. The foods served are often cold or at room temperature, for, according to Chinese ritual, steaming and boiling are allowed, but no frying or baking is permitted on the holiday. Knives and all cutting instruments are put away as well. Even brooms, dust pans, and dusters are not used before noon because throwing out dust or garbage on New Year's Day is compared to gathering and throwing away gold.

Today, in modern China, the New Year's holiday officially lasts three days, but in ancient China, the celebration continued for two weeks until the Feast of the Lanterns, a festival that falls on the fifteenth day of the first month.

CHINESE NEW YEAR'S BANQUET

Pang Pang Cucumbers

Pan-Fried Meat Dumplings

Littleneck Clams in Black Bean Sauce

Beggar's Chicken

Whole Red-Cooked Fish Smothered in Black Mushrooms and Garlic Cloves

Stir-Fried Asparagus and Mushrooms with Lettuce in Oyster Sauce

Three-Treasure Winter Melon Soup

Sweet Date Soup with Lychees

Almond Cookies

Pang Pang Cucumbers

8 gherkin or pickling
  cucumbers, or 3 gourmet
  seedless cucumbers
1½ teaspoons salt
2 ounces bean threads
  (cellophane noodles)

Bean Thread Seasonings
½ teaspoon salt
1 teaspoon sesame oil

Pang Pang Sauce
¼ cup chunky peanut butter
3 tablespoons soy sauce, or a
  little more to taste
1 tablespoon sugar
2 tablespoons sesame oil
2 teaspoons Chinese black
  vinegar
1 teaspoon chili paste
4 to 6 tablespoons chicken
  broth or water
1 tablespoon minced garlic
1 tablespoon minced
  gingerroot

1 tablespoon minced scallion
  greens

*Most connoisseurs of classic Sichuanese cooking are famil-
iar with* pang pang *chicken, a cold chicken salad dish
with a spicy sesame paste–based sauce. I like to substitute
peanut butter for the sesame paste and use the resulting
sauce to dress noodles, or vegetables such as sliced cucumbers or celery. This dish is excellent as a cold appetizer or as a vegetable side dish with assorted accompany-
ing entrées.*

1 Rinse the cucumbers and drain. Trim the ends
and slice each one lengthwise in half. Scoop out the
seeds and cut each half crosswise into 2-inch
lengths. Cut the pieces lengthwise into thin slices,
about ¼ inch thick. Place the slices in a mixing
bowl, add the salt, toss lightly, and let stand for 20
minutes. Drain off any liquid that has collected,
lightly rinse the cucumbers, and drain thoroughly.

2 Place the bean threads in a bowl with warm
water to cover for 10 minutes, to soften. Drain and
cut into 3-inch lengths. Blanch the bean threads by
briefly (for 10 seconds) dipping them in boiling
water; remove, drain, and refresh in cold water.
Drain thoroughly and mix with the **bean thread
seasonings**. Arrange the seasoned bean threads on
a serving platter. Arrange the cucumber slices on
top.

3 In a blender or a food processor fitted with the
steel blade, combine the ingredients of the **pang
pang sauce** and mix until smooth. The sauce should
be the consistency of lightly whipped cream. Before
serving, pour the sauce over the cucumbers and
sprinkle the top with the minced scallion greens.
Serves six.

Pan-Fried Meat Dumplings

冬

鍋

貼

4 cups chopped Chinese
  cabbage (Napa)
1 teaspoon salt
1¼ pounds ground pork
2 cups chopped Chinese
  chives or leeks

Dumpling Seasonings
1½ tablespoons soy sauce
1 tablespoon rice wine
1½ teaspoons sesame oil
1½ teaspoons minced
  gingerroot
1 teaspoon minced garlic
1 tablespoon cornstarch

36 dumpling skins (*goyoza*)
2 tablespoons safflower or
  corn oil
1 cup hot water
½ tablespoon flour

According to the Chinese Tasty Tales Cookbook *by Gary Lee, pan-fried meat dumplings, or pot stickers, were first invented because of a mishap in the Imperial Palace kitchens. A cook who was making boiled dumplings neglected to check them. The water in the dumpling pot had evaporated, leaving the dumpling bottoms fried to a crusty brown. The distraught chef decided to serve them nonetheless and, happily, they were a smashing success. This is my rendition of that northern classic.*

1 Place the chopped cabbage in a mixing bowl, add the salt, toss lightly to mix evenly, and let stand for 20 minutes. (This will draw out the water in the cabbage so the filling will not leak through the skin later.) Taking a handful of cabbage, squeeze out as much liquid as possible. Place in a bowl and repeat the same procedure for the rest of the cabbage.

2 Lightly chop the ground meat until fluffy. Add to the cabbage, along with the chives or leeks and the **dumpling seasonings.** Stir vigorously in one direction to combine evenly.

2 Place a heaping tablespoon of the filling in the center of one dumpling skin. (Keep the remaining skins covered with a damp cloth.) Spread a little water along the edge of the skin with your fingers and fold over the skin to form a half-moon shape. Press the edge tightly to seal so that the filling is completely enclosed. Repeat for the remaining dumplings.

3 Heat a wok or a well-seasoned skillet. Add the safflower or corn oil and heat until hot. Arrange the dumplings, in circular rows, to line the bottom of the pan. They should be packed fairly closely. This may be done in two batches, if necessary. Fry the dumplings over medium-high heat, until the bottoms are a deep golden brown. Mix the hot water with the flour and add to the dumplings. Partially cover and cook for 10 minutes, or until the dumplings are cooked and the liquid has evaporated. Uncover, and cook until the bottoms of the dumplings are very crisp. Add a little more oil if necessary. Use a spatula to loosen any dumplings that seem to

be sticking to the bottom. Invert the pan and un-
mold the dumplings directly onto a serving platter.
Serve with one of the dipping sauces. ***Makes about
thirty-six dumplings.***

Traditional Dipping Sauce

½ cup soy sauce
3 tablespoons Chinese black
  vinegar
2 teaspoons sugar
1 tablespoon finely shredded
  gingerroot

Combine the ingredients, stirring until the sugar
dissolves. Transfer to a serving bowl, and serve.

Spicy Dipping Sauce

½ cup soy sauce
2 tablespoons Chinese black
  vinegar
1 teaspoon chili paste
1 tablespoon minced garlic

Combine the ingredients and transfer to a serving
bowl and serve.

Littleneck Clams in Black Bean Sauce

豆
豉
蛤
蜊

24 small littleneck or hard
shell clams
3 tablespoons safflower or
corn oil

Minced Seasonings
2 tablespoons fermented black
beans, rinsed, drained, and
coarsely chopped
1½ tablespoons minced garlic
2 tablespoons minced
scallions
1 tablespoon minced
gingerroot

Black Bean Sauce
¼ cup chicken broth or water
1 tablespoon soy sauce
1½ tablespoons rice wine
1 teaspoon sugar
¼ teaspoon freshly ground
black pepper

Thickener
1 teaspoon cornstarch
1 tablespoon water

*Since clams symbolize good fortune, they are a popular
Chinese New Year's delicacy. In this dish, the baby clams
are cooked in a fragrant black bean sauce, redolent with
garlic and ginger. Since the actual cooking time is minimal, it is best to prepare all the ingredients in advance
and position them near the stove. The dish will be ready
to serve in a matter of minutes.*

1 Rinse the clams thoroughly and, if necessary,
scrub them lightly with a brush to remove any
sand. Place them in a bowl with cold water to cover
for 1 hour. Remove and drain. Prepare the minced
seasonings, the black bean sauce, and the thickener.

2 Heat a wok until hot and add the oil. Add the
minced seasonings and stir-fry for about 15 seconds, until fragrant. Add the **black bean sauce** and
heat until boiling. Add the clams and cover. Cook
the clams over medium heat, shaking occasionally,
until they just begin to open, about 5 to 7 minutes.
Uncover and stir the clams in the sauce. When they
have opened a bit further, add the **thickener** and
stir until the mixture has thickened. Carefully toss
the clams in the sauce and transfer to a serving
platter. Serve immediately. ***Serves six.***

Beggar's Chicken

富
貴
鷄

1 whole roasting chicken, weighing about 4 to 4½ pounds

Chicken Marinade
2 tablespoons soy sauce
3 tablespoons rice wine
2 whole star anise, smashed lightly with the flat side of a cleaver
4 slices gingerroot, smashed lightly with the flat side of a cleaver
3 scallions, smashed lightly with the flat side of a cleaver

Dough
4 cups all-purpose flour
1 teaspoon salt
1 tablespoon safflower or corn oil
1½ cups warm water

Chicken Filling
½ pound boneless center-cut pork loin (fat removed), cut into matchstick-size shreds
1 tablespoon soy sauce
1 tablespoon rice wine
1 teaspoon sesame oil
3 tablespoons minced scallions
2 tablespoons minced garlic
1 cup matchstick-size shreds bamboo shoot, blanched briefly in boiling water and drained
¼ cup Tientsin preserved vegetable, rinsed and drained (available at Chinese grocery stores; can be omitted)
½ cup matchstick-size shreds Chinese black mushrooms (softened in hot water and stems removed before shredding)
1 tablespoon soy sauce
2 tablespoons rice wine
1 teaspoon sugar, or to taste

According to a Chinese legend, this dish originated many years ago in China when a beggar had "borrowed" a chicken from a local farmer and was roasting it on a spit for his dinner. Suddenly, he heard the thunder of approaching horses. To protect his meal, he wrapped the chicken in a lotus leaf and buried it in mud near the fire. Once the unwelcome visitors had come and gone, he unearthed the wrapped chicken and discovered that the mud had hardened and dried to create a clay casing. He smashed open the covering and discovered that the chicken had cooked to a glorious tenderness, basting in its own juices. In the classic recipe, potter's clay is usually used. I prefer to use a flour-and-water dough, as in this recipe.

1 Rinse the chicken and remove any fat deposits from the neck and cavity. Pat dry and place in a bowl. Combine the ingredients of the **chicken marinade** and rub over the surface of the chicken and inside the cavity. Stuff the seasonings from the marinade into the cavity, cover the chicken with plastic wrap, and let stand overnight in the refrigerator.

2 To prepare the **dough** for the casing, place the flour and salt in a mixing bowl. Add the oil and water, and mix to a rough dough. (Add a little more water if the dough feels dry and a little flour if it feels too wet.) Transfer the dough to a lightly floured surface and knead until smooth and elastic. Wrap it in plastic wrap and chill for 30 minutes.

3 Prepare the ingredients of the **chicken filling**, adding the soy sauce, rice wine, and sesame oil to the pork shreds. Toss lightly to coat, and place the other ingredients near the stove. Heat a wok until hot. Add 3 tablespoons of the safflower or corn oil and heat until very hot. Add the pork shreds and stir-fry until they have changed color and separated. Remove with a handled strainer and drain. Reheat the pan and any oil left in it, and add the remaining oil. Heat until very hot and add the minced scallions and garlic. Stir-fry for about 10 seconds and add the bamboo shoots, preserved vegetable, and black mushrooms. Stir-fry for about

5 tablespoons safflower or
  corn oil
2 dried lotus leaves, soaked
  for 1 hour in warm water to
  cover and drained (available
  at Chinese grocery stores;
  can be omitted)
1 whole egg, lightly beaten

15 seconds and add the cooked pork and the soy sauce, rice wine, and sugar. Stir-fry until thickened. Remove and let cool.

4 Preheat the oven to 350 degrees. Stuff the filling into the cavity of the chicken. Open up the lotus leaves and lay them out flat on a counter. Place the chicken, breast side down, on the lotus leaves and wrap it up in them. On a lightly floured surface, roll out the dough to a large rectangle about ½ inch thick. Roll the edges slightly thinner than the center. Brush the surface with some water and place the chicken, breast side down, in the center of the dough. Fold in the edges, from the sides and the ends, to enclose the chicken like a package. (You may use any extra dough to make a decoration.) Brush the surface of the dough with the lightly beaten egg. Place the chicken on a baking sheet, seam side down, and bake for 1 hour. Reduce the oven temperature to 250 degrees and bake for 1 hour longer, or until the casing is golden brown. Remove and cool slightly. To serve, cut through the dough lengthwise and then crosswise to expose the chicken, which should be very tender. Move the dough away from the chicken and cut it into pieces along with some of the meat and filling. Or you may spoon the filling into a bowl and serve it on the side. *Serves six.*

Whole Red-Cooked Fish Smothered in Black Mushrooms and Garlic Cloves

紅燒魚

1 whole, firm-fleshed white fish (such as baby haddock, red snapper, pickerel, or lake trout), weighing 3 to 3½ pounds

Fish Marinade
3 slices gingerroot, smashed lightly with the flat side of a cleaver
2 tablespoons rice wine
1 tablespoon soy sauce

Pork Marinade
1 tablespoon soy sauce
1 tablespoon rice wine
1 teaspoon sesame oil
1 teaspoon cornstarch
½ tablespoon water

Fish Braising Liquid
4 cups chicken broth
¼ cup soy sauce
2 tablespoons rice wine
2 teaspoons sugar
1 teaspoon sesame oil

½ pound boneless center-cut pork loin

½ cup safflower or corn oil

Fish Seasonings
10 to 12 whole garlic cloves, peeled
6 dried Chinese black mushrooms, softened in hot water for 20 minutes, stems removed, and caps shredded
12 1-inch scallion pieces, white part only

Thickener
1 tablespoon cornstarch
2 tablespoons water

½ cup matchstick-size shreds bamboo shoots, blanched briefly in boiling water and drained
2 tablespoons finely shredded gingerroot

For the Chinese, a whole fish symbolizes prosperity and wholeness, and it is standard banquet fare for the New Year as well as any auspicious occasion. As Chinese decorum dictates, the head of the fish always points toward the guest of honor, and it is this lucky person who usually has the privilege of eating the fish's cheeks (considered by many Chinese to be the most succulent eating). This dish takes a little time to prepare, but the final product is well worth the effort.

1 Ask the fishmonger to scale the fish and clean it through the gills, if possible, leaving the belly intact. Rinse thoroughly, and drain. Holding the knife at a 45-degree angle to the fish, make deep scores crosswise along the length of the fish, an inch apart, running from the dorsal fin to the tail. Pinch the gingerroot slices in the **fish marinade** repeatedly for several minutes to impart the flavor. Rub the marinade all over the outside of the fish and into the scores. Cover the fish with plastic wrap and let stand for 30 minutes. Discard the gingerroot and drain the fish.

2 Remove any fat or gristle from the pork loin and discard. Cut the pork, across the grain, into slices ⅛ inch thick. Cut the slices into matchstick-size shreds. Place the pork shreds in a bowl, add the ingredients of **pork marinade**, toss lightly, and let marinate for 20 minutes. Place the fish braising liquid, the fish seasonings, and the thickener near the stove.

3 Heat a wok, add the oil, and heat to 350 degrees. Add the garlic cloves and deep-fry until golden brown. Remove with a slotted spoon and drain. Reheat the oil to 400 degrees. Slowly lower the fish, scored side down, into the hot oil, ladling the oil over the fish, and fry over high heat until golden brown on the bottom side. Remove and drain. Remove the fish from the wok and remove all but 4 tablespoons of oil from the wok.

4 Reheat the wok and the oil until very hot. Add the pork, stir-fry over high heat until the shreds turn color, remove, and drain. Add one or two more tablespoons of oil and reheat. Add the **fish seasonings** (including the fried garlic), and stir-fry for about 10 seconds, until fragrant. Add the pork shreds and **fish braising liquid**, and heat until boiling. Add the fish, scored sided up, and heat until the liquid boils. Reduce the heat to medium, cover, and cook for 12 to 15 minutes, or until the fish flakes when prodded with a chopstick or a fork. Using two slotted spatulas, carefully lift out the fish and transfer it to a platter. Heat the liquid until boiling and add the **thickener**, stirring constantly to prevent lumps. When the sauce has thickened, add the bamboo shoots. Toss lightly and spoon the sauce over the fish. Sprinkle the shredded ginger-root over the fish and serve immediately. *Serves six.*

Stir-Fried Asparagus and Mushrooms with Lettuce in Oyster Sauce

蠔
油
蘆
筍

1½ pounds leafy or Boston lettuce
1 15-ounce jar or can white asparagus, drained
2 15-ounce cans straw mushrooms (unpeeled, if possible), drained
¼ pound snow peas, ends snapped and veiny strings removed
3 tablespoons safflower or corn oil

Lettuce Seasonings
1 tablespoon rice wine
¾ teaspoon salt
½ teaspoon sesame oil

Minced Seasonings
2 teaspoons minced gingerroot
2 tablespoons minced scallions

Oyster Sauce
½ cup chicken broth
2 tablespoons oyster sauce
1 tablespoon soy sauce
1 teaspoon sugar, or to taste
½ teaspoon sesame oil
1½ teaspoons cornstarch

This is a "rice-accompanying dish," whose role in a formal banquet menu is to indicate that the meal is beginning to reach an end. Since lettuce symbolizes prosperity, this vegetable platter is particularly fitting for the New Year's holiday. The lettuce may be stir-fried ahead of time and served warm or at room temperature.

1 Discard any wilted leaves from the lettuce and cut away any stem ends. Rinse the lettuce, drain thoroughly, and pat dry. Cut the leaves lengthwise into 1-inch strips. Blanch the asparagus and straw mushrooms separately for 10 seconds in boiling water, drain, and refresh in cold water. Drain again. Blanch the snow peas for 5 seconds in boiling water, refresh in cold water, and drain. Place these ingredients, as well as the lettuce seasonings, minced seasonings, and oyster sauce, near the stove.

2 Heat a wok, add 1 tablespoon of the oil, and heat until almost smoking. Add the lettuce and the **lettuce seasonings** and stir-fry over high heat for 1 minute, until the lettuce is slightly wilted. Arrange the lettuce around the outer edge of a serving platter.

3 Reheat the wok until hot. Add the remaining oil and heat until very hot. Add the **minced seasonings** and stir-fry for about 10 seconds, until fragrant. Add the asparagus, straw mushrooms, and snow peas. Cook briefly, until just heated through. Add the **oyster sauce** and cook until the sauce has thickened. Remove the mixture and arrange in the center of the platter. Serve immediately. *Serves six.*

....

Three-Treasure Winter Melon Soup

三
鮮
冬
瓜
湯

1 piece of winter melon, from the end of the melon, weighing 5 to 7 pounds
1 whole frying chicken, weighing 2½ to 3 pounds
10 to 12 dried Chinese black mushrooms
¼ pound Chinese ham or prosciutto, cut into paper-thin slices about 2 inches square
5 to 6 cups chicken broth, preferably homemade, heated until boiling (page 194)
¼ cup rice wine
4 slices gingerroot, smashed with the flat side of a cleaver
3 scallions, smashed with the flat side of a cleaver
1 teaspoon salt
¼ teaspoon freshly ground white pepper

Most Chinese banquets culminate in the serving of a soup, and few such dishes are more stunning in their presentation than a whole steamed winter melon. Once cooked, the tender melon meat should be scooped out and served with the broth, chicken pieces, black mushrooms, and Chinese ham or prosciutto. This soup has the added advantage of being able to be cooked in advance and re-steamed for 10 to 15 minutes before serving.

1 Rinse the outside of the winter melon and pat dry. Using a sharp, heavy knife, trim a tiny wedge off the bottom of the melon so that it will stand upright, and carve a decorative design around the outside top surface. You may also carve designs in the skin of the melon. Place the melon upright in a large heat-proof bowl or on a platter with a lip.

2 Soften the black mushrooms in hot water to cover for 20 minutes. Using a heavy chef's knife or a cleaver, cut the chicken, through the bones, into bite-size pieces. Drop the pieces in boiling water for 1 minute and rinse in cold water to remove any scum. Arrange the chicken inside the melon. Remove the stems from the mushrooms, discard, and place the caps inside the winter melon. Add the Chinese ham, chicken broth, rice wine, gingerroot, and scallions. The melon should be only about two thirds full. Cover the top with aluminum foil.

3 Into a wok or a deep pot large enough to hold the melon place about 4 cups of boiling water. Place a steaming stand or an empty tuna fish can in the center of the pot and carefully balance the filled melon on top. (The melon should not be in contact with the water.) Heat until boiling and steam for 2 hours, or until the melon is tender. Replenish the water every 20 to 30 minutes.

4 Carefully transfer the melon to a serving bowl and remove and discard the gingerroot and scallions. Add the salt and pepper, stir, and taste for seasoning. Serve immediately in soup bowls. **Serves six.**

Sweet Date Soup with Lychees

1 pound pitted, chopped dates
3 cups water
Juice of ½ lemon
1½ teaspoons ground cinnamon
1 tablespoon vanilla extract
2 15-ounce cans lychees, drained

Sweet soups provide a fitting ending to any meal, and Chinese chefs have developed a substantial repertory. Some of the most notable include those made with walnuts, jujubes (Chinese dates), and peanuts. In this dish, a fragrant date broth provides a delicious contrast for the sweet lychees.

Place the dates in a saucepan with 2 cups of the water and heat until boiling. Reduce the heat to low and simmer for 15 minutes, stirring occasionally. Transfer the mixture to a blender or a food processor fitted with the steel blade, and purée the date mixture until smooth. Return it to the saucepan with the remaining water, and continue cooking until the mixture has thickened to the consistency of heavy cream. Add the lemon juice, cinnamon, vanilla extract, and lychees. Heat until just boiling. Portion into bowls and serve. **Serves six.**

Almond Cookies

杏
仁
餅

½ cup unsalted butter or
  shortening, softened to
  room temperature
¾ cup granulated sugar
1 egg
1¼ cups all-purpose flour
½ teaspoon baking soda
½ teaspoon salt
1 cup finely chopped almonds
1 teaspoon almond extract
1 whole egg, lightly beaten
36 whole blanched almonds

While cookies (like other Western pastries) were not indigenous to China, once introduced, they were quickly embraced with a vengeance. Almond cookies have now become a staple sweet in Chinese bakeries from Boston to Hong Kong. In the traditional Chinese recipe, lard is used, but once again, my Western roots prevail and I adapt the recipe to substitute sweet butter.

1 Preheat the oven to 350 degrees. In a mixing bowl, cream the butter and sugar for about 5 minutes. Add the egg and continue beating until smooth. Sift together the flour, baking soda, and salt. Slowly add to the butter mixture and mix until smooth. Add the chopped almonds and the almond extract. Mix until smooth.

2 Drop tablespoons of the cookie batter onto lightly buttered cookie sheets, spacing them about 1 inch apart. Dip your thumb in some flour and make an indentation in the center of each cookie. Brush each cookie with the lightly beaten egg and place a whole almond in the center of each indentation. Bake for 10 to 12 minutes, until the cookies are golden brown and puffed. Let cool slightly; then transfer to a wire cooling rack. Serve when cooled. ***Makes about thirty-six cookies.***

NEW YEAR'S BUFFET

Candied Walnuts

Lotus Root Salad in a Scallion Oil Dressing

Baked Fish Packages with Chinese Ham and Black Mushrooms

Stir-Fried Chicken with Pine Nuts in Lettuce Leaves

Coin-Shaped Scallops and Vegetables with Noodles in Oyster Sauce

Poached Pears in Ginger Sauce

Tangerines

Candied Walnuts

1 pound shelled walnuts
1½ cups granulated sugar
4 cups safflower or corn oil

The appetizers for any multicourse banquet should only tease the palate and prepare it for the delicacies that will follow. Such is the case with these walnuts, which are lightly cooked in a syrup, tossed in sugar, and deep-fried until golden. Like most cocktail nuts, they can be addictive, but they are a delicious and fitting accompaniment to drinks.

1 Place the walnuts in a saucepan, add 2 quarts of water, and heat until boiling. Reduce the heat to medium and cook the walnuts for approximately 3 minutes. Drain thoroughly in a colander and place in a bowl. Add the sugar and toss lightly to completely coat the walnuts. Shake off the excess sugar, and arrange the walnuts on a tray to air-dry. Let stand for 1 hour, turning occasionally.

2 Heat a wok, add the oil, and heat to 350 degrees, or a little less. Add a third of the walnuts and deep-fry, turning constantly, until the sugar begins to caramelize and the walnuts turn golden. Remove with a slotted spoon and drain for about a minute in a handled strainer. Arrange the fried walnuts on a tray that has been lined with brown paper and let cool. Deep-fry the remaining walnuts in two batches and drain thoroughly. Once the walnuts have cooled, serve. Store in a tightly sealed jar. **Serves six.**

Lotus Root Salad in a Scallion Oil Dressing

2 pounds fresh lotus root
2 green peppers, halved and
    seeded

Scallion Oil Dressing
2 tablespoons safflower or
    corn oil
2 tablespoons sesame oil
½ cup shredded scallions
½ teaspoon salt
1 teaspoon clear rice vinegar
¼ teaspoon freshly ground
    white pepper

When I was studying in Taiwan, one of my chef mentors was from Shanghai, a city renowned for the delicacy and refinement of its regional cuisine. This chef refused to use sesame oil, claiming it had an overpowering and bitter flavor. Instead, he would infuse peanut or vegetable oil with the pungent taste of scallions, and use it in salad dressings or to finish sauces. This dish was inspired by that chef, who made a salad of fresh lotus root very similar to this one. If lotus root is unavailable, Jerusalem artichokes make an excellent substitute.

1 Rinse the lotus root, peel away the tough, outer skin, cut off the ends, and cut into slices about ⅛ inch thick. Immediately place the cut slices in cold water to prevent them from turning brown. Cut the green peppers into thin julienne strips.

2 Heat 3 quarts of water until boiling and add the lotus root slices. Cook for 3½ minutes and remove. Immediately immerse in cold water and drain. Place in a bowl with the green pepper strips.

3 To prepare the **scallion oil dressing,** combine the oils in a heavy pan and heat until smoking. Add the scallions and turn off the heat. Cover and let the mixture stand for 20 minutes. Strain the oil, discarding the scallions, and combine with the salt, rice vinegar, and pepper. Add to the lotus root slices and green peppers. Toss lightly to coat and transfer to a serving dish. Serve at room temperature. *Serves six.*

Baked Fish Packages with Chinese Ham and Black Mushrooms

2 pounds fillet of sole or
flounder, skin removed

Fish Marinade
1½ tablespoons rice wine
2 slices gingerroot, smashed
lightly with the flat side of a
cleaver
1 teaspoon salt

¼ pound Chinese ham or
prosciutto, cut into very fine
shreds about 3 inches long
6 dried Chinese black
mushrooms, softened in hot
water, stems removed, and
caps cut into very fine
shreds

Minced Seasonings
2 tablespoons minced
scallions
2 teaspoons minced
gingerroot

Sauce
¼ cup chicken broth
2 tablespoons rice wine
2 teaspoons soy sauce
1 teaspoon sugar
½ teaspoon salt
¼ teaspoon freshly ground
white pepper
¾ teaspoon cornstarch

2 tablespoons safflower or
corn oil
2 tablespoons sesame oil
6 12-inch squares parchment
paper or aluminum foil

*This dish was inspired by a Cantonese classic. In the
original recipe, a whole fish is scored, stuffed with thin
slices of Chinese ham and black mushrooms, and steamed.
In this adaptation, fillets of fish are garnished with
Chinese ham and black mushrooms, coated with a light
sauce, and baked in parchment packages. The dish lends
itself particularly well to buffet dining, since it may be
prepared almost completely in advance and the cooking
time is minimal.*

1 Cut the fillets into six pieces about the same size,
and place in a bowl. Prepare the **fish marinade** by
combining the ingredients and pinching the gingerroot slices in the rice wine repeatedly for several
minutes to impart the flavor. Add the marinade to
the fillets, toss lightly to coat, and let stand for 20
minutes. Discard the gingerroot slices. Prepare the
seasonings and sauce and place near the stove.

2 Heat a wok or a heavy skillet and add the safflower or corn oil. Heat until very hot and add the
seasonings. Stir-fry over high heat for 10 seconds,
until fragrant, and add the **sauce.** Cook until the
mixture thickens, stirring constantly. Remove and
let cool.

3 Preheat the oven to 450 degrees. Brush the surface of each square of parchment with the sesame
oil and fold over the square to form a triangle.
Open up the paper, with the oiled side up, and arrange a piece of fish on the lower half of the paper.
Sprinkle some of the black mushroom and Chinese
ham or prosciutto shreds on top. Spoon some of
the sauce over the fish and fold over the paper to
enclose the fish. Fold in and crimp the edge to seal
tightly. Repeat for the remaining fish and sauce and
place the packages on a heavy baking sheet. Bake
in the preheated oven for 8 to 10 minutes, or until
the fish flakes when prodded with a fork. Remove
the parchment packages from the oven and cut
away the crimped edges for presentation. Serve.
Serves six.

Stir-Fried Chicken with Pine Nuts in Lettuce Leaves

2¼ pounds boneless chicken breast meat, skin removed

Chicken Marinade
2 tablespoons soy sauce
1 tablespoon rice wine
1 teaspoon sesame oil
1 egg white, lightly beaten, or 2 tablespoons water
1½ teaspoons cornstarch

8 dried Chinese black mushrooms, softened in hot water, stems removed, and caps finely shredded
2 cups water chestnuts, blanched briefly in boiling water, refreshed immediately in cold water, drained, and thinly sliced
2 cups pine nuts, lightly toasted in a 350-degree oven until golden brown

Minced Seasonings
2 tablespoons minced scallions
1 tablespoon minced gingerroot

Chicken Sauce
3 tablespoons soy sauce
2 tablespoons rice wine
2 teaspoons sugar
1 teaspoon salt
¼ teaspoon freshly ground white pepper
1½ teaspoons sesame oil
½ cup chicken broth
1½ teaspoons cornstarch

2 cups safflower or corn oil
1 ounce thin rice stick noodles or bean threads (cellophane noodles)
1 large head leafy lettuce or 2 heads Boston lettuce, leaves separated, rinsed, drained, and flattened slightly with the flat side of a cleaver

For optimal flavor, most stir-fried dishes should be served as soon as they come out of the wok. This dish is an exception, since it is equally delicious whether served hot or at room temperature. For a buffet, it may be kept warm in a chafing dish or served at room temperature. The chicken is delicately seasoned and contrasts beautifully with the fresh lettuce leaves and buttery pine nuts.

1 Trim any fat or gristle from the chicken meat. Arrange the breasts, smooth side down, on a cutting board, and holding the knife at a 45-degree angle to the meat, cut the meat into very thin slices. Holding the knife upright, perpendicular to the meat, cut into thin, matchstick-size shreds, about 2 inches long. Place the shreds in a bowl, add the **chicken marinade,** toss lightly to coat, and let stand for 20 minutes. Prepare the minced seasonings and the chicken sauce. Arrange the lettuce leaves in a serving dish or bowl.

2 Heat a wok, add the safflower or corn oil, and heat to 425 degrees, or until almost smoking. Lightly separate the noodles, if they are in a cluster, and drop into the hot oil. Deep-fry on one side until puffed and pale golden. Turn over immediately and deep-fry for another second. Remove with a slotted spoon and drain on absorbent paper. Transfer to a serving platter and lightly break up with your fingers to form a bed for the stir-fried mixture.

3 Remove a cup of oil from the pan and add half the chicken shreds. Stir-fry, for about 1½ minutes, until the shreds change color and separate. Remove with a handled strainer, drain, and reheat the oil. Add the remaining chicken and stir-fry until cooked. Remove and drain. Remove all but 3 tablespoons of oil from the pan.

4 Heat the oil until very hot. Add the **minced seasonings** and stir-fry for 10 seconds, until fragrant. Add the black mushrooms and stir-fry for another 5 seconds. Add the water chestnuts and toss lightly over high heat for about 20 seconds to heat through. Add the **chicken sauce** and stir until slightly thickened. Add the cooked chicken shreds and the pine nuts. Toss lightly to coat with the sauce and arrange over the fried noodles. Serve. Each diner spoons some of the chicken mixture, with a bit of the noodles, into a lettuce leaf, rolls it up, and eats it with his or her fingers. *Serves six.*

Coin-Shaped Scallops and Vegetables with Noodles in Oyster Sauce

1 pound fresh sea scallops, rinsed lightly and drained

Scallop Marinade
2 tablespoons rice wine
2 slices gingerroot, smashed lightly with the flat side of a cleaver
½ teaspoon salt

3 fat carrots, peeled, ends trimmed
2 gourmet seedless cucumbers, peeled and halved
¾ pound spinach noodles
1 tablespoon sesame oil
1 tablespoon safflower or corn oil

Shredded Seasonings
1 tablespoon finely shredded gingerroot
2 tablespoons finely shredded scallions

Oyster Sauce
½ cup chicken broth or water
5 tablespoons oyster sauce
2½ tablespoons soy sauce
1 tablespoon sugar
1½ teaspoons sesame oil

Noodles symbolize longevity and they are served in some form, for their flavor and auspicious significance, at almost all special gatherings. This stir-fried noodle platter makes an excellent staple, as in this meal, but it is equally delicious as a meal in itself for a light lunch or dinner.

1 Holding a cleaver or chef's knife parallel to the cutting surface, slice each scallop in half through the thickness. Place the scallop slices in a bowl. Prepare the **scallop marinade** by combining the ingredients and lightly pinching the gingerroot slices in the rice wine repeatedly for several minutes to impart the flavor. Add the marinade to the scallops, toss lightly, and let marinate for 20 minutes. Discard the gingerroot slices. Prepare the minced seasonings and the oyster sauce, and place them near the stove.

2 Fill a large pot with 2 quarts of water and heat until boiling. Add the carrots and cook for about 3 minutes. Remove with a slotted spoon and immediately immerse in cold water. (Retain the boiling water.) Drain the carrots, and using a melon baller, scoop out carrot balls. Using the melon baller, scoop out cucumber balls as well. Reheat the water until boiling and add the cucumber balls. Cook for about 1 minute; then remove with a slotted spoon and immerse in cold water. Drain thoroughly and set aside. Reheat the water and add the scallops. Poach for about 1 minute, or until they are cooked; then remove with a slotted spoon and drain. Add 1 tablespoon of safflower or corn oil to the water and reheat. Add the noodles and cook for about 10 minutes, or until just tender. (Do not overcook.) Pour the noodles into a colander and lightly rinse in cold water. Drain thoroughly and toss in the sesame oil. Arrange the noodles in a bed on a platter. Arrange the carrot and cucumber balls in a circular row around the middle, and arrange the poached scallops in the center.

3 Heat a wok or skillet, add the safflower or corn oil, and heat until very hot. Add the **shredded seasonings** and stir-fry for about 10 seconds, until fragrant. Add the **oyster sauce** and heat until boiling. Cook for 2 to 3 minutes, until slightly thickened, and transfer to a serving dish. Before serving, pour the sauce over the noodles and toss, or serve on the side. *Serves six.*

Poached Pears in Ginger Sauce

6 slightly underripe pears,
   either Bosc or Anjou
4 cups water
1½ cups sugar
2 cinnamon sticks
6 slices gingerroot, smashed
   lightly with the flat side of a
   cleaver
1 tablespoon candied
   gingerroot cut into
   matchstick-size shreds
1 tablespoon lemon peel cut
   into matchstick-size shreds
   and blanched briefly in
   boiling water

*Most Chinese meals do not have what is normally consid-
ered a dessert. Instead, sweets may appear throughout the
meal and fruit is usually served at the very end. This
pear dish would satisfy the palate of Westerners and
Chinese alike. It is flavorful, soothing, and not overly
sweet. Serving the traditional New Year's fruit, tangerines, after the pears will impart a wish for "good fortune"
and provide a simple yet refreshing ending to this holiday
repast.*

1 Peel the pears and cut each in half, removing the
core. Rub the peeled halves with a cut lemon half
to prevent them from browning.

2 Place the water, sugar, cinnamon, and gingerroot
slices in a 2-quart saucepan and heat until boiling,
stirring constantly to dissolve the sugar. Simmer for
30 minutes over medium heat.

3 Add the pears to the syrup and heat until the
liquid almost boils. Reduce the heat to low and let
the pears poach for 12 to 15 minutes, or until just
tender. To test, pierce with a knife.

4 Remove the pears with a slotted spoon and arrange in a shallow serving dish with a lip. Remove
the cinnamon and the gingerroot slices from the
poaching syrup and discard.

5 Add the shredded candied gingerroot and lemon
peel to the poaching liquid and reduce to a thick
syrup over medium heat. Pour the thickened syrup
over the pears and serve warm, at room temperature, or cold. ***Serves six.***

THE LANTERN FESTIVAL

On the fifteenth day of the first month, the New Year's festivities culminate in the celebration of the Lantern Festival, or the Feast of the Lanterns. On this holiday, brightly colored lanterns, of all shapes and sizes, are strung from doorway to doorway and everyone savors the holiday delicacy of sweet rice balls (*yuan xiao*), stuffed with sweet and savory fillings.

The Lantern Festival is believed to have originated in the Han dynasty, over two thousand years ago, but at that time it revolved around ceremonial worship. It was some eight hundred years later that lanterns were first used in the celebration.

The role of lanterns in the festivities may have originated with the ancient Chinese respect for the stars, which were worshiped as deities. The Chinese believed that a star shone in the heavens for every human being on earth. The stars were also worshiped to ensure happiness and to protect from harmful influences; small lamps were lit in observance of this belief. Others maintain that lamps were hung from doorways to attract prosperity and longevity to the inhabitants within.

In ancient China, lanterns were extraordinarily varied and ornate. Some were shaped like red carp and goldfish; others were multifaceted good-luck lanterns resembling a water caltrop (a starchy root vegetable), whose name in Chinese sounds the same as the word for good luck. Lanterns shaped like sheep were also popular, since the Chinese word for sheep is the same as that for good auspices.

In the home, a ceremony involving 108 small lamps was performed. The lamps were arranged on a table in the shape of the Chinese character *shun*, meaning agreeable or smooth. In the center was a large lamp, representing the God of Longevity. The lamps were all lit as incense was burned and sweet rice balls were offered as favors to the gods.

Traditionally, sweet rice balls were made in a rather complicated process whereby a small piece of flavored sugar was repeatedly rolled in rice flour and dipped in water. The successive layers formed round, inch-thick balls. When the balls were boiled in water, the sugar center dissolved into a syrup. They were then served in a sweet soup.

Today many Chinese still hang lanterns in honor of the holiday, and *yuan xiao* remain the traditional holiday delicacy. Most cooks make a simplified version, stuffing the sweet rice balls with red bean paste, sweet crushed sesame seeds, or peanut paste. Families gather together to prepare the dish for the holiday, and as they stuff the balls and roll them, they are usually very careful to mention only good things. In this way, they believe, good luck will be guaranteed for the forthcoming year.

冬

MENU I

Salt-Baked Cornish Game Hens

Mongolian Fire Pot

Thousand-Layer Scallion Rolls

Sweet Rice Balls

Salt-Baked Cornish Game Hens

冬

3 whole Cornish game hens, approximately 1½ pounds each

Marinade
¼ cup rice wine
1 tablespoon salt
¾ teaspoon five-spice powder
½ teaspoon freshly ground black pepper
6 scallions, smashed lightly with the flat side of a cleaver
6 slices gingerroot, smashed lightly with the flat side of a cleaver

3 16-inch squares parchment paper, or cut-up squares of a large oven-roasting bag
4 pounds rock salt or kosher salt
2 tablespoons Sichuan peppercorns
3 whole star anise, smashed lightly with the flat side of a cleaver
1 tablespoon safflower or corn oil
1 pound spinach, trimmed and cleaned
1 tablespoon minced garlic
1½ tablespoons rice wine
¾ teaspoon salt
1 tablespoon sesame oil

Dipping Sauce
¼ cup chicken broth
1 teaspoon salt
1 teaspoon sesame oil
1 tablespoon shredded scallions
1 tablespoon finely shredded gingerroot

This dish is an adaptation of a classic recipe using a whole chicken. Salt has long been used as a cooking medium by both Chinese and European chefs. Like clay, the salt forms a hard coating, sealing in the juices and producing a succulently tender bird. The parchment paper used in the recipe to wrap the hens may be omitted. Its sole purpose is to catch the juices so that the salt may be used more than once.

1 Lightly rinse each Cornish game hen and remove any fat from the cavity and neck. Drain the hens thoroughly and place them in a bowl. Prepare the **marinade** by combining the ingredients and repeatedly pinching the scallions and gingerroot in the mixture to impart their flavors. Add the marinade to the hens and rub it inside the cavity and all over the skin of each one. Cover with plastic wrap and let the hens marinate, breast side down, for at least 2 hours, or overnight in the refrigerator. Remove the hens from the marinade and place, breast side down, in the center of each parchment square, folding in the sides and wrapping up like a package to enclose the hens.

2 Preheat the oven to 450 degrees. Heat a wok or a very heavy skillet and add the salt, Sichuan peppercorns, and star anise. Stir-fry over high heat, stirring constantly, until the salt is very hot and begins to pop. Spoon about a third of the salt into a 4-quart Dutch oven or casserole, shaping three shallow indentations. Place the wrapped hens, breast side down, with the wrapped edges pressed tightly against the hen, in the indentations, and cover with the remaining heated salt. Place the pot in the preheated oven and bake for 45 minutes. Place the dipping sauce ingredients in a saucepan.

3 Heat a wok until very hot. Add the safflower or corn oil and heat until smoking. Add the spinach and garlic, and toss lightly for about 10 seconds over high heat. Add the rice wine and salt. Cook, tossing constantly, for about 30 seconds, until the spinach is just wilted. Remove and portion the spinach into a small bed on each of six plates.

冬

4 Remove the pot from the oven and let it sit for about 10 minutes. Carefully dig out the hens (you can retain the seasoned salt, store it, and reuse it), and discard the paper. Using a sharp cleaver or chef's knife, cut each hen in half, down the back. Brush the skin lightly with the sesame oil so that it glistens, and arrange each half on top of a bed of spinach. Heat the **dipping sauce** until boiling and spoon some of it over each hen. Serve immediately, with the rest of the sauce on the side. *Serves six.*

冬

Mongolian Fire Pot

蒙古火鍋

1½ pounds boned leg of lamb, shank portion
1½ pounds minute steak or eye of the round

Meat Marinade
¼ cup soy sauce
3 tablespoons rice wine
2 teaspoons sesame oil

1 pound Chinese cabbage (Napa), stems removed and leaves cut into 2-inch squares
2 tablespoons safflower or corn oil
2 cloves garlic, smashed with the flat side of a cleaver

Soup Base
2 tablespoons rice wine
6 cups Chinese chicken broth (page 194)
1 teaspoon salt

2 ounces bean threads (cellophane noodles)
2 cakes bean curd, about 3 inches square and 1 inch thick
1 pound fresh button mushrooms, rinsed, drained, and stems trimmed
½ pound fresh spinach, cleaned and trimmed

Dipping Sauce (Per Person)
2 tablespoons soy sauce
1 tablespoon rice wine
1 teaspoon Chinese black vinegar
1 teaspoon sugar
½ teaspoon chili oil (optional)
½ tablespoon minced scallions
1 teaspoon minced gingerroot
1 teaspoon minced garlic
1 egg, lightly beaten (optional)

Fire pot is a classic New Year–Lantern Festival specialty. Generally, this dish is prepared with either lamb or beef. In this unusual rendition, both are used, resulting in a delicious variation. Mongolian fire pot is an unusually filling dish that may be served as a soup-entrée, or even by itself as a meal. If a traditional fire pot is not on hand, an electric wok or skillet, or a soup pot placed on a hot plate, may be improvised in its place.

1 Trim any fat or gristle from the lamb and beef. Separately cut both meats into paper-thin slices about 2 inches square. (You may partially freeze the meats to facilitate cutting.) Place the meat slices in separate bowls. Combine the ingredients of the **meat marinade**, and add half to each bowl. Toss lightly to coat the meats, and arrange the meat slices attractively on a platter.

2 Separate the harder cabbage pieces from the leafier ones. Heat a wok, add the oil, and heat until very hot. Add the garlic, stir-fry briefly, and add the harder cabbage pieces. Stir-fry for about 1 minute over high heat, adding a tablespoon of the **soup base**. Add the leafy cabbage pieces and stir-fry for another minute over high heat. Add the remaining soup base and heat until boiling. Reduce the heat to low and let simmer, uncovered, for 20 minutes.

3 Soften the bean threads for 10 minutes in hot water to cover. Drain, and cut into 6-inch lengths. Cut the bean curd into 1-inch dice. Arrange the bean curd, mushrooms, spinach, and bean threads attractively on several platters. Place the platters containing the meats and other ingredients on a table where a heated Mongolian fire pot has been set up. (If you do not have a Mongolian fire pot, use a pot and a hot plate, or an electric skillet, or an electric wok.) Put a bowl of dipping sauce at each diner's place.

4 Pour the stock into the fire pot and heat until boiling. Each diner takes a slice of meat, dips it into the hot stock until the meat is cooked, then dips the meat into the dipping sauce, and eats. The bean curd, mushrooms, bean threads, and spinach are placed in the stock a little at a time and cooked until done. The diners may help themselves to these ingredients, once again dipping in the sauce before eating. The bean curd, bean threads, and mushrooms will cook in about 10 minutes, but the spinach should take only a minute. Once all the ingredients have been eaten, the flavorful broth is also consumed. *Serves six.*

. . . .

Thousand-Layer Scallion Rolls

千
層
糕

3 cups all-purpose flour
1 teaspoon salt
2 tablespoons sugar
1½ teaspoons active dry yeast
1 cup lukewarm water
1 tablespoon safflower or corn oil
1 teaspoon baking powder
3 tablespoons sesame oil
¼ cup minced scallions greens or Chinese chives
2 tablespoons unroasted sesame seeds

Since Mongolian fire pot is a traditional northern dish, a steamed bun or wheat-based staple is appropriately served as an accompaniment. Northern cooks are renowned for their steamed bread specialties in which a simple flour-yeast-and-water dough is fashioned into myriad shapes, stuffed or garnished with sweet and savory ingredients, and steamed until light and fluffy. This recipe, with its "thousand layers," is a delectable example of one of these steamed bread variations.

1 Place the flour and salt in a large bowl, and stir to combine. In a measuring cup, dissolve the sugar and yeast in the water. Let the mixture stand for 10 minutes until it foams to a head. Add the yeast mixture and the oil to the flour. Mix to a rough dough. Turn out onto a lightly floured surface and knead for about 10 minutes, until smooth and homogeneous. (If the mixture is too dry, add a little water.) Place the dough in a lightly oiled bowl and cover with a damp towel. Let rise for 3½ to 4 hours, until tripled in bulk.

2 Punch down the dough and turn out onto a lightly floured surface. Make an indentation in the center with your fist and place the baking powder in the center. Gather up the edges to seal and to enclose the baking powder. Knead the dough lightly to incorporate the baking powder evenly throughout the dough. Let the dough rest briefly.

3 Using a rolling pin, roll out the dough to a rectangle measuring 8 inches wide and about 12 inches long. Mentally divide the rectangle lengthwise into thirds, and brush the middle third generously with 1½ tablespoons of the sesame oil. Sprinkle with the scallion greens or Chinese chives. Fold over the upper third to cover the middle section, and brush this surface with the remaining sesame oil; then sprinkle with sesame seeds. Bring the bottom third up and fold over to cover. Lightly pinch the edges and ends to seal. This is one "turn." Wrap in plastic wrap and refrigerate for 20 minutes.

4 Remove the dough and place on a lightly floured surface with the seam on the vertical (perpendicular to the table). Roll out the dough to a large rectangle, fold over the upper third, and then fold up the lower third to cover the middle section. Press the edges and ends to seal. Let the dough rest briefly and then cut crosswise in half. Arrange each half in a 12-inch steamer tray that has been lined with parchment paper and lightly brushed with sesame oil. Let rise for 10 to 15 minutes.

5 Fill a wok with water level with the bottom edge of the steamer tray and heat until boiling. Place one steamer tray with the dough over the boiling water, cover, and steam for 20 minutes over high heat. Remove and steam the other half for 20 minutes. Remove and cut each square into slices about 1½ inches thick. Serve with other fire pots and stir-fried dishes. To reheat, steam for 10 minutes. *Serves six.*

Sweet Rice Balls

元
宵

2 cups raw sesame seeds
1 tablespoon unsalted butter
  or lard
3 tablespoons sugar
1½ cups sweet rice flour
1 tablespoon safflower or corn
  oil
¾ cup boiling water

Soup
4 cups water
1 cup sugar
8 slices gingerroot, smashed
  with the flat side of a
  cleaver

No Lantern Festival gathering would be complete without a serving of yuan xiao, *the stuffed sticky rice balls that have become synonymous with this holiday. In this version, a sweet sesame paste is used in the filling, but peanuts or walnuts might also be substituted — as well as red bean paste or date paste. The sweet rice balls may be shaped in advance and cooked just before serving. The sweet filling implies a sweet wish of happiness and prosperity for the coming year.*

1 Preheat the oven to 350 degrees. Place the sesame seeds on a baking sheet and toast in the oven until golden brown, about 10 to 15 minutes. Shake the seeds periodically so that they cook evenly. Let cool. In a food processor fitted with the steel blade, or in a blender, chop the seeds to a powder. Add the butter or lard and the sugar and work into the powder, turning the machine on and off. Turn the mixture out onto a counter and knead lightly to bring together. Form the mixture into a long snakelike roll, and cut it into twenty-four pieces.

2 Place the sweet rice flour in a mixing bowl and add the oil and boiling water. With a wooden spoon, mix to a rough dough. Turn the dough out onto a clean surface and knead lightly until smooth. Form the dough into a long snakelike roll, and cut into twenty-four pieces. Roll each piece into a ball and flatten it to a circle. Using your fingers, pinch the edges so that the center is thicker than the edges. (Alternatively, you may use a tortilla press to make 3-inch circles.) Place a portion of sesame seed filling in the center of each rice flour circle, gather up the edges, and pinch to seal. Roll lightly to form a ball. Repeat for the remaining sesame seed filling and rice flour circles.

3 To make the **soup**: Place the water, sugar, and gingerroot in a pot. Heat until boiling, lower the heat, and cook for about 15 minutes. Add the rice balls and heat until boiling. Reduce the heat and simmer for 8 to 10 minutes, or until they float to the surface. Remove the soup from the heat and discard the gingerroot slices. Portion a few rice balls and some sweet soup into each serving bowl. ***Serves six.***

冬

MENU II

Assorted Seafood Fire Pot

Crispy-Skin Mandarin Duck

Steamed Acorn Squash with Black Bean Sauce

Poached Pears with a Ginger Mousseline Sauce

Assorted Seafood Fire Pot

1½ pounds fillet of haddock, red snapper, pickerel, or any other firm-fleshed fish, skin removed

½ pound medium raw shrimp, peeled and deveined

½ pound sea scallops, rinsed and drained

½ pint freshly shucked oysters, in their liquor

Seafood Marinade

¼ cup rice wine

4 slices gingerroot, smashed lightly with the flat side of a cleaver

2 teaspoons sesame oil

1 teaspoon salt

1 pound Chinese cabbage (Napa), stems removed and leaves cut into 2-inch squares

2 tablespoons safflower or corn oil

2 cloves garlic, smashed with the flat side of a cleaver

Soup Base

2 tablespoons rice wine

6 cups Chinese chicken broth (page 194)

1 teaspoon salt

2 ounces bean threads (cellophane noodles)

1 bunch (1 cup) fresh enoki mushrooms, rinsed lightly, drained, and roots trimmed (if unavailable, substitute canned ones, rinsed thoroughly and drained)

½ pound fresh spinach, cleaned and trimmed

Dipping Sauce (Per Person)

2 tablespoons soy sauce

1 tablespoon rice wine

1 teaspoon Chinese black vinegar

1 teaspoon sugar

Few dishes are as welcome on a chilly winter day as a boiling cauldron of hot soup — otherwise known as a fire pot. The beauty of the fire pot is not only in its versatility (all types of sliced meats, seafood, and vegetables may be used) but in its ease of preparation. And fire pots can easily constitute a meal in themselves. In this variation, assorted seafoods are the main ingredients for this filling, delicious soup.

1 Holding a cleaver or a chef's knife at a 45-degree angle to the fish, cut the fillets into paper-thin slices measuring about 2 inches long. Place in a bowl. Score each shrimp along the back so that it will butterfly when cooked, and place all the shrimp in another bowl. Holding the cleaver parallel with the cutting surface, slice the scallops in half through the thickness. Place the scallops and oysters in separate bowls. Prepare the **seafood marinade** by lightly pinching the gingerroot slices in the rice wine repeatedly for several minutes to impart the flavor. Portion the marinade among the bowls of seafood, toss lightly to coat, and let stand for 20 minutes. Discard the gingerroot slices. Arrange the seafood in an attractive pattern on a platter and place on the table.

2 Separate the harder cabbage pieces from the leafier ones. Heat a wok, add the oil, and heat until very hot. Add the garlic, stir-fry briefly, and add the harder cabbage pieces. Stir-fry for about 1 minute over high heat, adding a tablespoon of the **soup base**. Add the leafy cabbage pieces and stir-fry for another minute over high heat. Add the remaining soup base and heat until boiling. Reduce the heat to low and simmer, uncovered, for 20 minutes.

3 Soften the bean threads for 10 minutes in hot water to cover. Drain, and cut into 6-inch lengths. Arrange the bean threads, the enoki mushrooms, and the spinach attractively on a platter. Place the platters containing the seafood and other ingredients on a table where a heated Mongolian fire pot has been set up. (If you do not have a Mongolian fire pot, use a pot and a hot plate, or an electric skillet, or an electric wok.) Prepare the **dipping**

½ tablespoon minced scallions
1 teaspoon minced gingerroot
1 teaspoon minced garlic

sauce and put a bowl of the sauce at each diner's place.

4 Pour the stock into the fire pot and heat until boiling. Each diner takes a slice or portion of seafood, dips it into the hot stock until it is cooked, then dips the cooked food into the dipping sauce, and eats. The bean threads, mushrooms, and spinach are placed in the stock a little at a time and cooked until done. The diners may help themselves to these ingredients, once again dipping in the sauce before eating. The bean threads and mushrooms will cook in 5 or 6 minutes, but the spinach should take only a minute. Once all the ingredients have been eaten, the flavorful broth is also consumed. *Serves six.*

Crispy-Skin Mandarin Duck

1 whole duck, weighing about
 4 to 4½ pounds
10 cloves garlic, sliced in half
 through the thickness
10 slices gingerroot
4 mandarin oranges or
 clementines, peeled
¼ cup soy sauce
1 cup freshly squeezed orange
 juice
½ cup rice wine
3 tablespoons honey

This crispy duck is not only comparable in flavor to the classic dish Peking duck, it also makes better use of the smaller, fatty ducks generally available in this country. The two-temperature baking process in the dish is designed for the purpose of first rendering off the excess fat and then slowly cooking the meat until tender.

1 Preheat the oven to 425 degrees. Remove any fat deposits from the neck and cavity of the duck. Rinse lightly, drain, and pat dry. Using the blunt edge of a cleaver, lightly pound the garlic and gingerroot together for several minutes. Rub the seasonings over the skin of the duck and inside the cavity. Stuff into the cavity. Separate the orange or clementine sections and stuff them into the cavity. Rub 1 or 2 tablespoons of the soy sauce over the skin of the duck to color. Combine the remaining soy sauce with the orange juice, rice wine, and honey.

2 Place the duck, breast side up, on a cooling rack or a grill placed on a jellyroll pan and pour 1 cup of water into the pan so that the fat from the duck drips down into the water, reducing the smoke. Bake the duck for about 1 hour, turning once. Remove the duck from the oven, pour out the water and rendered fat, and reduce the oven temperature to 350 degrees. Prick the duck with a fork in the fatty places. Bake the duck for 45 minutes, turning several times (ending with the breast side up), basting repeatedly with the orange juice–rice wine mixture. Remove from the oven and let stand for about 10 minutes; then carve into pieces and serve. *Serves six.*

Steamed Acorn Squash with Black Bean Sauce

3 small acorn squash, each
   weighing ¾ to 1 pound

Minced Seasonings
2 tablespoons fermented black
   beans
2 tablespoons minced
   scallions
1 tablespoon minced
   gingerroot
1 tablespoon minced garlic

Sauce
2 tablespoons soy sauce
2 tablespoons rice wine
1 tablespoon sugar
½ cup chicken broth
1½ teaspoons cornstarch

2 tablespoons safflower or
   corn oil
1 tablespoon minced dried red
   pepper
2 tablespoons minced scallion
   greens

*In this unusual recipe, the sweet steamed squash meat
provides a delicious foil for the spicy black bean sauce.
Other types of squash — such as Hubbard, pumpkin, and
even summer varieties — may be substituted for the
acorn squash. This dish may be prepared in advance and
reheated just before serving, but care should be taken not
to overcook the squash.*

1 Lightly rinse the squash. Using a sharp cleaver or
knife, cut each one in half through the stem end.
Scoop out the seeds, and if necessary, cut a thin
slice from the bottom so that the halves will sit flat.
Arrange the squash halves, with the cut side up, in
the bottom of a steamer tray that has been lined
with parchment or wax paper. Prepare the minced
seasonings and the sauce and place near the stove.

2 Heat a wok or a skillet and add the safflower or
corn oil. Heat until very hot and add the **minced
seasonings**. Stir-fry for about 10 seconds, until fragrant, and add the **sauce**. Cook, stirring constantly,
until the mixture has thickened. Spoon the thickened sauce into the squash. Sprinkle the tops with
the red pepper. Cover the steamer.

3 Fill a wok with water level with the bottom edge
of the steamer tray and heat until boiling. Place the
steamer tray containing the squash over the boiling
water and steam the squash for 30 minutes, or until
tender when pierced with a knife or a chopstick.
Remove, garnish the squash with the minced scallion greens and serve. *Serves six.*

Poached Pears with a Ginger Mousseline Sauce

6 slightly underripe pears,
  either Bosc or Anjou
2 lemons
4 cups water
1½ cups sugar
2 cinnamon sticks
6 slices gingerroot, smashed
  lightly with the flat side of a
  cleaver

Sauce Mousseline

6 slices gingerroot, smashed
  lightly with the flat side of a
  cleaver
½ cup Madeira
4 egg yolks
¼ cup sugar
1 cup heavy cream sweetened
  with 1 tablespoon sugar and
  whipped until stiff

Poached pears are a delicious ending to any meal, but in this recipe the fluffy ginger mousseline sauce adds an extraordinary flavor to the cooked fruit. Apples and other fruits also may be poached and served with the moussline sauce. And for those with simpler tastes, the pears or poached fruit may even be served by themselves.

1 Peel the pears and cut each in half, removing the core and seeds. Rub the peeled halves with a cut lemon half to prevent them from turning brown.

2 Place the water, sugar, cinnamon, and gingerroot slices in a 2-quart saucepan and heat until boiling, stirring constantly to dissolve the sugar. Simmer for 30 minutes over medium heat.

3 Add the pears to the syrup and heat until the liquid almost boils. Reduce the heat to low and poach the pears for 12 to 15 minutes, or until just tender. To test, pierce with a knife. Let the pears rest in the syrup briefly before removing and arranging on plates.

4 While the pears are poaching, make the **sauce mousseline**: Place the gingerroot slices in the Madeira and lightly pinch them to infuse the wine with their flavor. Let marinate the gingerroot slices for a few minutes; then discard them. Place the egg yolks and sugar in a heavy saucepan and beat, by hand or with an electric mixer, until pale yellow and creamy. Place the saucepan over a pan of barely simmering water and add the Madeira, beating constantly. The mixture will become very creamy and will increase in volume — like a hollandaise sauce. This will take 10 minutes or longer. Remove from the heat and carefully fold in the whipped cream. Spoon over the poached pears and serve warm. *Serves six.*

SOUPS AND CASSEROLES

Most Westerners envision China as a tropical paradise, steamy hot throughout the year. In fact, many regions experience a winter season, when the air takes on a nippy edge. It is at this time, during the cooler months, that soups and casseroles are most appreciated.

The earliest Chinese soups were stewlike dishes (known as *keng*) and were made with a mixture of meat, seafood, and vegetables. They were popular offerings at both banquets and everyday meals, served with rice or millet. Years later, with the use of local ingredients and the expertise of regional master chefs, soups and casseroles became as refined and varied as those enjoyed in present times.

In modern China, as in other countries, soups play a prominent role in the daily diet. A Chinese soup may be a filling, meal-in-itself type of dish, served as a hearty lunch or supper. Or it may be light and soothing and sipped as a beverage in a home-style meal. And soups are often eaten as an entremets between courses of a full-scale banquet.

With all soups, light or heavy, the key factor is the quality of the broth — almost even more than the ingredients used. The broth forms the base on which everything rests, and if it is not of the best quality, then the flavor of the entire soup will suffer. It is well worth the effort to make the broth from scratch. Chicken and pork bones provide the main flavoring for most soups, with a little help from seasonings such as gingerroot, rice wine, and, occasionally, scallions.

Casseroles, like soups, figure prominently in Chinese cuisine. Traditionally, most Chinese casseroles are prepared in an earthenware pot known as a sandy pot. The pot is fashioned from a mixture of clay and sand fired at an extremely high temperature. Generally, the interior of the pot is glazed and the exterior is unglazed. Sandy pot dishes involve long, slow simmering or braising, and this design allows the pot to absorb, distribute, and retain heat as efficiently as possible. For those who don't own a traditional sandy pot, a heavy Dutch oven or casserole will work just as well.

The repertory of sandy pot or Chinese casserole dishes is extremely diverse and includes braised meat and vegetable stews, soupy noodle pots, steamed rice casseroles, rice and millet congees, and red-cooked (soy sauce–braised) meat and vegetable dishes. Most of these dishes constitute a meal in themselves and since they generally don't require elaborate preparation, reheat beautifully, and are economical and delicious, they are popular at all times of the year, though especially in winter.

CHINESE SOUPS AND CASSEROLES

Basic Chinese Chicken Broth

Hot-and-Sour Chicken Soup

Layered Fish and Spinach in Broth

Hunan Scallop Soup

Duckling with Orange Peel Soup

Emerald Dumplings in Broth

Chicken Ball and Snow Pea Soup

Fish Soup Pot with a Chinese Aioli

Abalone and Chicken with Vermicelli Noodles

Five-Treasure Noodles in Broth

Red-Cooked Chicken with Chestnuts

Spicy Fish in a Sandy Pot

Braised Beef Short Ribs with Red Wine

Spicy Lamb with Turnips

Eight-Treasure Duck

Chinese Cabbage Casserole

Braised Chicken with Star Anise and Red Wine

Basic Chinese Chicken Broth

1 whole roasting chicken, or
  chicken backs and necks,
  weighing about 3 pounds
10 cups water
½ cup rice wine
4 slices gingerroot, smashed
  lightly with the flat side of a
  cleaver

*This chicken broth forms the base for almost all Chinese
soups and sauces. It may be prepared in large quantities
and then just refrigerated or frozen and used as needed.
Once refrigerated, it will keep for up to a week, but after
this time has transpired, it should be reboiled or frozen.*

1 Using a heavy chef's knife or cleaver, cut the
chicken through the bones into 2-inch squares.
Blanch the pieces in boiling water for 1 minute.
Rinse in cold water and drain thoroughly.

2 Place the chicken pieces, water, rice wine, and
gingerroot in a heavy soup pot. Heat until the liquid is boiling. Reduce the heat to low and simmer,
uncovered, for 2 hours, skimming the surface periodically to remove any impurities. Strain the broth
through a fine-meshed strainer or through cheesecloth, removing the chicken pieces and reserving
them for another use. ***Makes about 6 cups.***

Hot-and-Sour Chicken Soup

酸
辣
鶏
湯

1 pound boneless chicken
  breast meat, skin removed,
  cut into very thin
  matchstick-size shreds

Chicken Marinade
2 teaspoons soy sauce
1 tablespoon wine
½ teaspoon sesame oil
1 teaspoon cornstarch

10 dried Chinese black
  mushrooms, softened in hot
  water for 20 minutes
2 cups finely shredded leeks,
  rinsed thoroughly and
  drained

Soup Base and Seasonings
5 cups Chinese chicken broth
  (above)
2 tablespoons rice wine
1 teaspoon salt
2 tablespoons soy sauce
3 tablespoons Chinese black

*Most lovers of Sichuanese cooking are familiar with the
classic hot-and-sour soup, which uses pork, bean curd,
and dried wood ears as its main ingredients. This recipe
is a slight revision of that classic, with chicken, black
mushrooms, and leeks. The result is a subtler — but no
less spicy — version, which even the great Chinese mas-
ters would probably enjoy.*

1 Place the shredded chicken in a mixing bowl, add
the **chicken marinade**, toss lightly to coat, and let
marinate for 20 minutes. Remove and discard the
stems from the black mushrooms and cut the caps
into fine, matchstick-size shreds. Place the **soup
base and seasonings** in a large soup pot. Prepare
the thickener.

2 Heat the soup base mixture until boiling. Add the
chicken, black mushrooms, and leeks. Heat until
boiling and cook for about 3 minutes, stirring to
separate the chicken shreds, and skimming away
any impurities from the surface. Add the **thickener**,

vinegar or clear rice vinegar
1½ teaspoons sesame oil
¾ teaspoon freshly ground
 black pepper
2 tablespoons finely minced
 gingerroot

Thickener
2½ tablespoons cornstarch
¼ cup water

2 large eggs, lightly beaten

stirring constantly, and cook until thickened. Taste for seasoning, adding additional salt, vinegar, or gingerroot as desired. Turn off the heat, and slowly add the beaten egg in a thin, circular stream around the edge of the soup. Carefully stir once or twice so that the cooked egg forms streamers. Transfer to a tureen and serve. *Serves six.*

Layered Fish and Spinach in Broth

1½ pounds fillet of any firm-
 fleshed white fish (such as
 haddock, red snapper, or
 halibut), skin removed

Fish Marinade
1 tablespoon rice wine
2 slices gingerroot, smashed
 lightly with the flat side of a
 cleaver
½ teaspoon salt

¾ pound spinach, watercress,
 or water spinach, stems
 removed, trimmed, rinsed,
 and drained thoroughly

Soup Base
6 cups Chinese chicken broth
 (page 194)
2 tablespoons rice wine
1 teaspoon salt
½ teaspoon freshly ground
 white pepper

1 tablespoon minced scallion
 greens
1 tablespoon finely chopped
 unsalted roasted peanuts

This Hunanese fish soup is one of the most traditional of the western regional dishes. Few soups are simpler to prepare, or more delectable. The lightly cooked fish slices combine with the fresh spinach and savory broth to create a soothing and refreshing soup.

1 Holding a very sharp cleaver or a chef's knife at a 45-degree angle to the cutting board, cut the fish, across the grain, into paper-thin slices about 2 inches square. Place the slices in a mixing bowl. Prepare the **fish marinade** by combining the ingredients and lightly pinching the gingerroot slices in the rice wine repeatedly for several minutes to impart the flavor. Add the marinade to the fish slices, toss lightly to coat, and let marinate for 20 minutes.

2 Arrange the spinach or watercress in a large soup bowl or tureen. Discard the gingerroot slices from the fish and arrange the fish slices in overlapping circular rows over the spinach.

3 Place the **soup base** in a saucepan and heat until boiling. Just before serving, slowly pour the boiling broth over the fish slices. They will cook immediately and float. Sprinkle the top with the minced scallions and chopped peanuts and serve.
Serves six.

冬

Hunan Scallop Soup

1 pound fresh sea scallops,
  rinsed lightly and drained

Scallop Marinade
2 tablespoons rice wine
2 slices gingerroot, smashed
  lightly with the flat side of a
  cleaver
½ teaspoon salt
½ teaspoon sesame oil

3 cups ¼-inch-wide iceberg
  lettuce shreds (remove core
  before shredding)

Soup Base
6 cups Chinese chicken broth
  (page 194)
2 tablespoons rice wine
1 teaspoon salt
½ teaspoon freshly ground
  white pepper

2 tablespoons minced roasted
  almonds
2 tablespoons minced
  scallions

Although most Americans associate spicy seasonings with Hunan cooking, few are aware that there are also a number of delicately seasoned recipes. This soup is a revised version of the classic layered fish and spinach in broth, and like the original, the flavor is extraordinarily delicate. The dish is also extremely easy to prepare and it may be assembled in advance up to the very last step. Before serving, the boiling broth is poured on top and the thin seafood slices cook immediately.

1 Holding a cleaver or a chef's knife parallel with the cutting surface, cut the scallops through the thickness into paper-thin slices. Place the slices in a bowl. To make the **scallop marinade**, combine the rice wine and gingerroot, pinching the gingerroot slices in the rice wine repeatedly for several minutes to impart the flavor; then add the remaining ingredients. Add the marinade to the scallop slices, toss lightly to coat, and let marinate for 20 minutes. Discard the gingerroot slices.

2 In a large soup bowl or tureen, arrange the shredded lettuce. Arrange the scallop slices in overlapping circular rows to cover the lettuce.

3 Place the **soup base** in a heavy pot and heat until boiling, skimming the surface to remove any impurities. Slowly pour the boiling broth over the scallops and lettuce. With a spoon, lightly press down on the scallop slices so that they will cook in the broth. Sprinkle the top with the chopped almonds and scallion greens, and serve. ***Serves six.***

Duckling with Orange Peel Soup

1 whole duckling, weighing about 4½ pounds
1 teaspoon salt
2 tablespoons soy sauce
2 tablespoons rice wine
1 whole star anise, smashed lightly with the flat side of a cleaver
6 slices gingerroot, smashed lightly with the flat side of a cleaver

Soup Mixture
8 cups Chinese chicken broth (page 194)
½ cup rice wine
10 strips dried clementine or orange peel, measuring about 1½ inches long and 1 inch wide, blanched briefly in boiling water

1 ounce bean threads (cellophane noodles), softened for 10 minutes in warm water, and cut into 3-inch lengths

Duckling is an excellent flavor base for any hearty soup, and the fat need not be a problem. The first step is to bake the duck in a very hot oven, giving it an attractive, golden brown color and rendering some of the excess fat. The additional seasonings of orange peel and star anise further enhance and complement the rich duck meat and broth.

1 Preheat the oven to 500 degrees. Lightly rinse the duckling, removing any fat deposits from the cavity and around the neck. Pat dry, and using a very sharp chef's knife or cleaver, cut the duck, through the bones, into ten or twelve pieces. Place the pieces in a bowl, and add the salt, soy sauce, rice wine, star anise, and gingerroot. Toss lightly to coat and let stand for at least 2 hours at room temperature. Drain the duckling pieces, reserving the juice and adding it to the soup mixture, and place the duckling pieces on a baking rack placed in a jelly-roll pan. Place the pan in the oven and add about 1 cup of water to it (to prevent the rendered duckling grease from smoking). Bake for 20 minutes, until some of the fat has been rendered and the pieces are golden.

2 Place the **soup mixture** and the duckling pieces in a large pot. Partially cover, and heat until boiling. Reduce the heat to low and simmer for 1½ hours, skimming the surface occasionally to remove any fat and impurities. The duckling should be tender and the soup fragrant. Discard the gingerroot slices and dried orange peel and skim off any fat from the surface. Add the bean threads to the soup. Simmer, uncovered, for 10 minutes and serve. You may serve the duckling pieces separately, if you wish. *Serves six.*

Emerald Dumplings in Broth

Dumpling Skins
¼ pound fresh spinach, stems removed, rinsed and drained
1 tablespoon minced shallots
1 tablespoon rice wine
1 large egg
1 tablespoon sesame oil
½ teaspoon salt
½ teaspoon freshly ground white pepper
1 heaping cup all-purpose flour

Dumpling Filling
½ pound ground pork
6 medium raw shrimp, peeled
¼ cup water chestnuts, blanched briefly in boiling water and drained
1 ounce pork fat, chopped to a paste, or 1 teaspoon sesame oil
1 tablespoon soy sauce
2 teaspoons rice wine
½ teaspoon salt
2 teaspoons sesame oil (reduce to 1 teaspoon if substituting sesame oil for pork fat)
1 tablespoon minced scallions
1½ teaspoons minced gingerroot
2 tablespoons minced coriander
½ egg white or 2 tablespoons water
1 tablespoon cornstarch

Soup Base
5 cups Chinese chicken broth (page 194)
3 tablespoons rice wine
1 teaspoon salt
1 teaspoon sesame oil
2 tablespoons minced scallion greens

Dumplings are a food dearly loved by all Chinese, and there are numerous variations, both in skins and fillings. Emerald dumplings have a rather traditional stuffing, made with ground pork, shrimp, and water chestnuts, but the skin is a real departure from the ordinary. This unusual recipe calls for spinach, which colors the wrapper a beautiful deep green.

1 To make the dough for the **dumpling skins**: Place the cleaned spinach, the shallots, and the rice wine in a saucepan and cover. Cook briefly over high heat, stirring several times, until the spinach starts to wilt. Remove and drain, spraying a little cold water over the spinach to preserve the color. Squeeze out as much liquid as possible. Place the spinach and shallots in a food processor fitted with the steel blade and pulse, turning the machine on and off, for 5 to 7 seconds. Add the egg, sesame oil, salt, and pepper, and process until smooth. Add the flour and pulse again, until the mixture forms small beads. Remove the dough and flatten onto a lightly floured piece of plastic wrap. Lightly sprinkle with more flour and wrap up the dough. Refrigerate for 30 minutes.

2 To prepare the **dumpling filling**: Place the ground pork in a large mixing bowl. Devein the shrimp, rinse lightly, and drain thoroughly. Place the shrimp in a linen dishtowel and squeeze out as much moisture as possible. Chop the shrimp coarsely and add to the bowl with the pork. Chop the water chestnuts coarsely and add to the bowl, along with the pork fat or sesame oil and the remaining filling ingredients. Stir vigorously in one direction to combine the ingredients.

3 On a lightly floured surface, form the dough into a long snakelike roll about 1 inch in diameter. Divide the dough into twenty-four pieces. Cover the pieces with a damp towel to prevent them from drying out. With a cut edge down, press each piece into a circle. Using a small rolling pin, or a lightly floured tortilla press, roll each to a 3-inch circle and cover the circles with a cloth.

4 Using a spoon or two chopsticks, place a heaping teaspoon of the filling in the center of each circle and fold over to enclose the filling and form a half-moon shape. Press the edges to seal. Place the finished dumplings on a tray that has been lightly dusted with cornstarch.

5 Bring 4 quarts of water to the boil and add the dumplings. Cover and cook for 5 to 7 minutes, or until they rise to the surface. Using a handled strainer or a slotted spoon, remove them and portion into six soup bowls. Combine the ingredients for the **soup base**, except the minced scallions, in a pot and heat until boiling. Ladle the hot mixture over the cooked dumplings and sprinkle the top with the minced scallions. Serve immediately. *Serves six.*

Chicken Ball and Snow Pea Soup

1 pound boneless chicken
    breast meat, skin removed
⅓ pound Chinese ham or
    prosciutto, finely chopped
1 ounce pork fat or 1
    teaspoon sesame oil

Seasonings
1 egg white, lightly beaten
2 tablespoons rice wine
¼ teaspoon freshly ground
    white pepper
1½ teaspoons minced
    gingerroot
1½ teaspoons minced
    scallions
2 tablespoons cornstarch

Soup Base
6 cups Chinese chicken broth
    (page 194)
⅓ cup rice wine
1 teaspoon salt

1 ounce bean threads
    (cellophane noodles),
    softened in hot water for 10
    minutes, drained, and cut
    into 3-inch sections
½ pound fresh snow peas,
    ends snapped and veiny
    strings removed

Thickener
2 tablespoons cornstarch
¼ cup water

1 teaspoon sesame oil
2 tablespoons minced scallion
    greens

This recipe was inspired by an eastern original — shrimp ball soup — but here a purée of chicken meat and seasonings, flavored with Chinese ham or prosciutto, is used for the balls. This soup is exquisite, whether served as an appetizer, in the Western style, or toward the end of the meal, a custom generally observed in the Orient.

1 Trim any fat from the chicken meat and cut the meat into 2-inch squares. In a food processor fitted with the steel blade, chop the chicken meat to a paste. Add the Chinese ham or prosciutto and the pork fat or sesame oil. Pulse, turning the machine on and off, to combine the ingredients. Transfer the mixture to a bowl and add the **seasonings**, except the cornstarch. Stir vigorously in one direction to combine. Add the cornstarch and stir again. Shape the mixture, a tablespoon at a time, into round balls.

2 Place the **soup base** in a large pot. Heat until boiling, and add the chicken balls and bean threads. Simmer for about 5 minutes, or until the balls float to the surface. Skim any impurities from the surface and add the **thickener**, stirring constantly to prevent lumps. Add the snow peas and sesame oil. Cook for 15 seconds, and portion into soup bowls. Sprinkle the top with the minced scallion greens and serve. *Serves six.*

Fish Soup Pot with a Chinese Aioli

1 head Chinese cabbage
(Napa), weighing 1½ to 2
pounds, cored and cut into
2-inch squares, separating
the tougher pieces from the
leafier ones
2 tablespoons safflower or
corn oil

Soup Base
6 cups Chinese chicken broth
(page 194)
¼ cup rice wine
1 teaspoon salt

1 halibut steak, weighing 1½
to 2 pounds
2 tablespoons rice wine
½ teaspoon salt
1 pint freshly shucked oysters

Oyster Marinade
1 tablespoon rice wine
2 slices gingerroot, smashed
lightly with the flat side of a
cleaver
2 scallions, smashed lightly
with the flat side of a
cleaver
½ teaspoon salt

2 squares soft bean curd,
measuring about 3 inches
square and 1 inch thick, cut
into thin slices

Chinese Aioli
2 pieces gingerroot, about the
size of a quarter and ¼ inch
thick
2 cloves garlic, peeled
2 large egg yolks, at room
temperature
¼ cup sesame oil
½ cup safflower or corn oil
¼ teaspoon freshly ground
white pepper

Occasionally French and Chinese foods form a natural marriage, and such is the case with this dish. A traditional Chinese fish soup pot, with its garnish of poached fish fillets and oysters, is the perfect foil for the spicy garlic mayonnaise. This "aioli" is like no other; it is made with garlic, egg yolks, and fragrant sesame oil.

1 Heat a wok or a heavy pot and add the safflower or corn oil. Heat until the oil is almost smoking and add the tougher cabbage pieces, tossing lightly over high heat. Add several tablespoons of the **soup base** and cover. Cook for about 2 minutes and add the remaining cabbage pieces. Toss lightly over high heat and add the remaining soup base. Cover and heat until boiling. Uncover, reduce the heat to low, and simmer for 1 hour. Transfer the mixture to an earthenware pot or a Dutch oven with a lid. Preheat the oven to 400 degrees.

2 Cut the halibut steaks lengthwise into strips about 1 inch wide. Holding the knife at a 45-degree angle, cut the strips across the grain into ¼-inch-thick slices. Place the slices in a bowl, add the rice wine and salt, and toss to coat. Let marinate for 20 minutes at room temperature. Place the oysters, with their liquid, in a bowl. Combine the ingredients of the **oyster marinade** and lightly pinch the scallions and gingerroot in the rice wine repeatedly for several minutes to impart their flavors to the mixture. Add the marinade to the oysters, toss lightly to coat, and let marinate for 20 minutes at room temperature. Discard the scallions and gingerroot.

3 Arrange the halibut slices and bean curd cubes over the cabbage in the pot, saving room for the oysters, which will be added later. Cover and bake in the preheated oven for 20 minutes.

4 Meanwhile, make the **Chinese aioli**: Drop the gingerroot pieces into a food processor fitted with the steel blade and pulse, turning the machine on and off to mince very finely. Place the minced gingerroot in a square of cheesecloth and squeeze out as much juice as possible. Retain the juice, discarding the gingerroot pulp. By hand with a mortar and pestle, or with a food processor fitted with the steel blade, pound or purée the garlic cloves to a paste. Add the egg yolks and continue beating to a creamy consistency. Combine the oils, and slowly, drop by drop, add to the egg yolk–garlic mixture. Once the mixture has become slightly stiff, like a mayonnaise, you may add the oil more quickly. Fold in the gingerroot juice and pepper.

5 Remove the pot from the oven, uncover, and add the oysters. Cover and cook for 5 minutes longer, or until the oysters are done. Remove and portion the soup into serving bowls. Add a heaping teaspoon of Chinese aioli and serve. *Serves six.*

Abalone and Chicken with Vermicelli Noodles

1 whole frying chicken,
weighing about 2½ pounds
1 one-pound can abalone,
drained

Soup Base
6 cups water
¼ cup rice wine
1½ teaspoons salt
6 scallions, smashed lightly
with the flat side of a
cleaver
6 slices gingerroot, smashed
lightly with the flat side of a
cleaver

1 tablespoon safflower or corn
oil
½ pound vermicelli noodles

Abalone and chicken are a popular pairing in Chinese dishes. The reasons are obvious: their flavors are delicate; their appearance is light and attractive; and their textures are uniquely suited, since the abalone is chewy while the chicken is succulently tender.

1 Remove any fat from the neck or cavity of the chicken. Using a cleaver or a sharp knife, cut the chicken, through the bones, into 2-inch squares. Drop into 2 quarts of boiling water and blanch for several minutes, until the water returns to the boil. Remove, drain, and rinse off the chicken pieces. Drain again and discard the water.

2 Place the **soup base** in a heat-proof pot or bowl. Add the chicken and cover with plastic wrap. Place in a steamer tray and cover. Fill a wok with water level with the bottom edge of the steamer tray and heat until boiling. Place the steamer tray over the boiling water and steam the chicken for 1½ hours.

3 Meanwhile, trim any hard edges from the abalone and cut the abalone into paper-thin slices. Heat about two quarts of water until boiling. Add the abalone slices and blanch for about 10 seconds. Remove with a slotted spoon and drain.

4 Remove the soup from the steamer tray and skim off any fat from the surface. Remove the scallions and gingerroot slices. Add the abalone slices and stir.

5 Heat 2 quarts of water and the safflower or corn oil until boiling. Add the noodles and cook for about 5 minutes, or until just tender. Remove and drain. Portion into six serving bowls. Ladle some of the chicken and abalone soup on top, and serve. *Serves six.*

Five-Treasure Noodles in Broth

三
鮮
湯
麵

1 pound center-cut pork loin

Pork Marinade
1 tablespoon soy sauce
1 tablespoon rice wine
1 teaspoon sesame oil
¼ teaspoon freshly ground
black pepper
1 teaspoon cornstarch

8 dried Chinese black
mushrooms, softened in 2
cups hot water for 20
minutes and the liquid
retained
18 dried tiger lily buds,
softened in hot water for 25
minutes, drained, and each
tied into a knot
2 carrots, peeled and ends
trimmed
½ pound spinach, trimmed,
rinsed thoroughly, and
drained

Minced Seasonings
1 tablespoon gingerroot
2 tablespoons minced
scallions

Sauce
3 tablespoons soy sauce
2 tablespoons rice wine
1 teaspoon sugar
1 tablespoon Chinese black
vinegar
½ teaspoon freshly ground
black pepper

⅓ cup safflower or corn oil
½ pound very thin noodles,
such as vermicelli

Soup Base
4 cups Chinese chicken broth
(page 194)
2 cups retained liquid from
soaking black mushrooms
3 tablespoons rice wine
1 teaspoon salt
1 teaspoon sesame oil

Soupy noodles are a popular dish in the Orient. The streets of almost every Far Eastern city are dotted with small food stalls that specialize in noodle-soup dishes and stay open day and night. These, however, are not your ordinary street noodles. The garnish is made with chicken, black mushrooms, carrots, and other vegetables, and the noodles are delicate vermicelli. This dish is equally fitting as a light lunch or dinner and as a hearty snack before bedtime.

1 Trim any fat or gristle from the pork loin and cut the meat into paper-thin slices about 1 inch square. Place in a bowl, add the **pork marinade**, toss lightly to coat, and let marinate for 20 minutes. Trim the stems from the black mushrooms and cut the caps, holding the knife at a 45-degree angle to the cutting surface, into halves or thirds. Cook the carrots for 3 minutes in boiling water, remove, and immerse in cold water. Drain thoroughly and cut lengthwise into quarters. Roll-cut the lengths into 1-inch pieces. Prepare the minced seasonings and the sauce. Place the **soup base** in a pot and heat until boiling, skimming the surface to remove impurities.

2 Heat 2 quarts water and 1 tablespoon of the oil in a pot until boiling. Add the noodles and cook until just tender, about 2 to 3 minutes; remove and drain. Portion the noodles equally into serving bowls, reserving some for second helpings.

3 Heat a wok, add the remaining oil, and heat until very hot. Add the pork loin and stir-fry, stirring constantly, until the meat changes color. Remove and drain. Remove all but 2 tablespoons of oil and reheat. Add the **minced seasonings** and stir-fry about 10 seconds, until fragrant. Add the black mushrooms and stir-fry for 10 seconds; then add the tiger lily buds and carrots. Toss lightly and add the pork and the **sauce**. Turn off the heat and let the mixture stand while cooking the spinach.

4 Drop the spinach into the hot soup base and cook for 15 seconds. Ladle some of the soup mixture over the noodles in the bowls, top with portions of the pork mixture, and serve. ***Serves six.***

Red-Cooked Chicken with Chestnuts

红
烧
栗
子
鷄

1 whole roasting chicken,
  weighing about 4½ pounds
1 tablespoon soy sauce
½ pound dried chestnuts
8 dried Chinese black
  mushrooms
2 cups safflower or corn oil

Braising Mixture
1 cup soy sauce
1 cup rice wine
¼ cup sesame oil
2 tablespoons sugar
3 cloves garlic, smashed
  lightly with the flat side of a
  cleaver
4 slices gingerroot, smashed
  lightly with the flat side of a
  cleaver
4 scallions, smashed lightly
  with the flat side of a
  cleaver

Eastern regional Chinese cuisine is known for its rich braised dishes, and this red-cooked casserole is one of the finest and simplest examples. Duck and seafood are also often prepared in this manner, in a soy sauce–based cooking liquid. The dried chestnuts, if unavailable, may be omitted.

1 Remove any fat from the chicken neck and cavity. Using a sharp knife or cleaver, cut the chicken, through the bones, into 1½-inch squares. Place the pieces in a bowl, add the tablespoon of soy sauce, and toss lightly to coat. Soak the dried chestnuts in hot water to cover for 3 hours, changing the water three times. Drain them and scrape away any dark skin in the crevices. Drain thoroughly. Soften the black mushrooms in hot water to cover for 20 minutes. Remove, drain, and remove the stems and discard. Cut the caps in half.

2 Heat a wok or a skillet, and add the oil. Heat the oil to 400 degrees. Drain the chicken pieces, reserving any soy sauce, and add half the chicken pieces to the oil. Fry over high heat until golden. Remove with a handled strainer or a slotted spoon and drain. Reheat the oil and add the remaining chicken pieces. Fry the remaining pieces until golden brown, remove, and drain. Reheat the oil and add the chestnuts, frying until golden brown. Remove and drain. Combine the braising mixture ingredients.

3 In a heavy 3-quart casserole or Dutch oven, place the chicken pieces, chestnuts, black mushrooms, reserved soy sauce, and the **braising mixture**. Heat until the mixture is boiling. Reduce the heat to low, partially cover, and simmer for 1 hour, until the chicken and chestnuts are very tender and the sauce has reduced to a thick glaze. Discard the seasonings and serve over rice. *Serves six.*

Spicy Fish in a Sandy Pot

1 midsection of a firm-fleshed fish, such as halibut or sea bass, measuring about 8 inches long and weighing about 2½ pounds

Fish Marinade
1 tablespoon soy sauce
1 tablespoon rice wine
2 teaspoons Chinese black vinegar

3 tablespoons safflower or corn oil

Minced Seasonings
2 tablespoons minced scallions
1½ tablespoons minced gingerroot
1½ tablespoons minced garlic

1 teaspoon hot chili paste, or to taste
4 cups Chinese cabbage (Napa) cored and cut into 2-inch squares
3 squares bean curd, measuring about 3 inches square and 1 inch thick, cut into 1-inch dice

Sauce
4 cups Chinese chicken broth (page 194)
3 tablespoons rice wine
1½ tablespoons soy sauce
½ teaspoon salt
½ tablespoon sugar
1 tablespoon Chinese black vinegar
1 teaspoon sesame oil

2 tablespoons minced scallion greens

I first tasted this dish on a raw, winter day in Taipei many years ago. My Chinese surrogate family had received a present of a whole, wriggling lake fish, and without a moment's hesitation, our stalwart maid had killed, gutted, and sectioned the fish. The head was used in a delicious, spicy casserole, which inspired the creation of this revised version, in which only fish steaks are used.

1 Lightly rinse the fish section, drain, and place in a bowl. Combine the **fish marinade** ingredients and rub the marinade over the surface of the fish. Let stand for 20 minutes at room temperature; then drain the fish, reserving the marinade. Prepare the minced seasonings and the sauce, adding the reserved marinade to the sauce.

2 Heat a heavy 3-quart casserole, sandy pot, or Dutch oven and add the oil. Heat the oil until almost smoking and slowly lower the fish into the pan, using the wok lid as a shield from the hot oil. Shake the pan gently to prevent the fish from sticking, and fry until golden brown. Turn the fish section over and continue frying until golden. Remove with a handled strainer and drain.

3 Preheat the oven to 350 degrees. Reheat the oil, add the **minced seasonings**, and stir-fry for about 10 seconds, until fragrant. Add the chili paste and continue frying for 5 seconds. Add the cabbage and toss lightly over high heat, adding several tablespoons of the **sauce**. Cook for about 4 minutes, or until the cabbage is slightly wilted. Add the rest of the sauce and heat until boiling. Place the fish section in the center of the casserole and arrange the bean curd around it. Cover. Place the casserole in the preheated oven and bake for 25 minutes, or until the fish flakes when prodded with a chopstick or a knife. Uncover, sprinkle the top with the minced scallion greens, and serve. ***Serves six.***

Braised Beef Short Ribs with Red Wine

6 pounds beef short ribs
5 tablespoons all-purpose flour
1½ teaspoons salt
1 teaspoon freshly ground black pepper
4 tablespoons safflower or corn oil
6 cloves garlic, peeled and smashed lightly with the flat side of a cleaver
4 large onions, peeled and quartered
10 baby carrots, scraped or peeled and cut in half lengthwise
2 whole star anise, smashed lightly with the flat side of a cleaver
1 cup rice wine
½ cup red wine
½ cup boiling Chinese chicken broth (page 194) or water

Star anise, with its pungent licoricelike flavor, is the primary seasoning in this unusual dish. Unlike its European cousin aniseed, star anise is from a tree of the magnolia family. This dish, served with a simple vegetable side dish and a staple, is excellent as a hearty lunch or dinner.

1 Preheat the oven to 325 degrees. Combine the flour, salt, and black pepper. Dredge the ribs in the flour mixture, coating all sides. Lightly squeeze the ribs to make the flour adhere to the surface.

2 Heat a heavy 4-quart casserole or Dutch oven, add the oil, and heat until very hot. Add a batch of ribs and fry until golden on all sides, over medium-high heat. Remove with a slotted spoon and continue frying the ribs until golden brown. Remove all but 2 tablespoons of the hot oil.

3 Reheat the oil and add the garlic, onions, carrots, and star anise. Toss lightly over high heat for about a minute; then add the rice wine, the red wine, and the boiling broth or water. Add the ribs and heat until boiling. Cover tightly and place in the preheated oven. Bake for 1½ to 2 hours, or until the rib meat is very tender.

4 With a slotted spoon, remove the ribs and vegetables, setting them aside for a minute. Skim off any fat from the sauce. Taste the liquid for seasoning and add salt if necessary. Return the ribs and vegetables to the casserole and serve. ***Serves six.***

Spicy Lamb with Turnips

紅
燒
羊
肉

3 pounds lamb shoulder or breast
3 tablespoons safflower or corn oil
1 teaspoon chili paste

Braising Mixture
5 cups Chinese chicken broth (page 194)
½ cup soy sauce
3 tablespoons rice wine
2 tablespoons sweet bean sauce
1 tablespoon sugar
1 whole star anise
3 strips dried orange or tangerine peel, about 1 inch wide and 1½ inches long, softened in hot water to cover for 20 minutes and drained

1 Chinese turnip or daikon radish, weighing about 1½ pounds, peeled and cut into 1½-inch squares
1 tablespoon chopped coriander (Chinese parsley)

The pairing of lamb and beef with turnips in Chinese casseroles originated with the ancients; one of the earliest favorites of Han cooks reputedly was a stew made with beef or lamb and turnips. This dish is equally popular with present-day Chinese. For a hearty, filling meal, serve this casserole with rice and a stir-fried green vegetable.

1 Trim the lamb, removing any excess fat or gristle, and cut the meat into cubes about 1½ inches square. Combine the braising mixture ingredients.

2 Heat a 4-quart casserole or Dutch oven and add the oil. Heat until very hot and add a batch of the lamb pieces. Fry, over high heat, until browned on all sides. Remove with a slotted spoon and reheat the oil. Fry the remaining lamb in batches over high heat until browned on all sides. Remove the meat and drain.

3 Remove all but 1 tablespoon of oil from the casserole and heat until hot. Add the chili paste and stir-fry for about 5 seconds, until fragrant. Add the **braising mixture** and the lamb pieces. Cover and heat until boiling. Reduce the heat to low, partially cover, and let simmer for 1 hour, until the lamb is very tender. Skim off any fat from the surface. Add the turnip pieces and continue cooking, partially covered, for 30 minutes, or until tender. Sprinkle the top with the minced coriander and serve directly from the pot. *Serves six.*

Eight-Treasure Duck

八
寶
鴨

1 duckling, weighing 4½ to 5 pounds
1½ tablespoons soy sauce
¾ cup glutinous (sweet) rice, rinsed thoroughly in cold running water and soaked in hot water to cover for 1 hour
2 tablespoons safflower or corn oil

Few dishes are as impressive or as sumptuously presented as a whole braised duck with an "eight-treasure" rice stuffing. And the flavor of this wonderful dish merely increases with reheating. For those more adventurous cooks, the duck may be completely boned, stuffed with the rice filling, and reshaped to re-create the duck shape. Long Island ducklings, which tend to be very fatty and not very meaty, are most commonly available in this country. Muscovy ducks, which range in weight from 6 to 7

Eight-Treasure Stuffing

1 cup ¼-inch-diced Chinese pork sausage

¼ cup dried Chinese black mushrooms, softened in hot water to cover for 20 minutes, stems removed, and caps cut into ¼-inch dice

½ cup peeled and ¼-inch-diced carrot

½ cup water chestnuts, blanched briefly in boiling water, refreshed in cold water, and cut into quarters

1 cup fresh peas (if unavailable, substitute frozen and thaw to room temperature)

Stuffing Seasoning

1 tablespoon soy sauce

1 tablespoon rice wine

1 teaspoon sesame oil

¼ teaspoon freshly ground black pepper

1½ cups Chinese chicken broth (page 194)

Braising Mixture

3½ cups water

¼ cup soy sauce

2 tablespoons rice wine

1 tablespoon sugar

1 whole star anise

3 scallions, smashed lightly with the flat side of a cleaver

3 slices gingerroot, smashed lightly with the flat side of a cleaver

Thickener

1 teaspoon cornstarch

1 tablespoon water

pounds, are far meatier and they are now sold in a number of butcher shops. If using a Muscovy duck, increase the braising mixture proportionally and add another 30 minutes to the braising time.

1 Lightly rinse the duck and remove any fat deposits from around the neck and cavity. Drain thoroughly and pat dry. Rub the soy sauce all over the outside of the duck and inside the cavity, and let the duck stand at room temperature for 15 minutes. Drain the rice and assemble the ingredients of the eight-treasure stuffing. Prepare the stuffing seasoning, the braising mixture, and the thickener by separately combining the ingredients.

2 To make the **stuffing**: Heat a wok, add the safflower or corn oil, and heat until fairly hot. Add the Chinese sausage and stir-fry over medium-low heat to render some of the fat. Add the remaining stuffing ingredients and stir-fry for 1 minute over high heat. Add the rice and the **stuffing seasoning**. Heat until the liquid boils, reduce the heat to medium, and cook until the mixture is dry, stirring constantly. Remove the stuffing and let cool to room temperature. Drain the duck, adding any soy sauce to braising mixture. Stuff the cavity and neck of the duck with the cooled stuffing. Sew up and secure the openings with a trussing needle and twine.

3 Preheat the oven to 475 degrees. Place the stuffed duckling on a cooling rack over a jellyroll pan. Pour about 1 cup of water into the pan (to prevent the drippings from smoking), and roast the duck, turning it once, for about 20 minutes, or until it is golden brown. Remove the duck and reduce the oven temperature to 375 degrees. Place the duck and the **braising mixture** in a heavy 4-quart casserole or Dutch oven. Cover and return to the oven. Bake for about 1½ hours, or until the duck is very tender. Remove the duck, cut away the twine, and spoon the stuffing into a serving dish. Carve the duck and arrange the slices and pieces on a serving platter. Skim any fat from the braising mixture and discard the seasonings. Heat until boiling and slowly add the **thickener**, stirring constantly. When the sauce has thickened, spoon some over the duck and pour the rest into a dish to be served on the side. *Serves six.*

Chinese Cabbage Casserole

燉
白
菜

1 head Chinese cabbage
(Napa), weighing about 2
pounds

Soup Base
6 cups Chinese chicken broth
(page 194)
⅓ cup rice wine
1 teaspoon salt

5 tablespoons safflower or
corn oil
2 cloves garlic, peeled and
smashed lightly with the flat
side of a cleaver
1½ pounds ground pork

Meat Seasonings
4 dried Chinese black
mushrooms, softened in hot
water for 20 minutes, stems
removed, and caps finely
chopped
2 tablespoons minced
scallions
1 tablespoon minced
gingerroot
1 tablespoon rice wine
1½ teaspoons salt
1½ teaspoons sesame oil
2 tablespoons cornstarch

Meat Coating
1 tablespoon cornstarch
1 tablespoon soy sauce
1 tablespoon water

This dish, with its richly seasoned meat balls, tender cabbage, and delectable broth, is guaranteed to satisfy even the heartiest appetite. This casserole becomes even more flavorful when reheated. Serve it as a meal by itself, or as a soupy entrée with another meat or seafood dish and rice.

1 Remove four outer leaves from the cabbage head, keeping them whole, and set aside. Remove the core from the cabbage and cut the leaves into 2-inch squares, separating the leafy pieces from the tougher ones. Lightly chop the ground pork until fluffy and place in a mixing bowl. Add the **meat seasonings** and stir vigorously in one direction. Prepare the soup base and the meat coating by combining the ingredients in separate bowls.

2 Preheat the oven to 350 degrees. Heat a 3-quart casserole or Dutch oven and add 2 tablespoons of the oil. Heat until very hot, and add the garlic and the tougher cabbage pieces. Toss lightly over high heat, adding a tablespoon of the **soup base,** and cook for about 1 minute. Add the remaining cabbage and a few more tablespoons of the soup base, and cook for 5 minutes, or until the cabbage is slightly wilted. Add the remaining soup base and heat until boiling. Reduce the heat to low and simmer, uncovered, for 20 minutes.

3 Heat a wok or a heavy skillet and add the remaining oil. Heat until very hot. Separate the meat into four portions and form them into oval shapes. Dip the meatballs in the **meat coating** and roll them around to coat evenly. Place in the hot oil and fry over medium-high heat, turning once, until golden on both sides. Add any remaining coating mixture to the casserole. Place the meatballs on top of the cabbage in the casserole and cover with the four cabbage leaves. Cover the casserole and bake in the preheated oven for 1 hour. Remove the lid and skim away any fat. Portion the meat, cabbage, and broth into serving bowls and serve. *Serves six.*

Braised Chicken with Star Anise and Red Wine

1 whole roasting chicken,
   weighing about 4½ pounds
2 tablespoons flour
½ teaspoon salt
½ teaspoon freshly ground
   black pepper
4 tablespoons safflower or
   corn oil
1 teaspoon minced garlic
12 small white onions, peeled
   and cut in half
½ pound fresh button
   mushrooms, rinsed lightly
   and stems trimmed
2 whole star anise
1½ cups red wine
½ cup boiling Chinese
   chicken broth (page 194) or
   water

In this dish, which could be called a Chinese coq au vin, chunky pieces of chicken are gently simmered in a star anise–red wine braising mixture. Serve this rich and fragrant casserole with a side vegetable and rice for a delicious and satisfying meal. Like many casseroles, this one improves with age and tastes even better when reheated.

1 Using a heavy knife or cleaver, cut the chicken, through the bones, into bite-size pieces, about 2 inches square. Mix the flour, salt, and pepper, and dredge the chicken pieces in the mixture, lightly coating the outside. Preheat the oven to 350 degrees.

2 Heat a large casserole or Dutch oven and add the oil. Heat the oil to 375 degrees and add half the chicken pieces. Sear the outside over high heat until golden brown, turning once. Remove. Add the remaining chicken pieces and sear them until golden brown on all sides. Remove and drain.

3 Remove all but 3 tablespoons of oil from the casserole and heat until hot. Add the garlic, onions, and mushrooms. Toss lightly over high heat until the garlic is fragrant and the onions are lightly golden. Add the star anise, the red wine, and the boiling broth or water. Heat the mixture until boiling, cover, and bake in the preheated oven for 1½ hours, stirring occasionally. Before serving, skim the broth to remove any fat, taste for seasoning, and portion into serving bowls. *Serves six.*

CHINESE MENU PLANNING

THE BASICS

For many Western cooks, one of the more intimidating aspects of Chinese cooking is designing the menu. Knowing how to select the necessary dishes for a correct, well-rounded Chinese meal appears to be the chief dilemma. For others, the execution of the various dishes so that they are ready for serving simultaneously — or spaced at reasonable intervals — presents another problem. Both menu planning and meal preparation involve the use of some basic rules, but before a further explanation is given, the distinction must be drawn between the main types of Chinese meals.

Chinese meals follow one of two forms: banquet and home-style. The major difference is the number of courses served and the complexity of the dishes prepared. Banquet meals typically consist of twelve to fourteen elaborate dishes, whereas a home-style meal usually includes the serving of four or five simple recipes. Occasionally, one dish is served as a complete home-style meal in itself.

Home-style meals are served on an everyday basis, and the focal point of the meal is some type of staple (rice, noodles, or steamed breads). The staple is the filler and the other dishes are designed to garnish and flavor it.

A banquet, which is a celebration of an auspicious occasion such as a wedding, a birthday, or a particular holiday, may consist of anywhere from ten to twenty-four courses, and a staple is not the main filler of the meal.

The menu and composition of the meal may differ greatly for these two situations, but the considerations involved in planning the appropriate dishes — whether for an informal or an elegant gathering — are exactly the same. The key words are *balance* and *practicality*.

The following guidelines should be considered in the planning of any Chinese banquet or home-style menu.

• Consider the seasonal ingredients that are available.
• Select dishes with contrasting cooking methods. A

variety of cooking techniques — stir-frying, steaming, braising, and deep-frying — should be used in preparing the meal. Similarly, the cooking methods should accent and highlight the individual ingredients: steam and stir-fry fresh vegetables and seafoods; braise heavy meats and vegetables.

- Choose dishes that contrast and complement one another in taste and texture. Plan a menu that includes a sweet-and-sour, a hot-and-spicy, a delicate, and a salty sauce. Serve the more delicately seasoned dishes earlier in the meal, and the spicier dishes later. Also, plan dishes with contrasting textures, such as pairing smooth bean curd with crunchy celery or water chestnuts.
- Consider the aesthetics of the overall menu. Select dishes that complement one another in terms of color and shape: prepare dishes with contrasting colors and ingredients cut in various shapes, such as shreds, dice, and slices.
- Highlight variety. A Chinese meal should be full of simple surprises, even in a home-style format. Avoid dishes that repeat the same ingredients and select those which use different products.

The key to successful meal preparation lies in practicality and organization. Before planning any menu, honestly assess the kitchen facilities and the cook's capabilities. Be realistic and try not to be overly ambitious. The following additional suggestions may also prove helpful:

- For easy meal presentation — particularly when entertaining — select as many dishes as possible that may be prepared in advance. Assemble cold dishes beforehand and refrigerate them. Braised casseroles and soups may be prepared a day earlier and reheated before serving. Whenever possible, complete the preparation of steamed dishes up to the final step of steaming. Deep-fry foods ahead, if you wish, reserve them at room temperature, and reheat in a hot oven before serving.
- In planning the menu, do not chose more than two stir-fried dishes, since they often involve extensive last-minute preparation. Much of the work involved in stir-fried dishes can be done in advance:
  - Precut all ingredients; marinate meats, poultry, or seafood; chop seasonings; mix sauces.
  - Precook vegetables if necessary. When time is of

the essence, the meat, poultry, or seafood may also be cooked ahead of time and reserved in a bowl at room temperature.

• Choose appropriate platters and serving pieces. Organize all of the ingredients in bowls and place them near the stove for easy access.

A TRADITIONAL HOME-STYLE MEAL

Any traditional home-style meal involves a combination of balance, practicality, and simplicity. As mentioned earlier, the four or five entrées in the meal are simple dishes made up of meat, chicken, seafood, bean curd, or eggs coupled with a seasonal vegetable. The main filler or staple of the meal usually is rice, noodles, steamed breads, or pancakes. A soup is also generally served, and it plays the dual role of a palate cleanser and a soothing beverage.

Unlike a banquet, which is served in courses, for home-style meals the dishes are served simultaneously. The entrées and soup are placed in the center of the table, and if rice is served, a full bowl is given to each diner. Everyone usually helps himself by deftly selecting prime morsels of the meat, seafood, or vegetables with chopsticks. Bites of these dishes are usually followed with mouthfuls of rice, and every now and then, a spoon is dipped into the soup and the broth is sipped.

After the last mouthful of food has been eaten, most diners like to fill their bowls with hot soup. The delicate broth of many savory soups — so the Chinese believe — soothes the stomach and aids digestion.

A typical menu for a traditional Chinese home-style meal might consist of the following dishes (recipes are included in the preceding chapters):

Red-Cooked Chicken Wings

Steamed Whole Fish with Black Bean Sauce

Sweet-and-Sour Cucumber Salad

Stir-Fried Beef with Leeks

Hot-and-Sour Chicken Soup

Steamed Rice

A TRADITIONAL CHINESE BANQUET

All traditional Chinese banquets follow an established formula. The dishes may vary from region to region, depending on the ingredients and the specialties of the chef, but the basic format is always the same. While the home-style meal is designed with the staple as the focal point, a banquet consists of a series of courses, served one after the other, which vary in tone and character. The number of courses can range from ten to twenty-four, but the meal generally includes the following courses:

Cold Platter (leng pan):

Every Chinese banquet opens with the serving of an appetizer cold platter. In some areas, a number of small dishes are served simultaneously and placed in the center of the table, for diners to nibble on. Choice sliced, cooked meats and seafood, pickled vegetables, and crispy fried nuts are all part of the opening course. The ingredients are often arranged in ornate, still-life designs in the shape of a dragon, a phoenix, a panda, or selected flowers. The food usually has been cooked in advance and is served at room temperature. The beauty of opening the meal with this course is twofold: It gives the cook time to prepare other courses and encourages the diners to savor the food in a leisurely way.

Wine-Accompanying Dishes (jiu cai):

Before the entrées are sampled, a mandatory ritual of any Chinese banquet is toasting the guest of honor, host or hosts, and other guests, in turn. The toasting period may last for the entire first part of the meal, but it would be considered inappropriate for anyone to become intoxicated. Accordingly, small dishes designed to complement spirits are served to offset the debilitating effects of alcohol. These "wine-accompanying dishes" may be dry and crisp, such as cashew-coated chicken, or savory, such as stir-fried beef or baby shrimp. One to four courses or dishes may be served, depending on the sumptuousness of the banquet.

Chinese Menu Planning

Main Dishes (da cai):

The middle and focal point of a banquet is the serving of the "main dishes." They are the most impressive platters of the meal and might be Peking duck, roast suckling pig, or some type of whole fish. The arrival of these dishes (as many as four may be served) alerts the guests that the high point of the banquet is at hand, and, traditionally, the drinking and toasting reach a climax. Once the main platters have been removed, the meal begins its gradual dénouement and the drinking winds down as well.

Rice-Accompanying Dishes (fan cai):

Although rice does not play a major role in a banquet meal, it may be served toward the end. This last series of courses includes dishes that are much humbler than the main platters. They may be made of vegetables, bean curd, or eggs. Some hosts like to serve rice at this point as a symbolic gesture, implying that if the diner, for some inconceivable reason, has still not had his fill of food, the rice will assuage any hunger pangs. Rice-accompanying dishes are soothing to the stomach and foretell the ending of the meal.

Entremets:

Soups and sweet and savory pastries are served between the sections of the meal to soothe and freshen the palate. These dishes also serve the purpose of subtly notifying the diner that the meal is about to enter a new phase.

Fresh, cut-up fruit generally is served at the end of a banquet. Many hosts serve tea and hot towels to their guests to revitalize their sagging energies. It is also a tradition to apologize to your guests for the meagerness of the display of hospitality, no matter how sumptuous or lengthy the meal may have been. For a detailed menu of a traditional banquet, and a revised buffet, refer to the menus presented for Chinese New Year in the Winter section of this book.

THE CHINESE PANTRY

CONDIMENTS, SEASONINGS, SPICES, AND STARCHES

Any serious Chinese cook inevitably keeps the necessary condiments and spices on hand. With few exceptions, many of the basic ingredients described here may be stored at room temperature, in a cool, dry place. Pastes and sauces that come in cans should be transferred to tight-fitting jars after opening, and stored in the refrigerator.

Condiments: Basic Sauces, Spirits, Oils, and Pastes

Chili Paste and Hot Bean Paste

Both chili paste and hot bean paste impart a fiery flavor to Chinese dishes. Chili paste, or sauce (depending on the manufacturer), is made with mashed chili peppers, vinegar, and assorted seasonings — invariably garlic. Hot bean paste contains the same ingredients, with the addition of soybeans. Many cooks use these two sauces interchangeably, but some canned bean pastes are very salty. Both chili paste and hot bean paste will keep indefinitely, stored in the refrigerator, though they tend to lose their punch with the passage of time.

Chinese Rice Vinegar

Chinese cooks are partial to grain vinegars, which tend to be lighter and sweeter than Western vinegars. Because of these differences, American and European vinegars are not acceptable substitutes. The three main types of Chinese vinegar are white (clear), red, and black. Clear rice vinegar is used most frequently as a flavoring for sauces, pickling mixtures, and dressings; red vinegar is used most frequently as a dipping sauce for seafood; and Chinese black vinegar, which has a flavor somewhat similar to Worcestershire sauce, is commonly used as a flavoring in sauces, as well as a dipping sauce. Black vinegar with the Chinkiang label is imported from China and is the best tasting of the bunch.

Duck (or Plum) Sauce

Fruity and thick, with a sweet-and-sour flavor, duck sauce is made from a blending of plums, apricots, vinegar, and sugar. Although it has become a staple condiment at many Chinese restaurants in the United States, this sauce is traditionally used by the Cantonese as a dipping sauce with barbecued duck or goose.

Hoisin Sauce

Each region has its individual variety of bean sauce, and in southern China it is known as hoisin sauce or barbecue sauce and made with fermented mashed beans, salt, sugar, garlic, and occasionally pumpkin. The ingredients and flavor vary with the manufacturer. Like sweet bean sauce, its northern cousin, hoisin sauce is used in marinades for barbecued and roasted meats, as well as for a dipping sauce.

Oyster Sauce

Pungent and rich, oyster sauce is made from a concentrate of oysters, salt, soy sauce, and assorted seasonings, which have been cured over a lengthy period. On its own, oyster sauce has a strong flavor, but when mixed in sauces, it accentuates the taste of delicate ingredients such as vegetables and seafood. Oyster sauce will keep indefinitely in the refrigerator.

Rice Wine

In Chinese cooking, the all-purpose wine used for seasoning is rice wine, or yellow wine. The best type is known as Shaohsing and is imported from eastern China and Taiwan. Many Chinese supermarkets also now sell Chinese rice wine for cooking, which usually contains salt. If Chinese rice wine is unavailable, substitute Japanese sake, Scotch, or a dry white vermouth.

Sesame Oil

Amber-colored and pungently nutty, sesame oil is extracted from roasted seasame seeds. Unlike the light-colored, cold-pressed sesame oil found in many health food stores, Chinese sesame oil is primarily used as a seasoning and not as a cooking oil. It smokes at a very low temperature and has an overpowering taste.

Sesame Paste

A thick, pungent butter made from roasted sesame seeds, sesame paste is primarily used as a base for cold salad and noodle dressings. It is available at most Chinese grocery stores, but if it is unobtainable, peanut butter may be substituted. Mix sesame paste thoroughly before using and store in the refrigerator.

Soy Sauce

There are three grades of Chinese soy sauce: light; medium or thin; and thick, heavy, or dark. Light soy sauce, which is lighter in consistency, is usually reserved for seafood, vegetable, and chicken sauces. Medium-grade soy sauce is darker and slightly thicker. It is all-purpose and used for most cooking. Heavy soy, which is colored with molasses, is used to barbecue and roast meats, and in red-cooked or braised dishes.

Sweet Bean Sauce

The northern Chinese version of hoisin sauce, sweet bean sauce is made from a fermentation of soy beans, flour, salt, and water. It is primarily used as a flavoring for sauces and marinades, and as a dipping sauce — most notably with Peking duckling. Other kinds of bean sauce include those made with brown beans and yellow beans. Although they vary in flavor and texture, they may be used interchangeably. Sweet bean sauce will keep indefinitely stored in the refrigerator.

Seasonings and Spices

Chili Peppers

Chili peppers are grown in several parts of China, but the hottest varieties and the greatest abundance are found in Sichuan and Hunan provinces. In these areas, chili peppers, both fresh and dried, are used to infuse sauces with a fiery flavor. And chili oil, made from dried chili peppers, is added to dressings and used as a dipping sauce. When small, fresh red chili peppers are unavailable, substitute green jalapeño peppers. Although chili oil is sold in bottles in Chinese supermarkets, it is best if it is homemade. To make chili oil: Heat ½ cup safflower or corn oil and ½ cup sesame oil until smoking in a heavy pan with a tight-fitting lid. Add 1 tablespoon Sichuan peppercorns, ⅓ cup one-half-inch pieces dried red peppers, 6 scallion stalks, and 6 gingerroot slices. Turn off the heat, cover, and let stand for 30 minutes. Strain out the seasonings and transfer the oil to a jar. Use as directed in individual recipes and store indefinitely in a cool, dry place.

Chinese Cinnamon Bark

Westerners are probably more familiar with rolled cinnamon sticks, but Chinese cooks usually prefer thin slices of bark from the cassia, or Chinese cinnamon, tree. The flavors are quite similar and they may be used interchangeably. Chinese cinnamon or cassia bark is used as a pungent seasoning in braised stews and casseroles. It is also ground and used in five-spice powder.

Chinese Ham

The Chinese cure ham using a method similar to that used for Smithfield ham, thereby creating a pungent, salty seasoning. Chinese ham is sold in most Chinese supermarkets and is used as a flavoring or garnish for soups, seafood, poultry, and vegetable dishes. If it is unavailable, substitute prosciutto or Smithfield ham.

Chinese Sausage

Most Chinese supermarkets sell two types of Chinese sausage — pork and liver. Pork sausage, which is made with pork loin and seasonings, has a sweet, meaty flavor. Liver sausage, which is made with pork or duck liver, tends to be brown and has a grainy texture. For the majority of recipes, pork sausage is preferred. Chinese sausage will keep indefinitely, wrapped tightly, in the refrigerator.

Dried Chinese Black Mushrooms

For Chinese cooks, nothing compares with the pungent, smoky flavor of dried shiitake mushrooms — even fresh shiitake, which are now widely available in the Orient. They are used as a prominent seasoning in many Chinese soups, as well as meat, fish, poultry, and vegetable dishes. As any visit to a well-stocked Chinese market will reveal, they come in a variety of grades, and prices vary accordingly. Mushrooms of the highest grade, with a thick, full cap and a small white star design in the center, are generally reserved for expensive banquet dishes, where the caps are used whole. The thinner, less expensive varieties are usually used when the mushrooms are to be cut up. Dried Italian porcini mushrooms may be substituted if dried Chinese mushrooms are unavailable. Store dried mushrooms, tightly wrapped, in the freezer.

Dried Oysters and Scallops

In China, both oysters and scallops are dried and used to flavor soups, vegetable dishes, and stews. Dried scallops, in particular, are considered a delicacy and are sold by the ounce, with other treasured seasonings, at Chinese supermarkets. Dried scallops should be rinsed, steamed for 30 minutes with equal parts rice wine and water to cover, then shredded by hand. Dried oysters should be soaked overnight in hot water to cover and rinsed thoroughly to remove any shells. Both dried scallops and oysters will keep indefinitely when tightly wrapped and refrigerated.

Dried Shrimp

Miniature shrimp, which have been preserved in a salty brine and dried, are often used as a seasoning in soups and vegetable dishes. They are extremely pungent, so they should be used sparingly. Stored in a plastic bag in the refrigerator, dried shrimp will keep indefinitely.

Dried Tangerine or Orange Peel

Zesty and sharp in flavor, dried tangerine or orange peel is used as a seasoning in both stir-fried and braised dishes. According to cooking authorities in China, the older the peel, the more prized the flavor. Usually the peel is reconstituted in hot water before use. Since store-bought peel tends to be bitter, it should be blanched in boiling water before using. To make homemade peel, simply air-dry tangerine or clementine peels for several days. Wrapped tightly in plastic bags, the peel will keep indefinitely in a cool, dry place.

Fennel Seed

Traditionally, fennel seed is used in numerous braised dishes, in stews, and in tea-smoking. It has a pungent, licoricelike flavor. If it is unavailable, aniseed may be substituted. Chinese pharmacologists recommend fennel seed for stomach maladies.

Fermented Black Beans

One of the oldest seasonings developed by the Chinese, fermented (or salted) black beans are made from beans that have been preserved in a salty brine, then dried and fermented. Though the beans themselves are salty and pungent, when mixed with other flavorings and used in sauces, they tend to accentuate delicate foods including poultry, seafood, meat, and vegetables. The beans are available in plastic bags and cans. Packed in an airtight container and refrigerated, they will keep indefinitely.

Five-Spice Powder

This fragrant mixture is made with a number of different spices, including star anise, cinnamon, nutmeg, Sichuan peppercorns, cloves, fennel, and licorice root. The blend and flavor vary with the manufacturer, but it is usually a combination of five of these spices (hence the name). Five-spice powder is used as a seasoning in marinades, and when mixed with salt, as a dipping salt for deep-fried foods.

Garlic

One finds a liberal use of garlic all over China and the fresh green stalks are used as frequently as the cloves. Chinese chefs never use a garlic press, but prefer to preserve the integrity of this pungent seasoning by mincing or slicing it. Garlic is considered to have warming properties and is credited with prolonging life, as well as strengthening the body. Garlic chives are another popular seasoning in Chinese dishes. See "Chinese Chives" in the following section, "Selected Fresh, Dried, and Preserved Chinese Vegetables."

Gingerroot

A knobby stem (tuber rhizome) that grows underground, developing knuckles or lobes, gingerroot is one of the most basic and popular Chinese seasonings. It is usually available in two forms: spring and mature. Spring gingerroot, which is available sporadically throughout the year in Chinese supermarkets in the United States, has a papery skin, a delicate flavor, and pink tips. It is served in soups, pickled in sweet-and-sour dressings, and sprinkled on dishes as a garnish. Mature gingerroot, which has a thick skin and a much stronger flavor, is used mainly as a seasoning to flavor and remove strong tastes, particularly in seafood. Gingerroot is also said to cure colds, aid digestion, and revitalize the body. In buying gingerroot, select fat roots with smooth, unwrinkled skin. Store gingerroot buried unpeeled in a jar of sand, or peeled in a jar of rice wine in the refrigerator. When a slice of gingerroot is called for in recipes, it should be about the size of a quarter.

Scallions

Scallions are another prime seasoning in Chinese cooking. The white part is usually minced, chopped, sliced, or shredded, and used as a seasoning; the greens are usually used as garnish. A fresh scallion stalk also comes in handy for testing the temperature of hot oil for deep-frying. At 350 degrees, the bubbles emerging from the end of a scallion stalk submerged in the oil are quite small and slow-moving. At 375 degrees, the bubbles are bigger, they appear more quickly, and there is a slight sizzling noise. At 400 to 425 degrees, the bubbles are still bigger, they emerge at a furious pace, and there is a distinctive sizzling noise. The tip of the scallion stalk will also turn brown.

Sichuan (Szechuan) Peppercorns

Reddish-brown, open-husked peppercorns with a slightly numbing flavor, Sichuan peppercorns are used as a seasoning in marinades, dressings, and sauces. Toasted lightly, pulverized, and mixed with salt, they become a dipping powder for deep-fried foods. Store indefinitely, wrapped in plastic, in a cool, dry place.

Star Anise

An eight-pointed star with a distinct licoricelike flavor, star anise is used as a seasoning in marinades, braised dishes, and stews. Unlike European anise, which is from a bush, star anise comes from a tree of the magnolia family. Some Chinese also suck star anise as a breath freshener. It will keep indefinitely wrapped in plastic and stored in a cool, dry place.

Starches

Cornstarch

A starch extracted from the endosperm of a corn kernel, cornstarch has become the foremost thickener in Chinese cooking. In some parts of the Orient, however, tapioca starch (see below) is used just as frequently in thickening sauces. Cornstarch is also used as a coating in deep-fried dishes, and in marinades. Potato starch and arrowroot are acceptable substitutes.

Sweet Rice Flour

Glutinous, or "sweet," rice is often ground to a powder and used in batters and coatings, as well as in a variety of cakes and dumpling skins. It is available in most Chinese markets and will keep indefinitely in a cool, dry place.

Tapioca Starch

Derived from the cassava root or manioc plant, native to the West Indies, tapioca starch is popularly used to make dumpling skins, as well as for a thickener. Once cooked, the white powder turns translucent. In some recipes, cornstarch may be used as a substitute. Tapioca starch is available in all Chinese markets, and will keep indefinitely, tightly wrapped, in a cool, dry place.

Water Chestnut Flour

The starch extracted from fresh water chestnuts is dried and used by Chinese cooks as a coating for foods, and as a thickener. Water chestnut flour is also used to make the famous Cantonese *dim sum* steamed water chestnut pudding. It is sold in Chinese markets and will keep indefinitely, tightly wrapped, in a cool, dry place.

Wheat Starch

The powder remaining from flour once the gluten has been removed is known as wheat starch. Its primary use in Chinese cooking is in the making of dumpling skins, but it also may be used in batters and in preparing certain *dim sum.* It should be stored in a cool, dry place and is available in most Chinese markets.

SELECTED FRESH, DRIED, AND PRESERVED CHINESE VEGETABLES

Over the past five years, the availability of Chinese produce has vastly improved. Today almost every Chinese market offers an extensive selection of fresh vegetables, which changes seasonally, and even Western supermarkets offer a modest supply. In buying fresh Chinese vegetables, the first consideration is to select those of the highest quality available. The next step is to use them to their best advantage.

Traditionally, Chinese vegetables are classified into three major families: roots, leafy vegetables, and fruits. Root vegetables include carrots, taro, daikon radish, bamboo shoots, water chestnuts, lotus root, and gingerroot. Leafy vegetables encompass assorted Chinese cabbages, watercress, amaranth, and spinach. Fruit vegetables include tomatoes, eggplant, winter melon, bitter gourd, and cucumbers. To eliminate confusion, I have adapted these categories to the following groups: Leafy Vegetables and Cabbages; Root Vegetables and Gourds; Beans and Legumes. Also included here is a glossary of the more prominent dried and preserved vegetables.

Leafy Vegetables and Cabbages

Amaranth, or Chinese Spinach (xian cai)

In the West, this leafy plant with varying shades of green and red is considered merely decorative. In the Orient, its tender leaves and stems are relished as a delectable vegetable. The flavor of amaranth is somewhat like spinach, with a little additional spice and sweetness. It is commonly stir-fried or used in soups and is most widely available during the summer.

Chinese Broccoli (gao lan cai)

Chinese broccoli differs from its American cousin in flavor and shape. The stalks are quite slender, usually ending with green leaves and tiny yellow flowers, and the taste is fresh, but somewhat bitter. Before cooking, the stalks should be trimmed of any tough or dried leaves. Chinese broccoli is most commonly stir-fried and is widely available during the spring, summer, and fall.

Chinese Chives (jiu cai)

Chinese chives, otherwise known as garlic chives, have long, slender, flat leaves and a pungent, garlicky flavor. Occasionally, chives appear in markets with small buds at their tips, which are also edible. Yellow chives, which are grown in the dark, are also sometimes found in Chinese markets. Although similar in taste to the green chives, yellow chives are used primarily in stir-fried dishes. Green chives, on the other hand, are used to flavor soups, dumpling fillings, and stir-fried dishes. Chinese chives are available sporadically throughout the year.

Coriander (xiang cai)

Coriander, Chinese parsley, and cilantro are all names for a flat-leaf parsley with a pungent, musky flavor. (Some people maintain that there is a slight difference in flavor between cilantro and coriander, but they may be used interchangeably.) This seasoning is avidly relished in soups, salads, and cold platters. Some Westerners find the flavor unpleasant, so it should be used with discretion. Coriander will keep for over a week, refrigerated with its roots resting in water. It is usually available year round.

Chinese Cabbage (bai cai)

The Chinese cabbage family is varied and extensive. Fortunately, though only one or two varieties used to be available, now many are. Since it is primarily a cool-weather vegetable, the largest selection will be found during the late fall and winter. The following types are most widely available in the United States.

Bok Choy

Bok choy is considered by some to be the quintessence of Chinese cabbage, mainly because it was widely available — courtesy of Cantonese immigrants — long before other types of Chinese cabbage. This variety is sold in a number of different forms. The largest, and most common, has a thick, stalky body with leafy stems and is best stir-fried, used in soups or casseroles, or pickled. Miniature bok choy or tiny hearts of white cabbage are delectable stir-fried, or braised in casseroles. For both types, tough, outer stalks should be removed before cooking.

Chinese Cabbage (Napa)

Oval in shape, with broad leaves and a firmly packed head, Napa usually has a sweet, non-cabbagey flavor. Its juicy leaves are primarily used in dumpling fillings, soups, casseroles, pickles, and stir-fried dishes. It is also now sold in the produce section of many American supermarkets.

Chinese Celery Cabbage

A close relation to Napa cabbage (many group the two varieties together), celery cabbage has a much longer, thinner, and more closely packed head than Napa. The flavor may not be dissimilar, but the texture — firm and crunchy — is different from Napa. Accordingly, it is best stir-fried, pickled, braised, or cooked in soups.

Chinese Flowering Cabbage

If you notice a bunch of greens tied together with slender stalks, leafy branches, and small yellow flowers, you have discovered Chinese flowering cabbage. It has a fresh, very mild cabbagey flavor, and is best stir-fried. Make certain to select tender stalks and trim away old leaves and tough stalks before cooking.

Mustard Cabbage

This vegetable resembles a small, tightly wrapped oval head of celery hearts. The flavor of mustard cabbage is distinctly bitter, but delicious. Mustard cabbage is generally braised or stir-fried, and served in soups. The tough outer stem and leaves should be trimmed prior to cooking. It is most abundant in winter, but is also available through the spring.

Chinese Chrysanthemum (tong hao cai)

Unlike its Western counterpart, which is used primarily for decoration, Chinese chrysanthemum, or garland chrysanthemum, is relished for its spicy-sweet flavor. The dark-green chrysanthemum leaves are often sold in bunches in Chinese markets and their appearance is suggestive of dandelion greens. Chrysanthemum greens from the home garden that have not been sprayed with insecticides are an acceptable substitute. The greens, which are available in the late fall and winter, are used fresh to garnish soups; in their dried form, they flavor tea and wines.

Chinese Water Spinach (keng xin cai)

The Chinese name "empty heart vegetable" aptly describes this spinachlike green, with thin, hollow stalks. The flavor of water spinach is so fresh, and the texture so delightfully crisp, that it is relished by many Chinese. It is excellent stir-fried with a little oil and garlic and served as a vegetable side dish. Chinese water spinach is at its peak through the summer but is also available in the fall.

Root Vegetables and Gourds

Bamboo Shoots (xun)

Fresh bamboo shoots are not available in this country, even in well-stocked Chinese supermarkets. This is unfortunate, since the flavor of the canned product pales in comparison to that of the fresh. In markets in the Orient, there are numerous kinds of bamboo shoots, varying in size, shape, and season — from the delectable slender shoots of early summer to the substantial meaty shoots of winter. In selecting canned bamboo shoots, choose those labeled the winter variety; they are generally superior in quality. Always blanch canned shoots briefly in boiling water and refresh them in cold water before using, to remove the tinny flavor.

Chinese Eggplant (qie zi)

Chinese eggplant is stunningly beautiful, with its slender, shapely body and deep purple color. This vegetable easily stands out in any produce bin. And there is its ivory-white cousin with a stout, shorter body. Both varieties have sweet meat, edible skins, and decidedly fewer seeds than their Western counterparts. Chinese eggplant lends itself to a number of preparations: it may be steamed, deep-fried, stir-fried, or braised. In buying eggplant, choose those with firm, smooth skins. Chinese eggplant is usually sold year round, but if it is unavailable, substitute the small Italian variety.

Daikon Radish (bai luo bo)

The daikon radish, or Chinese turnip, may be similar in texture to the Western radish, but that is where the resemblance ends. Daikon radishes have a long, white body (occasionally with a greenish tinge) and their flavor is sweet, but stronger than their Western counterpart. They are relished in soups, salads, stews, savory pastries, and pickles. Daikon radishes are also popularly sold dried and salted, in long strips. Select fresh radishes with a smooth, unblemished surface and firm center. They are available year round, but are at their best during the cooler months.

Lotus Root (lian e)

Fresh lotus root looks like a muddy, bulbous root. It is a starchy vegetable with a sweet taste and crisp texture. Like a potato, once it is peeled it will darken very quickly. Chinese cooks blanch this vegetable and serve it in salads, cooked in soups, or stuffed and steamed with sweet rice or red bean paste. Select firm, whole roots, with an unblemished skin. It is available fresh in the summer and fall, and in the winter around Chinese New Year.

Melons or Gourds

Like the cabbage family, the family of melons is quite extensive, including both fruit and vegetable varieties. Many of the different types are only available seasonally; some are obtainable year round. The most prominent varieties found in the United States are the following:

Bitter Melon (ku gua)

Bitter melon or gourd is a vegetable relished by most Chinese. Westerners may find the bitter flavor unpleasant. The vegetable has a green, blistered skin and a round body with a pointed end. The greener the melon, the more bitter the flavor. It is usually steamed, stir-fried, or stuffed and braised. Make certain to remove the seeds and trim the ends before cooking. This vegetable is available in late spring and throughout the summer.

Hairy Melon (mao gua)

Some say that hairy, or fuzzy, melon is the smaller cousin to the winter melon. The flavors are so similar that the two may be used interchangeably. As its name implies, hairy melon has a light fuzz all over its rind, which should be rubbed off before cooking. The sweet, mild flesh is best steamed, braised, stir-fried, or cooked in soups. It is available throughout the summer and into the fall.

Luffa Squash (si gua)

Luffa squash is also commonly known as Chinese okra, and its ridged, green, okralike body readily explains why. All similarity to okra ends with the appearance, however, since the flesh of the luffa squash is firm and sweet. Choose the smaller squashes, as the larger ones tend to become tough. Before cooking, use a vegetable peeler to remove the ridges, leaving some skin. Steam in slices, or stir-fry with a little oil and garlic. Luffa is available periodically throughout the year, but its peak season is during the summer.

Winter Melon (dung gua)

Most Chinese vegetables may seem miniature in comparison to the massive winter melon. Some melons reach a weight of up to a hundred pounds. Most winter melons are sold in sections by the pound; you merely indicate how much you want. This melon has a green outer skin, which is often tinged with a frostlike coating. The interior is white and fleshy, with seeds that should be removed before cooking. Winter melon may be carved out and used as an edible bowl for soups, or the meat may be stir-fried, steamed, or cooked in soups. Although the name implies otherwise, its prime season is during the warmer months.

Taro (yu tao)

Like the potato, taro is a starchy, slightly bland vegetable. There are a number of kinds of taro, but only two are commonly available in this country. Both are oval-shaped, with brown, hairy skin and pinkish-purple meat. One variety is 2 to 3 inches in diameter; the other is usually about the size of a coconut. It is first peeled and then the flesh may be shredded and deep-fried to form nests, or steamed in sweet and savory pudding dishes, dumplings, or cakes. Select firm, unblemished roots. Taro is available throughout the year but mainly during the winter.

Water Chestnuts (pi chi)

A tuber of the sedge plant, fresh Chinese water chestnuts have become a common sight in Chinese markets, as well as in the produce sections of many Western supermarkets. The sweet flavor of the fresh chestnuts is far superior to that of the canned variety. Fresh water chestnuts must be peeled with a sharp knife and placed in water, since they turn color quickly. For savory dishes, they are usually precooked in boiling water for 10 minutes, then refreshed in cold water. For sweet dishes, they are peeled and used as is. Canned water chestnuts should always be blanched in boiling water briefly and refreshed in cold water. This extra step will remove any tinny flavor. In selecting fresh water chestnuts, choose firm, unblemished specimens. Fresh water chestnuts are available year round.

Beans and Legumes

Bean Sprouts

There are two main types of bean sprouts used in Chinese cooking, although Westerners may be familiar with only one.

Mung Bean Sprouts (lu do ya)

Mung bean sprouts are the smaller, more familiar sprouts usually found in Western supermarkets and in salad bars. They are sprouted from green mung beans and are admired for their crisp texture and fresh taste. Purists trim the end of each one to remove the sprout and bitter tip. Select crisp-looking white sprouts and avoid any soggy, brownish tips. Mung bean sprouts are primarily used in stir-fried dishes, or in salads. They are available year round. If fresh bean sprouts are unobtainable, omit. Canned bean sprouts are not an acceptable substitute.

Soybean Sprouts (mao do ya)

Soybean sprouts are thicker and longer than mung bean sprouts. For positive identification, merely look at their sprouted tip: soybean tips are much larger than those of their mung bean cousins. The flavor is also stronger, but most Chinese love them in stir-fried dishes, soups, and braised stews. Like mung bean sprouts, soybean sprouts are also available year round. They will keep for about a week in the refrigerator.

Fava Beans (mao do)

Fresh fava, or broad, beans are one of the most popular kinds of small green beans consumed by the Chinese. Some liken the appearance of the fava bean to the lima bean; once cooked, however, the flavor is more like that of fresh peas. Fava beans are frequently used in stir-fried dishes and soups. They are most widely available in the fall.

Snow Peas (lan do)

Chinese pea pods, or snow peas, have become a staple in most produce sections, in both Western and Chinese supermarkets. Their delicate, fresh flavor and crisp texture make them a popular ingredient in stir-fried dishes, salads, and soups. If possible, select smaller peas; they generally tend to be more tender. Before using, snap both ends and remove the veiny string along each side of the pod. In the Orient, snow peas are only available during the winter. In the West, they are available year round, but prices usually drop in the fall and late spring.

Yard-Long String Beans (qing gong dou)

These string beans are much longer than Western green beans; often they do measure as long as a yard. In flavor, they are similar to the French *haricot vert*, but if they are unavailable, Western green beans may be substituted. Stir-fried or deep-fried, and tossed in a sauce, or served cold in a salad, they are delicious. Yard-long string beans are available year round in most Chinese markets.

Dried and Preserved Vegetables

Dried Wood Ears or Black Fungus

Edible black fungi, which resemble leaves, are collected and dried for the Chinese market. Before use, they are reconstituted. The larger black fungi, known as cloud ears, are slightly rubbery in texture; the smaller variety, called wood ears, are crunchy and a little more delicate. Both have a slightly smoky flavor. Store tightly wrapped in plastic in a cool, dry place. They will keep indefinitely.

Pickled Cucumbers

Pickled cucumbers are popularly used as a seasoning in salads, soups, and stir-fried dishes. They are also served by themselves as a crisp pickle. Tea cucumbers, which are long and thin, are seeded, cut into strips, and preserved in a soy sauce brine. They are available in cans and will keep indefinitely if transferred to a jar and refrigerated.

Red-in-Snow

This spinachlike vegetable is preserved in salt, giving it a pungent, sour taste. Although preserved, the vegetable retains its original pleasing texture. Whole or minced, it is used as a flavoring in stir-fried dishes, soups, and steamed dumplings and buns. In some Chinese supermarkets, red-in-snow is available fresh. It is always available in cans. Packed in a tightly covered jar in the refrigerator, it will keep indefinitely.

Sichuan (Szechuan) Preserved Mustard Greens

The Sichuanese preserve the central heart of a variety of cabbage greens in salt, chili pepper, and assorted seasonings. Left to sit for several months, the knobby stems still retain their crisp texture but acquire a hot, spicy flavor. The pickle is then used in soups and stir-fried dishes, or sprinkled on top of cold platters. Sichuan preserved mustard greens are sold in cans or by weight from huge earthenware pickling crocks in Chinese grocery stores. They will keep indefinitely if refrigerated in a closed container.

Tianjin (Tientsin) Pickled Vegetable

In northern China, cabbage is salted and dried, creating a slightly sweet but pungent pickle known as Tianjin pickled vegetable. It is used as a seasoning in soups, dumpling fillings, and, most notably, in the stuffing of Beggar's Chicken, a classic eastern dish. It is sold in clay crocks and will keep indefinitely in the refrigerator.

CHINESE BEVERAGES

● ● ● ● ● ● ● ● ● ● ● ● ● ●

CHINESE BEVERAGES

The modernization of China has brought a number of changes to the Chinese table, and Western influence seems particularly strong in regard to beverages. In ancient China, according to Pearl S. Chen, author of *Everything You Want to Know About Chinese Cooking*, the only liquids served at a meal were soup and grain-based wines. The soup broth quenched the thirst and cleansed the palate, while wine generally was used for toasting fellow guests or as an offering to the gods.

Today, soup is still the most popular beverage for a home-style meal, but beer and grape wines (both of which were introduced from the West) have become staple drinks at more formal meals. And it is not unusual to see bottles of Coca-Cola and Orange Crush appear at the most elegant banquet gatherings. Tea customarily is served before and after meals in China (unlike the Western custom of serving it throughout a Chinese meal), and it remains the ubiquitous beverage. It is ritually served throughout the day with *dim sum* — teatime snacks — or it may be brewed and savored informally whenever the urge demands.

Teas

The first bowl — how soothing to the throat!
The second bowl — all feeling of loneliness vanishes;
The third bowl — I start searching my soul, to find five thousand volumes of ancient tomes;
The fourth bowl — a slight perspiration which washes away all unhappy things;
The fifth bowl — my bones and muscles all cleansed;
The sixth bowl — I establish communication with the immortal spirit;
The seventh bowl — this must not be taken,
Already a cool ethereal breeze
Emanates from underneath my arms.
                    — Lu Tung, a poet of the Sung dynasty

For most Westerners, tea is synonymous with China. Considering its lengthy history in the Far

East, this is not such an inappropriate association. Tea plants were believed to grow wild in east Asia, and the first tea bushes were cultivated by the Chinese around A.D. 350.

The mythical Imperial ruler Shen Nung has been credited with inadvertently brewing the first pot of tea some five thousand years ago. According to the tale, he was innocently boiling water one day when a few leaves randomly floated down from a nearby tree into his pot. He drank the resulting brew, discovered it to his liking, and introduced it to his subjects. From then on, tea became a popular drink, but it was relished more for its reputed pharmacological benefits than as a beverage.

It was Lu Yu, a poet of the T'ang dynasty (618–907), who wrote the definitive treatise on the subject, titled *Classics of Tea*, and established himself as the revered authority on tea and tea-making. For Lu Yu, mountain water was essential for the perfect cup of tea — as were the proper pots and vessels. Lu Yu also maintained that boiling the leaves was a necessary step. Later, during the Sung dynasty (960–1279), when tea-making achieved the refinement and cultural appeal of modern times, this method was revised to allow steeping.

Today the Chinese serve tea to guests as a preliminary to any social ritual — whether it's a simple household visit or the partaking of a twelve-course feast. Tea is rarely served alone but is accompanied by some form of savory or sweet tidbit. Chinese teahouses, where customers gather for business discussions and informal socializing, serve small snacks, or *dim sum*, along with an extensive selection of teas.

Tea plants flourish in the subtropical temperatures of southern and eastern China. The plant may grow to a height of thirty feet but is customarily pruned back for maximum yield. The first picking, usually in early spring, is considered the most precious. Frequently, for the first picking, the leaves are not yet full grown and contain a whitish down, called *pai hao*, from which the word *pekoe* derived. A second picking is done when the bush is in full bloom. Then the leaves are dried or cured to produce three main types of tea: black, or "red," tea; semifermented tea; or green tea.

Black teas, which are made from fully fermented leaves, are generally robust and full-flavored. The most notable types of black teas are Pu Erh, from Yunnan province; Keemun, from eastern China; and Lapsang Souchong, a distinctively smoky tea from Fujian in eastern China.

Semifermented, or oolong, teas generally are from eastern and southern China and are not as sharp, and are more subtle in flavor. Some of the noted varieties include Black Dragon oolong and orange pekoe.

Green teas are merely dried leaves that have not been cured. Although they are not as well liked in the West, green teas are favored by many Orientals. They are generally slightly astringent, cleansing and soothing the palate, particularly after oily foods have been eaten. The most precious green tea, reputed to be made from the top three leaves of each branch, is Dragon Well tea from eastern China.

For those intent on brewing a good pot of Chinese tea, the following guidelines should be observed:

- Use spring water, ideally, or fresh tap water for each pot.
- The teapot and cups should be made of porcelain, earthenware, or glass. The Chinese believe the I-Hsing pots, made from a natural rust-colored clay, are best for brewing tea.
- Freshen the pot and cups with boiling water before brewing tea.
- Add one teaspoon of loose tea per cup to the pot. Heat the water until just boiling. Do not boil the water for too long, or it will taste flat. Once the water is poured, cover the pot, and steep the tea for four to five minutes before serving.

Wine, Liquors, and Beers

Like other brilliant mishaps that have occurred throughout Chinese culinary history and supposedly led to the invention of a new food or drink, rice wine — so it is said — was first created by a neglectful cook who left some rice to soak in water in a covered earthenware pot. Some time later, he returned to find a strong brew that was rather flavorful and created a pleasant, euphoric feeling. He sampled the contents, enjoyed it immensely, and christened the drink *jiu*, or yellow wine.

Early brews of *jiu* were made from other grains besides rice. Millet and sorghum also provided a flavorful base for fermentation. These spirits were used in religious rituals, as offerings to the gods; in social ritual, for the toast-making that accompanies every banquet; and as tonics for improving the health. Many fermented grain wines were fortified and flavored with assorted Chinese herbs and seasonings, including Sichuan peppercorns and cassia blossoms or bark (Chinese cinnamon).

The most highly reputed yellow wine is fermented in Shaohsing, a city in eastern China. It serves a dual purpose, as a cooking wine and as a drinking wine. For banquets, Shaohsing generally is heated briefly before serving and garnished with paper-thin slices of lemon or pickled plums.

Grape wine was introduced from the West and enjoyed as early as the Han dynasty (206 B.C.–A.D. 220). Soon afterward, grapes were transplanted to provinces in northern China, where they thrived. It was not long before grape wine was produced domestically in China. It is still made today, primarily in Shandong province, but Chinese grape wine has never been outstanding and production is limited. Other wines are made from an assortment of fruits and flower blossoms.

Strong distilled liquors, made from sorghum and other grain mashes, also became popular during the early dynasties. Ranging in strength from 100 to 150 proof, they are still popular today. The most noted are *mao tai*, *gaoliang*, and *bai gar*. These drinks are primarily used for toasts at banquets, but are also remedies prescribed for a variety of illnesses. The Chinese also make flavored liqueurs with fruits such as pears, plums, quince, and chrysanthemum and rose petals.

Though undistinguished as great grape wine makers, the Chinese more than make up for this failing with their beers. Chinese beers are light, full-bodied, and beautifully thirst quenching. Beer is the most popular beverage served at banquets, aside from rice wine. It was the Germans, during the early nineteen hundreds, who first brought beer to China, building breweries in northern China. Today, the most popular beer, Tsingtao, hails from the north, but many areas in China have their own local breweries.

When selecting the appropriate beverage for a Chinese banquet, be it Chinese rice wine, beer, or European or domestic grape wines, there are a few considerations to keep in mind. (If your guests insist on drinking tea, then by all means indulge them, but tea is more properly served before and after the meal.)

• Consider the food with which the beverage is being served. The drink should be complementary to the food, and stand up to the flavors of the prepared dishes.

• The beverage should be appropriate for its particular role in the meal. At a banquet, rice wine or a potent, distilled liquor is served for toasting, and beer or soda for quenching the thirst and cleansing the palate between courses.

Bibliography

The sources listed here were consulted in preparing much of the background material on the holidays as well as the glossary of Chinese ingredients. They are also highly recommended for additional reading and insight into Chinese food and culture.

Aero, Rita.
Things Chinese.
Garden City, N.Y.: Dolphin Books, 1980.

Ball, J. Dyer.
Things Chinese.
Hong Kong: Oxford University Press, 1982.

Bodde, Derk.
Festivals in Classical China.
Princeton: Princeton University Press, 1975.

Bredon, Juliet, and Igor Mitrophanow.
The Moon Year.
Hong Kong: Oxford University Press, 1982.

Burkhardt, V. R.
Chinese Creeds and Customs.
Hong Kong: South China Morning Post Ltd., 1982.

Chang, Cecilia Sun Yun, as told to Allan Carr.
The Mandarin Way.
Boston: Little, Brown, 1974.

Chang, K. C., ed.
Food in Chinese Culture: Anthropological and Historical Perspectives.
New Haven: Yale University Press, 1977.

Chen, Pearl Kong, Tien Chi Chen, and Rose Tseng.
Everything You Want to Know about Chinese Cooking.
Woodbury, N.Y.: Barron's, 1983.

Dahlen, Martha, and Karen Phillips.
A Guide to Chinese Market Vegetables.
Hong Kong: Yee Tong Printing Press Ltd., 1980.

Dahlen, Martha, and Karen Phillips.
A Further Guide to Chinese Market Vegetables.
Hong Kong: Yee Tong Printing Press Ltd., 1981.

Harrington, Geri.
Grow Your Own Chinese Vegetables.
Pownal, Vt.: Garden Way Publishing, 1978.

Huang, Su-Huei.
Chinese Cuisine.
Translated by Nina Simonds.
Taipei: Wei-Chuan Publishing Company, 1974.

Huang, Su-Huei.
Chinese Snacks.
Translated by Nina Simonds.
Taipei: Wei-Chuan Publishing Company, 1974.

Keys, John D.
Chinese Herbs.
Rutland, Vt.: Charles E. Tuttle Company, 1976.

Lai, T. C.
At the Chinese Table.
Hong Kong: Oxford University Press, 1984.

Lai, T. C.
Chinese Food for Thought.
Hong Kong: Hong Kong Book Centre, 1978.

Lai, T. C., Husein Rofe, and Phillip Mao.
Things Chinese.
Hong Kong: Swindon Book Company, 1971.

Lamb, Corinne.
The Chinese Festive Board.
Shanghai: The Willow Pattern Press, 1938.

Lee, Gary.
Chinese Tasty Tales Cookbook.
San Francisco: Chinese Treasure Productions, 1974.

Leeming, Margaret, and May Huang Man-Hui.
Chinese Regional Cookery.
London: Rider, 1983.

Lin, Hsiang Ju, and Tsuifeng Lin.
Chinese Gastronomy.
London: Thomas Nelson and Sons, Ltd., 1969.

Lo, Kenneth.
Peking Cooking.
New York: Pantheon Books, 1971.

Lo, Kenneth.
The Complete Chinese Cookbook.
Glasgow: William Collins Sons & Co. Ltd., 1974.

Lowe, H. Y.
The Adventures of Wu.
Princeton: Princeton University Press, 1983.

Passmore, Jacki, and Daniel Reid.
The Complete Chinese Cookbook.
New York: Exeter Books, 1982.

Perkins, David W., ed.
Hong Kong & China Gas Cookbook.
Hong Kong: The Hong Kong & China Gas Co. Ltd., 1978.

Shou, Tuan-Hsi.
Chinese Homemade Dishes of Four Seasons.
Taipei: Hilit Publishing Co. Ltd., 1982.

Simonds, Nina.
Classic Chinese Cuisine.
Boston: Houghton Mifflin Company, 1982.

Tun, Li-Ch'en.
Translated by Derk Bodde.
Annual Customs and Festivals in Peking.
Hong Kong: Hong Kong University Press, 1965.

Williams, C. A. S.
Outlines of Chinese Symbolism & Art Motives.
New York: Dover Publications, 1976.

Yeh, Cheng-Huei, ed.
Translated by Nina Simonds.
Chinese Cuisine II.
Taipei: Wei-Chuan Publishing Company, 1980.

Zee, S. Y., and L. H. Hui.
Hong Kong Food Plants.
Hong Kong: The Urban Council of Hong Kong, 1981.

Index

Cabbage
bok choy, 234
casserole, Chinese, 210
Chinese, 234–35; celery, 235
Chinese flowering, 235
with crabmeat, stir-fried,116
hot-and-sour, 80
mustard, 235
rolls, stuffed, 44
Candied walnuts, 168
Cantonese-style
chicken wings, 131
spring rolls, 39; wrappers, 38
Carrot salad with fresh coriander, 84
Carrots, spicy Sichuan, 7
Casserole(s), 191–92; list, 193
beef short ribs braised with red wine, 207
Chinese cabbage, 210
eight-treasure duck, 208
red-cooked chicken with chestnuts,205
spicy fish in a sandy pot, 206
spicy lamb with turnips, 208
Celery hearts with peppercorn dressing, 83
Chicken
and abalone with vermicelli noodles, 203
ball and snow pea soup, 200
beggar's, 160
braised with star anise and red wine, 211
broth, basic Chinese, 194
chrysanthemum fire pot, 114
and ham, in a light mustard dressing with pancakes, 14
and leeks, stir-fried noodles with, 22
livers, tea-and-anise-flavored, 12
noodle salad, spicy, with chili oil dressing, 89
red-cooked with chestnuts, 205
salad, hacked, with noodles in a spicy peanut dressing, 66
sauce, 56, 171
sausage and rice wrapped in lotus leaves, 56
skewered with almond coating, 137
soup, hot-and-sour, 194
soup, triple-shred, 101
spring rolls, 36
steamed in melon soup, 55
stir-fried with pine nuts in lettuce leaves, 171
tea-smoked with red pepper dressing, 60
wings, Cantonese-style, 131
wings, red-cooked, 6
wontons, deep-fried, 133
Chile
oil, 226
oil dressing, spicy chicken noodle salad with, 89
paste, 223
peppers, 226

Home-style meal, 215–17
    traditional, menu, 218
Honey-coated crispy pine nuts, 126
Hot bean paste, 223
Hot-and-sour cabbage, 80
Hot-and-sour chicken soup, 194
Hunan scallop soup, 196

Juicy buns, steamed, 142

Lamb
    kebabs, spicy, 73
    spicy, stir-fried with sweet bean sauce, 42
    spring, in sesame vinaigrette, composed salad with, 26
    with turnips, spicy, 208
Lantern festival, 175–76
    menus for, 177, 185
Layered fish and spinach in broth, 195
Leeks, stir-fried beef with, 41
Leeks and chicken, stir-fried noodles with, 22
Lemon sauce, fresh, steamed scallop rolls with, 139
Liquor, Chinese, 248
Littleneck clams in black bean sauce, 159
Longevity buns, 23
Loquats
    and lychees stuffed with duck in a fresh orange sauce, 135
    and melon balls in candied ginger syrup, 62
    and strawberries sweetened with plum wine, 15
Lotus
    buns, steamed, 68
    leaves: chicken, sausage, and rice wrapped in, 56
    root, 237
    root salad in scallion oil dressing, 169
Luffa squash (Chinese okra), 238
Lumpia skin. *See* Spring rolls, Wrappers
Lychee(s)
    and loquats stuffed with duck in a fresh orange sauce, 135
    -strawberry ice, 29
    sweet date soup with, 165

Mandarin pancakes, 40
Meat. *See also* Name of meat
    dumplings, pan-fried, 157
    ground and black bean filling for savory turnovers, 144
    ground and black beans, stuffed bell peppers with, 134
    in salads, 77
Melon(s)
    balls and loquats in candied ginger syrup, 62
    or gourds, 237–38
    soup, chicken steamed in, 55
    varieties, bitter, 237; hairy, 237; winter, 238

Menu(s). *See also* Festival menus, Seasonal dishes
    for Chinese barbecue, 65, 71
    -planning, about, 215–17
    for traditional Chinese banquet, 219–20
    for traditional home-style meal, 218
Mongolian barbecue, 67
Mongolian fire pot, 180
Moon cakes
    about, xi
    savory, 102
    sweet, 104
Mung bean sprouts, 240
Mushroom(s)
    and asparagus, stir-fried, with lettuce in oyster sauce, 163
    black
        baked fish packages with, 170
        Chinese bisque, 106
        dried Chinese, 227
        and garlic, red-cooked fish smothered in, 162
    dried duxelle filling for flaky turnovers, 146
    drunken, 82
Mussels and asparagus, ginger noodles with, 92
Mustard greens, preserved (Sichuan), 242
Mustard sauce. *See* Sauces and Dressings

New Year banquet, Chinese, 155
New Year's buffet, menu for, 167
Noodle(s). *See also* Rice noodles
    in broth, five-treasure, 204
    chicken salad, spicy, with chili oil dressing, 89
    ginger with mussels and asparagus, 92
    scallops and vegetables in oyster sauce with, 172
    silver pin, 87
    stir-fried with chicken and leeks, 22
    vermicelli, abalone and chicken with, 203
    zucchini with a spicy dressing, steamed, 28

Okra, Chinese (luffa squash), 238
Orange sauce, fresh, loquats and lychees stuffed with duck in, 135
Orange or tangerine peel, dried, 228
Oyster sauce, 163, 172, 224
Oysters and scallops, dried, 227

Pancakes. *See also* Roll-ups
    crispy scallion-ham, 127
    Mandarin, 40
    shredded ham and chicken in a mustard dressing with, 14
Pang pang cucumbers, 156
Pantry, Chinese, 223–48
Peanut(s)
    dip, spicy, vegetables sticks with, 129

Nancy Belford, *who designed this book, trained in both the United States and Switzerland. Her work combines form and color with a minimalist aesthetic. Belford Design is in Boston.*

Johanna Chao, *calligrapher, was born in Shanghai, China. Since childhood, she has been inspired and disciplined in the art of calligraphy. She lives in Newton, Massachusetts, with her husband and three children.*